An ABC of Nostalgia

An ABC of NOSTALGIA

From Aspidistras to Zoot Suits

E. S. TURNER

with illustrations by
John Jensen

MICHAEL JOSEPH
LONDON

First published in Great Britain by Michael Joseph Ltd
44 Bedford Square, London WC1
1984

British Library Cataloguing in Publication Data
Turner, E. S.
    An ABC of Nostalgia
    1. Great Britain – Social life and customs – 20th century
    I. Title
    941.083 DA566.4

ISBN 0 7181 2386 7

Filmset by J & L Composition Ltd. Filey, N. Yorkshire
Printed in Great Britain by Hollen Street Press, Slough.
Bound by Dorstel Press Ltd, Harlow

The entries on Bird-Nesting, 'Bullets', the Electrophone, Libraries (1),
Meccano, Sweets and Ventriloquism have appeared in different form in
Punch and those on Journalism (1) and (2) in *The Listener*. Four lines
from 'The Waste Land' by T. S. Eliot are reproduced on p.110 from
Collected Poems 1909–1962 by permission of Faber and Faber.

CONTENTS

PREFACE

This book is a haphazard cruise up the Amazon of nostalgia, sometimes in the main channel, sometimes in the shallows and backwaters. For some, nostalgia means the 1960s and the first mini-skirts; for others, the inter-war years of the charabanc and the *palais de danse*, or the 'ocean greyhounds'; for a happy few, it means the years before the wars, when old ladies had their money washed by the servants and straw was laid on the roads for those dying or giving birth. As one who was born in the year Blériot flew the English Channel, I find myself hankering for the inter-war years, but nostalgia does not confine itself to any fixed period.

There is much in these pages on childhood delights and adolescent obsessions – from bicycling to bird-nesting, from car-spotting to forlorn attempts at voice-throwing and frustrated quests for the Facts of Life. The book deals with the birth pangs of the gramophone, the forgotten Electrophone (for listening to plays and sermons), the 'rag and bone' crystal set, the coming of the air circus and the talkies (much resented by film critics). It looks at cults like those of the Silly Ass, Froth-Blowing, Couéism and Eurhythmics. It explores the neglected subject of special trains. It casts a friendly eye on chorus girls in their heyday and remembers the once-universal office boy. It takes a sober look at what used to happen or not happen, during the Two Minutes' Silence.

Much of the detail is from the lumber of my own memory, but I have not hesitated to quicken, and supplement, remembrance by looking things up – browsing in old Meccano handbooks, back copies of the *Children's Newspaper*, old hymnals and catalogues, cuttings from the publications on which I worked, ships' newspapers brought back from the North Atlantic and so on. It is obvious I can have no personal memories of Black Ascot, which was staged in my infancy, but my elders talked about this macabre festival and it was

11

essential to satisfy my curiosity about it; as about other things which formed part of their world, like life-preservers and the Bible in Pitman's Shorthand.

Not everyone may think the things recalled here deserve the passing tribute of a sigh. All I hope to arouse is a mixture of recognition, incredulity and, perhaps, relief – relief at being born too late to wear a dunce's cap or to be pierced by hat-pins.

E. S. Turner
London, 1983

ABERDEEN JOKES
Direct From The Factory

There was the Aberdonian who cured his stutter by making a Transatlantic phone call . . . and the Aberdonian who held sea-sickness at bay by clenching a sixpence between his teeth . . . and the Aberdonian who, on Christmas Eve, fired a shotgun behind the woodshed and told his children Father Christmas had committed suicide . . . and the Aberdonian who plucked a fly from his whisky and wrung it out . . . and there was the headline, 'Two Taxis Collide in Aberdeen: 57 Hurt'.

The Aberdeen joke reached an astonishing peak of popularity in the 1920s. When that roving writer H. V. Morton published *In Search of Scotland* in 1929 he devoted more than four pages to a description of life in a closely-guarded joke factory housed in a granite block in Aberdeen. Spoofs are dangerous exercises, especially those with a wealth of circumstantial detail, and it may be that many a reader, faced with Morton's final tongue-in-cheek pronouncement

13

about this factory, 'I am sure it exists!', felt equally sure that it was based on reality.

Punch had already published a full-page skit about conditions in the Aberdeen joke factory, showing hangdog and exhausted staff trudging home after a hard day's grind. The magazine, a joke factory itself, had been tilting intermittently at the frugality of the Scots for most of its career. In 1868 appeared the famous verdict of a Scots visitor to London: 'E-eh, it's just a ruinous place, that! Mun, a had na' been the-erre abune twa hoours when – *bang* – went saxpence!!!' This visitor was not, in fact, an Aberdonian but, according to the caption, a 'Peebles body'. Nor was he called MacTavish, a name which eventually became a trigger for an instant laugh ('No MacTavish / Was ever lavish.' – Ogden Nash).

Sir Harry Lauder, a Lowlander, deliberately drew on himself a reputation for meanness, but by his time the public had become mysteriously convinced that the real home of skinflints was Aberdeen. If the city had no joke factory, how could one account for all those comic postcards (notably one showing a deserted Union Street captioned 'Aberdeen on a flag day'), those cracker quips, those books called 'Canny Tales Frae Aberdeen' and 'More Canny Tales Frae Aberdeen', those daily jokes on the tear-off calendars? According to H. V. Morton the real Aberdeen joke was the publicity given to the city by those who spread jokes about it. By this reasoning, the city was animated by the spirit of its townsman who gave his fiancée lipstick for her birthday because he knew he would get it all back. But did jokes about Aberdeen really bring cash-spending tourists flocking to Deeside to see if all the tales were true? Well, Henry Ford is supposed to have encouraged 'Tin Lizzie' jokes because they helped sell his cars.

In any event, why Aberdeen and not Peebles or Dundee? Cuthbert Graham, in *Portrait of Aberdeen and Deeside*, says the city's reputation for meanness arose from the extreme frugality of life in the past. 'Suddenly in the first or second decade of this century the shifts of ruthless hoarding and saving to which their ancestors had been put began to seem comic to Aberdonians themselves. And thus the Aberdonian joke was born.' Graham quotes the Aberdeen City Analyst as saying, 'as late as 1922', that Aberdeen was (note: not 'has') 'a factory working day and night – especially at night – manufacturing jokes about Aberdeen.' Not that it had become a spendthrift city: the annals show that in 1920 a visitor to Aberdeen could play six holes of golf for a penny, completing the course for three-pence.

The explanation by Cuthbert Graham is fair enough as far as it goes, but why should Aberdeen in particular have felt this revulsion against a skimping past? Is there any truth in the theory advanced by the comedian Jimmy Logan that the legend sprang from the year 1817, when the city, having seriously overspent on improvements, declared itself bankrupt? If so, the legend took nearly a hundred years to gather real momentum. Perhaps all this is like asking why, out of all the land-locked towns in Lancashire, Wigan was saddled with jokes about its pier.

In recent years Aberdeen has been transformed by oil wealth. Yet Paul Theroux, describing the town in *The Kingdom by the Sea* (1983), claims to have found a residual 'tartan tight-fistedness' which made him think of an Aberdonian as one who would extract a halfpenny from a dunghill with his teeth.

AEOLIAN HARPS
'Delicious Surges'

'A sound-box with strings tuned in unison, sounding harmonics in a current of air.' This source of celestial Muzak, a great plaything of the Romantic poets, was revived as a minor cult in the 1960s, when the instruments could be bought in London for £30. The cult soon died, perhaps because an Aeolian harp calls for a sharpish draught from an open window, perhaps because our sensibilities have become blunted, and perhaps (as some say) because it was never a very good idea.

Sir Edward Elgar had an Aeolian harp, which on a not-too-breezy day he professed to find soothing. As Coleridge could have told him, much depended on the strength of the wind. A stiff gust could produce shrill discords, giving way to more amiable strains as the wind abated and ending in little more than a sigh. The sound of a Lakeland gale attacking Coleridge's Aeolian harp, 'placed length-ways in the clasping casement', struck him as devilish to a degree.

'Mad Lutanist!' he cries in his poem 'Dejection'; but in another poem, written in calmer conditions, he praises 'the long sequacious notes' which 'over delicious surges sink and rise'. The Romantics fell over each other to praise the 'harp of the winds' and raided its performance for metaphors; Schiller, for instance, thought that Hope and Fear could set woman trembling like an Aeolian harp.

The device was sometimes found twanging away in noblemen's parks. For good service it had to be kept tuned. A do-it-yourself enthusiast could construct a serviceable instrument without too much difficulty; alternatively, any reliable harp-maker could run one up. The usual number of strings was six or eight, but Anna Seward, 'the Swan of Lichfield', had one with twenty-two. It was modelled on a harp she had seen, in 1795, in the Gothic cottage of the 'Ladies of Llangollen', two well-born eremites who lived in a state of what Miss Seward calls Davidean friendship. The Llangollen harp had given Madame de Genlis a stimulating night – 'it was not music but an indistinct and celestial harmony which penetrated my soul ... I listened with transport.' According to Miss Seward, the multi-string harp by far 'transcended, both in quantity and quality, the general order of this airy instrument'.

Through the Victorian age the Aeolian harp gradually went out of favour, though it still turned up in unlikely places, as on the verandahs of Jamaica and attached to hurtling cars in fairgrounds.

The word Aeolian remained in currency. It was used by a leading manufacturer of player-pianos, in which an artificial wind was directed at the perforations on moving music-rolls.

AIRGUNS
'Boy, That's A Daisy!'

It is an education to sit down with a copy of today's *Airgun World*, that prosperous-looking magazine which caters for 'airgun nuts' – young men with blackened faces, wearing stormtrooper motley, who use wicked-looking weapons with silencers and light-capturing telescopic sights to shoot sitting vermin. The advertisements stress that 'all weapons are as powerful as legally permitted.' One of them features a 'limited edition' of the centenary BSA air rifle, marketed in 1982.

The BSA air rifle! That was the prize for which we pined in vain, a weapon with a vaunted muzzle velocity of 530 feet per second. Instead, we saved up for the much-advertised, seven-and-sixpenny Daisy airgun, without which the pangs of puberty would have been insupportable. Whatever its shortcomings, the Daisy was a great leap forward from the water-pistol, which in turn had been a gratifying advance on the pea-shooter and the home-made potato gun (discharging sections of potato or turnip through a quill).

The Daisy was a weapon of American origin, its rather silly name being blameable on a manufacturer who exclaimed to the inventor, 'Boy, that's a daisy!' It was spring-operated and fired the usual range of hollow slugs, ball shot or tufted darts. One of its defects was that the trigger-piece became worn and if it was not fired within a few seconds of being cocked and loaded it would go off of its own accord, which gave an extra dimension of excitement. During the German invasion scares before 1914 the makers commended the Daisy to parents as a means of training sons to defend the home. Unlike the Lord Roberts air pistol advertised in *The Gem* it was never held out as capable of killing 'one hundred birds or rabbits at a cost of ninepence only'.

The 'airgun misuse' which is occasionally deprecated in *Airgun World* certainly flourished among us. Weathercocks and chimney-pots were among the inanimate targets. In *The Buried Day* Cecil Day-Lewis describes how he and Nicholas Llewellyn-Davies – one of 'Barrie's boys' – used to pepper pedestrians with an airgun from an attic of Barrie's house in Campden Hill Square, London.

Perhaps it is no excuse to plead that 'airgun misuse' used to flourish in the Pavilion at Brighton in the Prince Regent's day. The Prince encouraged his guests to practise in the map-room, but Lady Downshire succeeded in hitting a fiddler in the dining-room. Some years later the Prince was potted by airguns as he rode through London, by which time he was an unmissable target.

APACHE DANCES
Echo Of The Guillotine

One of the odder *divertissements* on the stage in the years between the wars was the Apache Dance. The setting was a low café of the Montmartre type. The male dancer, a lean, mean brute with side-whiskers, a knife in his red sash and a handkerchief round his neck, yanked his female partner from the table where she had been sulking in her slit black skirt and striped jumper. He then began to cuff her about the stage, pulling her hair and variously abusing her until finally he threw her in a heap on the floor, abject if not unconscious. This unchivalrous performance must have appealed to something deep-seated in British audiences, whose applause was never grudged. Occasionally it was the woman who threw the man about, but nobody in those days wanted to see a man kicked in the groin. The cult of the *apache* even extended to the wearing of *apache* hats by women, *très chic, très féroce*.

Today many would be hard-stretched to define an *apache*, other than the Red Indian kind. The *apaches* who horrified tourists in Paris

early this century were ruffians of a particularly debased stamp, for whom the guillotine was kept sharp and poised. They lived by robbery and murder, their special target being policemen; but they also fought among themselves, duelling with knives in the street (the nearest approach to a real-life *apache* dance). Among their weapons were spiked leather wrist-guards akin to those worn by Bank Holiday roughs today. From time to time police with savage dogs conducted raids on public parks and old fortifications where *apaches* lurked, flushing them out like wild animals. The dogs were normally muzzled, but in Brussels, which also had its *apaches*, it was apparently the custom to unmuzzle them when in hot pursuit. In France it sometimes happened that an *apache* was half-lynched by the crowd; one victim facing this fate cried out that he was Oscar Wilde.

Apaches had a sharp warning when, in 1909, four murderers' heads rolled in quick succession into the guillotine basket outside Bethune Gaol. The crowd howled and cheered as the bodies were taken away to Lille for dissection. But even *apaches* had their defenders. The editor of *La Guerre Sociale* was gaoled for four years for glorifying the murder of a policeman by the *apache* Liaboeuf; and when Liaboeuf was executed in 1910 the editorial staff of *La Guerre Sociale* trooped to La Santé prison with a wreath hailing him as '*victime des Apaches des Moeurs*'. The French Army was unhappy about the admission of hundreds of *apaches* into its frontier regiments. Conceivably, there are bones of *apaches* in the great ossuary at Verdun.

ASPIDISTRAS
Cast-Iron Splendour

'**O**ften regarded as a symbol of dull, middle-class respectability', as the dictionary says, the aspidistra – once Britain's favourite pot plant – made its way without help from an Aspidistra Marketing Board.

John Damper Parks brought back the first aspidistra from China in the early 1820s. As it was found to thrive on cold, thirst, exhausted soil, smoke, dust, musty air and sneers it became known as the cast-iron plant; none of which reflects much credit on the middle classes whose parlour emblem it became. The more humane householders wiped its leaves tenderly and whispered encouragement. In *Sorrell and Son*, the best-selling novel of the 1920s by Warwick Deeping, the demobbed Captain Sorrell MC got a job as a handyman in the Angel Inn at Staunton where 'a cynical slovenliness prevailed . . . a sly filthiness', yet even in this slum it was the custom to wash down the aspidistras in the yard, a task possibly invented for Sorrell to bring home to him his degraded state.

The mockery of aspidistras received a fillip when George Orwell published his novel *Keep The Aspidistra Flying* in 1936. Its anti-hero, a poetry-writing bookshop assistant, tries to kill off his landlady's aspidistra, epitomising as it does everything he loathes, but after severe tribulations sells his soul to an advertising agency, recognises the aspidistra as 'the tree of life' and, in a far-fetched final scene, seeks to bring one into the house over his young bride's pregnant body.

Gracie Fields made a hit with her song 'The Biggest Aspidistra in the World', a title later used, rather mysteriously, by Peter Black for his history of the BBC. The motto of the Royal Air Force was sometimes perverted by wags into *Per ardua ad aspidistra*. But ridicule could never stop readers of old-fashioned women's magazines from writing in to boast of the number of leaves borne by their aspidistras. The *Guinness Book of Records* says the biggest aspidistra in Britain was grown by Gertie James in Staveley, Chesterfield: 50 inches tall, spanning five feet and bearing more than 500 leaves.

Today pot plants have become vastly more varied and sophisticated, but we really should keep the aspidistra flying, if only to atone for all those generations of neglect. When, incidentally, will a travel writer come back from China, or the Himalayas, enthusing about the limitless vistas of aspidistras?

AUDIPHONES
And Conversation Tubes

The ear trumpet was supposed to funnel sounds to the ear, but (as Evelyn Waugh discovered in a court of law) it was none too efficient. An alternative aid to hearing, in the early years of this century, was the Audiphone, which transmitted sound through the teeth. It consisted of a curved vulcanite sound-concentrator attached to a mouth-piece. 'The instrument,' said the instructions, 'may be used at the side of the mouth, thus displaying it, and rendering it unnecessary to remove the Audiphone while speaking.'

There were also conversation tubes, with one end to fit the ear and the other end for passing to one's neighbour at dinner (or even to one's next neighbour but one). In an age noted for bizarre dinner-table equipment there was a peculiarly fashioned 'receiver', placed at the centre of the table, which was supposed to draw in sound and redistribute it to the hard-of-hearing through conversation tubes running under the table cloth. Alas, one never reads of it in accounts of life with the great hostesses.

AUNT SALLIES
For Fun And Exercise

An Aunt Sally is now no more than a metaphor for an unpopular institution, or politician. What we have forgotten is that it used to be a wooden, black-faced figure of an old woman with a pipe in her mouth, set up in a fairground, and the idea was to hurl short heavy sticks and knock the pipe from between her lips. There is an excellent model of an Aunt Sally in the Bethnal Green Museum of Childhood, along with an extract from a Victorian manual extolling the sport as an athletic exercise. 'Though there is really nothing in the game,' we are told, 'the players contrive to get a considerable amount of fun and merriment out of it . . . and cannot fail to gain health in the exercise.' The idea of hurling sticks at an old woman did not seem to worry anyone; she had a black face, anyway.

BIBLE IN SHORTHAND
Onward And Upward With Pitman

Who were the young men and women who sat down nightly to wrestle with that formidable work, *The Holy Bible in Pitman's Shorthand*? If one was pledged to read a chapter of the Bible every day there was something to be said for learning a trade at the same time. Yet, if the Lord God was a jealous God, would He not resent the fact that He was receiving divided attention? Would He not grow exceeding wrath that His word was being downgraded to a mere learning aid?

Most young women who learned shorthand did so in classes run by ladies with names like Miss Jellaby or Mrs Horsfall. Discipline was said to be strict, but it is unlikely to have been reinforced by a crash course of devotional grammalogues. Almost the only young men who learned shorthand were aspiring to be reporters and they were the least likely to be found brushing up their skills on the Scriptures. Yet one likes to think there were clerks in the mould of Mr Pooter who, having zealously learned shorthand the scriptural way, in later life yielded to the temptation of conducting family prayers with the Pitman Bible, partly to keep their hands in, partly to impress their offspring (and the servants) with their virtuosity. One sees Mr Pooter setting out confidently to read the lesson and, after a buoyant start, becoming slowly trapped in a sequence of names like Aholibamah and Jeush, yet snappishly rejecting any attempt by someone with an ordinary Bible to prompt him ('I am managing perfectly well, my dear fellow, thank you').

Sir Isaac Pitman was not the first to put the Bible into shorthand. As a boy Daniel Defoe helped his 'honest but over-frighted' elders to accomplish this task, so that if popery triumphed they would still retain an uncorrupted text. But whereas Defoe gave up after transcribing the Pentateuch, Pitman worked through the entire Bible more than once. He also published a special version of the 'Song of Solomon' and a *Pitman Book of Psalms*, which one likes to think were used at Pitman rallies and reunions – the sort of function at which the faithful bought those £2 busts of the Great Stenographer, in white Parian marble, sculpted by the Royal Academician, Thomas Brock.

Pitman also transcribed into his system *Paradise Lost*, *Pilgrim's Progress*, and *Robinson Crusoe*; and, for good measure, tales about Sherlock Holmes and Jeeves. In 1953 clerks may have fallen about on the Clapham omnibus reading the shorthand version of *Three Men In A Boat*, published that year. Jerome could have written a pretty fancy on the subject.

How very agreeable it must have been, at a literary party, when fellow writers were boasting about being published in Braille, or about having sold half-a-dozen passages for use on eye-testing cards, to mention that one had just disposed of first British and Commonwealth shorthand rights.

BICYCLING
(1) The Step – And All That

One of the arresting sights of childhood was an old gentleman mounting a bicycle. He did so by surprising it from the rear, with the aid of a device now obsolete, if not illegal: a step. This was a short cylindrical projection which took the place of the left-hand rear hub nut. Standing behind the machine, with his outstretched arms gripping the handlebars, the rider made a short run, placed his left foot on the step and then lifted his body forward until in a position to subside not ungracefully on to the saddle. One slip, and the injury to the rider's pelvic region, and to his self-esteem, would have been extremely painful, but these old gentlemen knew what they were doing. This was how bicycles, notably the penny-farthing, had always been mastered.

Boys also had steps on their cycles, but they used the fitting in a way never intended; that is, by allowing a passenger to stand on it, with his hands clutching the rider's shoulders. It was a precarious form of progress and for that reason discouraged.

Some cycles had no free-wheel, which meant that the pedals revolved constantly, even when going downhill. The trick then was to raise the feet to the rests provided and let the pedals get on with it, recovering them only when momentum slowed, as explained in a much-quoted but indifferent poem by Canon H. C. Beeching called 'On Going Down Hill On A Bicycle'. It was decidedly not the way to descend steep hills, since panic-stricken attempts to recapture the pedals in order to decrease speed could produce heavy bruising. However, fixed-wheel cycles were preferred by many seasoned men of the road, who claimed that, properly ridden, they gave more control, more exercise and enabled faster speeds to be maintained. Such riders could afford to laugh when they saw the owner of a free-wheel cycle pedalling furiously to no effect, the ratchets in the device having stuck – a defect sometimes cured by dipping the back wheel in a friendly river.

Some of us had cycles with a back-pressure brake, operated by reversing the direction of the pedals. Others had two-speed or three-speed gears, which the rest greatly envied while jeering at such devices as mindless foppery. As it was, we were reduced to climbing hills by tacking to and fro, with the worn chain creaking in protest, mocked by posters which showed girl cyclists effortlessly floating uphill into sunlit uplands (as described in Jerome K. Jerome's *Three Men On The Bummel*). There was a theory that the sign 'This Hill Is Dangerous To Cyclists' should have been erected at the foot of an ascent, to deter riders from straining their hearts while trying to mount it.

Another way of ascending a hill was to cling with one hand to the rear corner of a lorry, a parasitic habit which many cyclists adopted even on the level. Lorry drivers took no more kindly to this practice than did cab drivers when they became aware, usually from cries of 'Whip behind!', that boys were riding on the rear.

Cycles were much abused by their owners, some of whom liked to strip off superfluous items like mudguards and brakes, preferring to slow with a foot against the front tyre. Cycles were also stripped in order to facilitate such acrobatic feats as the Simple Standstill (setting the front wheel at an angle and then balancing the machine by rocking the wheel back and to with the feet); the Wheel Stand (standing on the front wheel, set at an angle, and rocking it as required); and the spectacular Flying Angel (hands on handlebars, one knee on the saddle, the other raised high in the air). For really advanced stunts, as performed in music halls, a cycle might be fitted with four steps, two to each wheel.

Fancy feats often led to buckled wheels, which made riding a peculiar agony. Roy Hattersley has told how his father rode twenty miles to work with a bent wheel which caused him to travel in two dimensions all the way. Most wheels, if not riders, would have disintegrated under this treatment.

Bicycles spent much time upended on their saddles, the position for adjusting chains and mending punctures. All but the worst tyre gashes yielded to the famous John Bull Puncture Repair Kit, replete with assorted patches, sulphur sticks and french chalk (a pop group called itself the John Bull Puncture Repair Kit). Had we known it, the upended position of the cycle was the one recommended by a French military writer to cyclist troops faced with a cavalry charge. Rapid revolution of the wheels, he wrote, would frighten the horses, the more so if bright sunlight glinted on the spokes. As a back-up defence a few cycles were to be laid flat in the path of the attack so that the horses' feet would be trapped.

25

The idea of cyclists hanging on to motor vehicles was at one time encouraged by the British Army. For safety reasons, saluting from the saddle was forbidden. Another regulation said that an officer's sword was to be kept strapped to the machine until the time came to use it.

BICYCLING
(2) The 'Kuklos' Way

In the 1920s the bicycle began to be slimmed down and the size of the frame and wheels reduced, so that the rider had no need to keep dismounting in traffic and could simply use one foot as a support. He could mount by holding it still and throwing one leg over it.

A strong-minded advocate of these simplicities was the cycling correspondent of the *Daily News*, Fitzwater Wray, who wrote as 'Kuklos' (Greek for wheel). His column was a great refreshment and so was his *Kuklos Annual*. For the women's swoop-frame cycle he had great contempt; it was unstable and ten pounds heavier than the male model. He saw no need for elaborate dress guards and gear cases, since skirts no longer reached the working parts. Cheap gear cases particularly annoyed him – 'laced-up things of bad leather and celluloid are worse than useless.' They were supposed to hold oil but leaked it when the machine was upended for repairs. Only bad chains, he maintained, needed coddling in oil baths.

Women, in his view, ought to wear decent breeches to cycle and he had a style designed for them. If they were ashamed of their legs they should stay at home. He would have admired the lazy grace with which trousered Chinese girls ride today, though he would have been horrified at the sight of their high old-fashioned machines, complete with chain-cases.

On the subject of saddles, 'Kuklos' was endlessly helpful. Cyclists were not to give up riding just because they had undergone serious operations. 'After a clean and successful excision of the prostate, cycling may be resumed if a saddle is used with a central slot or opening along its full length,' said the *Kuklos Annual*, which then

26

proceeded: '*Fistula in ano*. After a thorough operation by incision and if the wound is completely healed and dry, cycling may be resumed on a dry and soft saddle which has the slot described.' The saddle sounds very like the one mentioned in *Three Men on the Bummel*. This was 'constructed on anatomical principles' and divided to resemble a pair of kidneys, so that 'every time you went over a stone or a rut it nipped you; it was like riding on an irritable lobster.'

When it came to touring, 'Kuklos' was all for travelling light. 'A shirt is good for a week, even when worn day and night,' he pronounced; a view also held, if memory is correct, by the Army in World War Two. A damp bed could be detected by slipping a mirror between the sheets to see whether it misted (pocket hygrometers were once marketed for this purpose). Nobody, 'Kuklos' thought, ought to pay more than six shillings a night for bed and breakfast. The more usual rate was five shillings, but going below that carried the risk, as one well remembers, of finding someone else in the bed in the morning (in those days doubling up was not thought to be reprehensible). Temperance hotels were plentiful and 'Kuklos' recommended them, though not so heartily as did one's parents. In some Commercial Rooms the members might object to cyclists (something to do with shirts, perhaps?), but as 'Kuklos' said, a courteous word would always put things right.

What 'Kuklos' could never forget was a cycle marketing racket which apparently flourished just before World War One. Cheap machines were specially manufactured to be advertised in local newspapers with baits like 'Must sell: urgent, officer ordered abroad (Alexandria)'; or the excuse might be 'professional, engaged for Tropics' or 'bought Daimler car'. Circulars were distributed in order to try to induce people to take two or three bicycles into their homes while advertisements were put in their local paper. 'All you have to do is just show them to callers and sell them and then send the cash on to us by Postal Order. We will allow you five shillings on every machine sold. We shall then send others in their place and so on throughout the season. In this way you will sell about 100 machines.'

There must have been many worse rackets. It all seems like a great deal of work and risk for very small profits.

BIMBASHIS
Strong, Silent, Extinct

Nostalgia for Empire will be muted, perhaps cravenly so, in these pages. There will be no regrets for Empire Day, or for the map of the world that was three-parts red, or for the men who played the Great Game, or even for the District Officer. Let us, however, shed a sigh for an unsung figure in the ranks of strong, silent men who were to be found, as Maugham put it, 'everywhere that is a long way off': namely, the *bimbashi* – the British *bimbashi* – who held the peace on the River Nile. It is something to have met and shaken hands with this military hybrid, before he became extinct.

Young Britons acquired this rank by being seconded to the Egyptian Army, like the fag Wake in *Stalky and Co.* The word was a Turkish one, a left-over from Ottoman rule, and a *bimbashi* was supposed to be the lord of a thousand men. Gladstone held the rank in low esteem, denouncing *bimbashis* as the agents of atrocities visited on the Bulgarians. When the Sudan Defence Force was founded in 1924 British *bimbashis* were attached to it, as 'senior majors'. They were still to be seen in the 1950s, on the parade-grounds of Khartoum, sun-helmeted, with a crown and pip on their shoulders. *Bimbashis* could also be found serving in splendid isolation for up to six months at a time, in wild regions like Equatoria and Kordofan. The rank was highly anachronistic by then, but it was a great *Boy's Own Paper*-and-*Blackwoods* sort of job. With 'sudanisation' it vanished.

The ranks above *bimbashi* were *kaimakam* (lieutenant-colonel) and *miralai* (colonel). That very funny novel, *A Time To Laugh*, by Laurence Thompson, in which the Sudan Defence Force is lightly disguised as the Buna Defence Force, opens with this sentence: 'El Miralai Masterson Bey, called the Elephant Strangler, came to Loweyn in the cool of the evening, having been chased up a tree by a lion.' 'El' as a prefix and 'Bey' as a suffix looked very splendid in daily orders. One of Thompson's *bimbashis* is a 'Gabardine swine' from Cairo, another a keen Eighth Army man. It is sad to read that there were *bimbashis* from Warrington and Surbiton who would rather have remained British Army subalterns and served where there were fewer flies.

28

BIRD-NESTING
'Leave The Bird A Stone'

Nowadays those who write autobiographies rarely admit to having gone bird-nesting in youth; they would be as likely to confess to ratting or cat-skinning. It is one of many boyish pastimes which are now illegal. As the Royal Society for the Protection of Birds says: 'The taking of just one egg of a common bird such as a blackbird or robin could result in a fine of £50.' The practice, says the Society, 'is rather pointless and selfish', and the thing to do is to *watch* birds. Try telling anglers to watch fish.

We junior oologists rather prided ourselves on our humanity, enshrined in the rule that only one egg was to be taken from any one nest. We had it on good authority that birds could not count, but were ready to concede that even the dimmest mother bird would notice the difference between four eggs and one, which was why we never left her with just a singleton. One school of thought held that it was all right to take the last egg and substitute a marble. Certainly we felt superior to an earlier generation of boys who took not only eggs

29

but birds as well, setting themselves up as foster parents to fledglings. Village boys would provide 'live' nests for a fee. Anyone could buy clap nets, nooses, springes or trammels, and bird lime was advertised in *Cage Birds*, 'guaranteed to hold a pigeon; money back if not satisfied.'

There were manuals on the art of bird-nesting, laying down that 'rational curiosity' or 'the rational intention of making a collection' excused almost anything; really serious collectors were entitled to take an entire clutch of eggs, because clutches often had peculiarities of their own. 'Try to be kind-hearted boys and with God's blessing you will become merciful men,' wrote a clergyman, one of the school who thought it callous to remove eggs without substituting stones.

Aids to bird-nesting were advertised in the Army and Navy Stores catalogue. The issue for 1915 depicts spiked climbing irons; egg drills, with plain or 'rosed' points; blow-pipes, in brass or glass; egg-lifters, or 'oologists' forceps'; and grand multi-drawered egg cabinets. Only very vulgar collectors threaded their eggs on a string.

Blowing eggs was a tense and often frustrating operation. 'Don't teach your grandmother to suck eggs' ran the puzzling adage; it should have been 'Don't teach your grandfather to blow eggs', because the older male generation had all the know-how. Blowing was performed by making tiny holes at each end of the egg with a needle, which was then used to stir the contents. With the lips against the smaller hole, one blew gently, and then hard. Slowly a tiny lucent blob would emerge; then, with luck, out would plop the entire contents. This was done over a bowl of water, in case the egg was dropped. Eggs could also be emptied through a single hole amid-ships, sucking with a straw or blow-pipe.

The trouble came with 'hard-set' eggs or eggs which were half-way to becoming a chick (these floated in water, whereas fresh eggs sank). Often all thoughts of further blowing had to be abandoned, with suitable shudders. However, those in possession of minute forceps would extract even the most advanced embryo piecemeal. It was no use trying to blow plovers' eggs bought in the local market, because they were hard-boiled. (In *Hansard* for 4 December 1953 one may read of a dealer who sold up to 25,000 plovers' eggs in a year, mostly to children at sixpence; a statistic extremely hard to believe.)

As every ex-predator will admit if he is honest, bird-nesting was a pastime of strong excitements, not without a whiff of danger. Pluck was needed to climb an elm and slither down with an egg in the mouth, which was the safest way of carrying it, though an addled egg bursting on the tongue was a fearful punishment. Every season boys had to be rescued from cliff faces as they tried to emulate those much-written-up Flamborough Head heroes who dangled on ropes high above rock-fanged waters, angrily buzzed by the birds whose eggs they snatched as soon as they were laid. Rational curiosity drove us into swamps and ragwort jungles, as well as into barns, tunnels, culverts and graveyards. There were routine, though never serious, clashes with farmers, owners of shrubberies and old ladies (whose cats mangled more nests than boys did). Mostly the game of wits was between boy and bird, with many a bird winning on points; there were thrushes which 'sat close' on the nest and faced out an intruder only a foot away.

It was a rare sensual pleasure to reach up and over the edge of a nest and delicately count the warm eggs with the finger tips. In theory one could always count the eggs with a mirror fastened to a stick, but that was not easy in practice. No device could enable one to count eggs in holes and crevices, though there were dubious wire contraptions for lifting out unseen eggs. Rookeries posed the hardest problem: how did anyone ever obtain a rook's egg from the high-swinging tree-tops? Another dream, never realised, was to find a cuckoo's egg. Yet the BBC's 'Birdman', Henry Douglas-Home, tells in his autobiography how a cuckoo obligingly laid its egg every year in a sparrow's nest under a balustrade of the ancestral home. The Birdman admits he used to feast on magpies' eggs, 'as delicious as a plover's' (he was a bird-*watcher*, but magpies had to be kept down). Somehow he had all the luck. Probably he used to come across girls trying to hatch eggs in their bosoms, like that minx in Hardy's *Jude the Obscure*.

In 1953 Parliament discussed bird-nesting, which Lady Tweedsmuir described as 'not only a most exciting pleasure, but one which gives a lasting interest in wild life' (she had her own collection, complete with ostrich egg). Their lordships said they would hate to see bird-nesting made a criminal offence, but a criminal offence it now is. It is even a criminal offence to sell a collection of birds' eggs without a licence from the Department of the Environment. In 1979 the Women's Voluntary Services were warned not to dispose of birds' eggs at jumble sales.

31

BLACK ASCOT
The Elegance Of Gloom

A h, if only one could have been a spectator at Black Ascot! Was it the silliest social function of the century, or a superb *concours d'élégance*? Or both?

King Edward VII had died in May 1910, a date uncomfortably close to Ascot Week but not so close as to warrant calling off the meeting. The Turf had its own imperatives, as the late King would have recognised. Clearly the Royal Family could not attend, so the royal stand was left empty with blinds drawn. All round, in the paddock and royal enclosure, surged Society in the blackest of finery. Women wore giant cartwheel hats decked with black plumes, big puffs of black tulle or black sheaves of corn and barley. Some had white or mauve flowers tucked in at the waist and one daringly sported a large horseshoe of orchids on her corsage. Gentlemen in the Royal Enclosure wore black frock coats or morning coats with very dark trousers, tall hats with mourning bands and black suede gloves. Black was almost universally worn, too, by the coach parties reverently picking the winners from a race-card edged in black.

The *Daily Mail* said it was the gloomiest race meeting ever seen; even the result of the Royal Hunt Cup was received in mournful silence. However, a lady commentator in *The Tatler* thought the feminine crowd had never looked more elegant. 'There is no doubt,' she wrote, 'that English women seldom appear to greater advantage than in sombre attire, though it is extremely rare that they can ever be forced to dress themselves in anything but garish colours and an overabundance of garish trimmings. Their complexion being generally the most noticeable part of their renowned beauty, it certainly never shows itself off half so well as when framed in black or dark shades. Thus it was that the paddock and the enclosure looked smarter than it has done for years . . .'

A correspondent of *The Graphic* also thought that mourning did much to save Englishwomen from the worst excesses. However, other commentators found the scene impossibly sombre, even with so many women wearing ear-rings, necklaces and brooches. A common complaint was that it was impossible to locate one's friends, since everyone looked alike. One lady informed *The Tatler* that this was not necessarily a disadvantage. 'I like black,' she said, 'because I can always say afterwards to anybody I don't want to be bothered with, "I was looking for you everywhere, but of course it was imposs-ible to find you." '

The gossips noted that ministers and ambassadors had stayed away, as had intimates of the Throne, but the top strata of the nobility were by no means unrepresented. The Turf ranked with the Opera as a legitimate recreation in times of grief. In fact the opera at Covent Garden was enjoying a boom since, as *The Tatler* said, 'to listen to music may be compatible with the severest grief when to watch a comedian might be considered bad taste.' Evidently, to back horses was also compatible with the severest grief.

A woman diarist in the *Illustrated London News* noted that the ear-rings were shorter at the racecourse than at the opera; these 'swinging censers of light', as somebody had called them, shed a welcome radiance beside that famous English complexion.

Whether a tasteful black outfit, with ear-rings, would have flattered the brides of that mournful Spring we cannot know, since the new King had directed that he did not expect mourning to be observed at weddings.

BLACK BORDERS
Grief From The Press

A newspaper in mourning is an uncomfortable and faintly comical sight. By now there is an adult generation which has never seen *The Times* with its columns confined in black borders to mark the death of a sovereign.

How the tradition of putting the press into 'weepers' began is hard to discover. The thick borders are created simply by reversing the rules which divide the columns, so that a broader surface takes the ink. The result affords solemnity of a sort, but does not help legibility.

The first opportunity presented to *The Times* to honour a monarch in this manner was when George III died. Mad he might have been, but if soldiers were to reverse arms in his honour, why should not journalists reverse whatever they had to hand? The edition of 31

January 1820 was deeply grief-stricken, with a black grid-work on each page and a particularly thick outer border. All the issues until 17 February, by which time the King was buried, were printed in the same fashion. When George IV died a similar procedure was followed. The parade of grief did not prevent the leader-writer, in the first issue after the King's death, chastising him for his sins, deploring his debts, mocking his women and reviling his taste in architecture ('tawdry childishness of Carlton House . . . mountebank Pavilion'). William IV was accorded non-stop black-bordered issues until he was buried, but when Queen Victoria died the black borders were reserved for the issue containing the initial announcement and then suspended until the lying-in-state and funeral. Substantially the same system was followed for Edward VII and the last two Georges.

Only royalty qualified as of right for these sombre attentions. When the Duke of Wellington died one small announcement announcing the fact appeared in a thick black border on the main news page, and the front and back pages on the day of the funeral were black-bordered. Tennyson received no black lines in *The Times*, nor did Churchill, though the Churchill coverage eclipsed almost anything ever given to royalty.

The popular papers have always made their own mourning rules. Whether, when the occasion next arises, the tabloids will run black rivulets round their frivolities and indecencies is something we must wait, preferably a long time, to see.

BONA FIDE TRAVEL
'Where Are You From?'

Everyone will remember the discomfiture of Mr Pooter when, with three companions, he called for refreshment at the 'Cow and Hedge' after a long Sunday walk in the Hampstead area. A man on duty at the public-house raised his arm and asked him, 'Where from?' On his replying 'Holloway' he was refused admission. Stillbrook, one of his companions, was asked the same question and boldy replied 'Blackheath', thus establishing himself as a *bona fide* traveller entitled to a drink on a Sunday. So Stillbrook and the two others went into the 'Cow and Hedge' for brandies, while the honest Pooter sulked outside.

That system vanished in England in 1923 but continued in Scotland. The object of the law was a quite simple one: to put difficulties in the way of Sunday drinking. A *bona fide* traveller was one whose lodging-place during the preceding night was at least three miles from the place where he demanded to be served with liquor, such distance being calculated by the nearest public thoroughfare. All this restriction did was to encourage the nation to lie and cheat on a heroic scale. Critics never tired of producing anomalies. A party of climbers might set off from an inn at Fort William to climb Ben Nevis. On their return they would be refused refreshment because they were not *bona fide* travellers; yet a party who had travelled by charabanc from a few miles away would be entitled to anything they wanted. A *Punch* drawing had a variation on this theme: 'Landlady: Hae ye been travellin' by rell? – No, I have been walking – 14 miles. – Na, na, nae drink will ony yin get here who's been pleesure-seekin' on the Sawbath.' James Cameron has described (in the Angus McGill anthology, *Pub*) how the system caused a Sunday interchange of populations between the adjacent townships of Forfar and Kirriemuir. One Sunday, in the early 1950s, the globe-trotting Cameron was refused a drink in a station hotel in Glasgow, despite a plea that he had just returned from Korea via Japan and India.

The *bona fide* traveller had such companions in humbug as the *bona fide* hotel resident and his *bona fide* guests (for whose drinks the 'resident' paid, having earlier collected the money from them). There were also *bona fide* members of recreational clubs, which opened when the pubs closed, notably in Wales. Those Welshmen who did not care to drink in such clubs went on charabanc trips – to beauty-spots in England.

'BOY WANTED'
(1) Smudging The Letters

Telegraph boys, in jaunty pill-box caps, riding red bicycles, have now passed into history, along with chimney boys and link boys. They were part of a grand army of boys who, earlier this century, were hired to lick stamps, to hold reins, to 'ride tiger' on carriages, to knock on doors for old ladies, to sweep the roads, to polish shoes, to shout sensational news through the suburbs, to lather chins, to blow bugles on liners, to scour pots and spittoons, to whack bullocks and to scare birds. The 'wanted' advertisements called for 'Boy (presentable)', 'Boy (intelligent)', 'Boy (well-educated)' and 'Boy (strong)'. On the whole it was a cheerful, willing army and if it was also a cheeky one the skinflints who exploited it deserved all they got.

The biggest division in this grand army was made up of office boys, now a much-dwindled species, thanks to mechanisation and the preference of management for having young girls about the place. In the big commercial cities the office boy at fourteen sometimes wore the bowler hat and dark suit that would be his uniform for life. His duties were to fill the ink pots, answer bells, work the telephone switchboard, keep the letter register and copy the newly-typed letters on to moist flimsy with the aid of a heavy mechanical press. This process imparted smudgy edges to the typescript, as if it had been left out in the rain, and sometimes letters had to be re-typed, or even re-handwritten. Typists, who held office boys in great scorn, complained that their letters were ruined out of sheer incompetence, if not malignity. Only the coming of carbon paper brought these tensions to an end.

The office boy delivered local letters to save postage, often being treated as a lazy pariah by liftmen. However, the chore gave him a chance to dawdle about the streets and meet his equals. If he hand-delivered a dozen letters a day he saved his employers the cost of his wages, and they could hardly complain if he frittered away the rest of the day, though complain they did. As a popular butt the office boy ranked almost with the seaside landlady: a freckled, snub-nosed, inky imp for ever begging time off to attend his grandmother's funeral. The comics which were said to be his staple reading often ran a mis-spelled feature with a heading like 'Our Offiz Boy's Dairy', or failing that the editor's own diary would be eked out with jokes about Our 'Orace or the Wily Wilfrid.

The office boy had a powerful friend in H. G. Wells, who made him a hero of his novel *The Dream* (1924). This features a firm of publishers which churns out rubbish for the illiterate and finds that promoted office boys are the best judge of what the market will bear. (Edward Lloyd, the Victorian publisher of 'penny dreadfuls', reputedly tried out doubtful manuscripts on the office boys.) University men, as Wells took great pleasure in explaining, were useless at the job, lacking enthusiasm, boldness and a desire to know things and impart things. One of the firm's spokesmen says: 'On the one hand were these office boy fellows, with an intellectual courage and vigour – oh! of Aristotle and Plato, whatever the quality of their intellectual equipment might be; on the other, the academic man, affectedly Grecian, like the bought and sold learned man of Roman slavery . . .'

Lord Northcliffe was one who looked for eager young men with uncluttered minds, but he was not amused when Lord Salisbury described the *Daily Mail* as a paper written by office boys for office boys. However that may be, newspaper offices employed dozens of boys – boys to fetch the tea for the sub-editors, boys to put the sub-edited copy in the pneumatic tubes, boys to escort visiting shoplifters who were anxious to have their court cases suppressed. In the bigger newspaper offices the foyer might boast a whole row of uniformed boy messengers, sitting like starlings on a telegraph wire, waiting for the snap of the fingers which would send them off on an outdoor errand. Their finger-nails and hair-cuts were inspected daily and they did not find this degrading. Today they have been replaced – all too often – by bitter elderly men who are determined not to be put upon.

'BOY WANTED'
(2) California Here I Come

Of boys in uniform, the most numerous were the telegraph boys. That story for young readers, *Post Haste*, by R. M. Ballantyne (see also POST HASTE) describes the adventures of Phil, a paragon of Post Office messengers, 'trained in the ways of righteousness and having the word of God as his guide', securely armed against the temptations of drink and the 'thickets of speculative philosophy'. Not all boy messengers were as strong-minded as Phil, or as capable of resisting the temptation to kick noisy objects along the street; nor were they all bright enough to become postmen or sorters. There were often rows in Parliament about the wastage among telegraph messengers turned adrift in their mid-teens.

In time of war the sight of a telegraph boy in the street was a heart-stopper. Did one tip the boy (or, later, girl) who brought the news of a son's death? Apparently one did, like H. G. Wells's Mr Britling. In time of peace there could be doorstep dramas too, but at least the messenger never had to sing his telegrams, in Western Union style. Under the rules, he might have to deliver a person; occasionally reporters would try out this service, presenting themselves as individuals to be escorted. Reporters also had the exclusive use of messengers to ferry telegrams from football and cricket matches.

In London the telegraph boy had a rival, also wearing a pill-box cap. The District Messenger Company was launched in 1890, the year of the scandal involving the male brothel in Cleveland Street, where telegraph boys were debauched by members of the nobility. The Company had aristocratic patronage of a more acceptable sort, with Gartered dukes taking an active supervisory interest in its affairs. Unfortunately the Post Office behaved badly towards the Company, trying to put it out of business on the grounds that letter-carrying infringed its monopoly, and exacting a royalty on every transaction. The public rebelled at this bullying and the Company was given a safe lease of life which carried it into the 1950s. Which did not stop the Post Office trying to duplicate many of its services.

The blue-uniformed District Messengers, whose motto was 'Swift and Sure', not only carried urgent letters, including love letters, but queued for theatre tickets, escorted old ladies, accompanied diplomats, carried babies and even led the occasional circus elephant across London. One messenger, William Jaggers, earned fame by sailing to America and delivering letters with great expedition in New York, Chicago and Philadelphia; on a later occasion he left London for California on an hour's notice.

The Company had its own call-boxes installed in hotels, railway stations, clubs and offices. By moving a pointer in the box a caller could connect electrically with the Company's head office in St Martin's Lane, to indicate that a messenger was needed.

The aristocratic patrons gave prizes and badges to the smartest messengers. In return they expected to be entertained at annual meetings with gymnastic, boxing and fife-and-drum displays. On suitable occasions church parades were held and the older lads were encouraged to join the Territorials – anything to preserve them from West End temptations and speculative philosophy. Today's dashing motor-cycle messengers, emblazoned with names like 'Pony-Express', would find the system decidedly oppressive.

Nowadays boys in pill-box hats and buttons are found, as a rule, only in very grand hotels. Yet at one time it looked as though there might be a career for the page boy in the air. When the Daimler air lines began to operate out of London in the post-1918 years, a cabin boy in buttons formed part of the crew. It was a job to swank about, even though in practice there was little to do except look brave at all times and watch the passengers being airsick. Other air liners also hired cabin boys, but a fatal crash in which a boy in buttons was killed seems to have discouraged the fashion. The 'air hostesses' did not arrive until the 1930s.

BRILLIANTINE
For A Scented Kiss

The antimacassar, as is well-known, was introduced as a defence against Rowland's Macassar Oil, that 'elegant, fragrant and pellucid' vegetable product which dominated the hair-oil market for most of the Victorian era. As the new century neared, Rowland was up against a powerful mineral rival, brilliantine, which went to (and on to) men's heads in a big way. The Edwardians had a score of

brands to choose from, including one by Atkinsons, the bear's-grease people. A sleek crown like patent leather, with a parting on the left, was now the *beau idéal*, and would remain so for another generation, even though it gave men a pin-headed, tape-worm appearance, as in the humorous drawings by Lewis Baumer. The glossy top was to be seen on monocled knuts, on the new breed of car salesmen, on matinee idols, on young men in the City and on pear-shaped philanderers in night-clubs, on cavalrymen and, in due course, Buchmanites; in short, on all who fancied themselves in the swim. That included schoolboys, who felt deep shame if their hair was the kind which refused to lie flat under a lustrous dressing. An advertisement for 'Icilma' brilliantine in *The Captain* showed a smug shiny-topped schoolboy standing beside one with a scarecrow thatch; a headmaster, cane in hand, was torn between approval of the one and detestation of the other.

Brilliantine was for 'imparting brilliance to the hair' – no nonsense about nourishing the roots or conquering dandruff. It smelled of violet, honey, almond, white lilac and even less masculine fragrances, contrasting strongly with that of the cocoanut oil favoured by down-to-earth fathers (their method was to melt the solidified oil in the palm, then rub it vigorously into the protesting child's hair and scalp). Mothers hated brilliantine and in self-defence retained the antimacassar. Brilliantine, however, was an excellent defence against the sort of young woman who liked rumpling her admirer's hair. It was possible for a girl to receive a brilliantined kiss, for the dressing came in two categories: one for the hair, one for the moustache.

As time passed brilliantine acquired a bounderish, Valentino-type image, associated over-much with jazz bandsmen and co-respondents. Other products came along, offering virtues brilliantine had never claimed. In World War Two the Royal Air Force were known as the 'Brylcreem Boys'. They used so much of the product that the manufacturers took space in the newspapers urging other people to 'go easy' with it so that our airmen should not suffer.

'BULLETS'
Bottomley's Best Idea

Few will now believe there was a time in Britain when good clean wit could fetch £1,000 a word.

Horatio Bottomley is remembered chiefly for his sins, yet it was he who, in 1912, launched in the weekly *John Bull* the literary contest known as 'Bullets'. This ran for almost sixty years and put nearly two millions into the pockets of word-jugglers (though in the very early days some of the prize money was collusively returned to the old rogue himself). All the competitors had to do was to choose a phrase from a list provided and add to it up to four words of original comment. In 1932 a reader who took the phrase 'If we want peace' and followed it with 'Let meek greet meek' was paid 4,500 guineas. In the following year a prize of 5,000 guineas was awarded for this high-minded pun: 'For Services Rendered – King "Pinned On Cross." '

At the outset easy money was to be picked up by flattering *John Bull's* editor, as with: 'Borrowed Plumes – Sermons From Bottomley's Articles'. The words 'Horatio Bottomley' were often included in the list of phrases and so were the words 'Winston Churchill'. In 1954 Odhams, who had taken over *John Bull*, issued a booklet of 167 prize-winning lines based on Churchill. A 1944 winner was: 'Round Hitler – Ashes. Round Churchill – Ash.'

In 1913 £500 went to the sender of a line which became a popular classic: 'Wedding March – Aisle Altar Hymn.' The early judges were willing to reward even such puns as 'Fee – Nominal' and 'Angus Tourer.' Over the years their tastes became more exacting, but they never baulked at extravagances of sentiment like: 'Every Morning – Let Marmalade Recall Orange-Blossom.' In 1934 £5,000 was won by: 'Peak of Success – "Happy, Mary?" "Yes, John." ' This award was not universally acclaimed; loyal subjects would probably have preferred George to John. Mild cynicism did not go unrewarded as in: 'Seldom Works – Admiring Wife's Old Hat'; or: 'Hand In Glove – If Men Wore Wedding-Rings.' But on the whole entries which extolled old-fashioned virtues were more in favour, like: 'Be A Man And – Bear Pain Like Woman.'

Right from the start a tribe of professional line-writers battened on to 'Bullets' and rival literary contests. Their tipster-like advertisements supported a succession of journals. In 1915 the *Competition Prize Winner* justified this professionalism on the grounds that competitors who lacked 'the time, ability or inclination necessary to secure the big prizes' needed solutionists to help them. This journal also argued that professionals raised the level of entries, while admitting there was 'an augean stables of duplicating solutionists'.

Professional line-writers charged their clients so much a line – anything from a penny to a shilling – and claimed twenty to twenty-five per cent of wins over £1. A man might go round boasting that he had won £500 for: 'Boarding-House Philosophy – Let Bygones Be Rissoles'; but his neighbours could always ascertain, by reference to the competition press, whether he had written it himself. That line was claimed by a solutionist of Harrow.

Many professionals listed long strings of three-figure and four-figure wins. In 1920 Miss Jane Louise, 'the lucky little lady of Deal', with five £1,000 prizes to her credit, printed as one of her prize-winning lines: 'Hard to Explain – Why Tipster Isn't Millionaire.' Why, then, did line-writers not become millionaires? All, it seems, preferred to help the struggling; none more so than King of Ilford who claimed to have won 'Bullets' £1,000 prizes three weeks running.

The professionals did not pretend that they wrote all their own lines. Continually they advertised for line-writers ('state terms per

100 lines you require') and apparently had no trouble in enlisting them. Why, then, did not the line-writers submit their own efforts? The snag was that each competitor had to send in a fee with his entry. So the curious situation arose that Smith would write a line to send to Jones who sent it to Robinson to enter as his own work (and the line might be one of those which preached the virtue of self-help). If the line was a winner the man who wrote it would expect a cut from his employer's commision.

One line-writer styled himself Professor. Another had a picture of himself wearing a mortar-board. A sporting parson charged higher rates than some for 'work emanating from a cultivated "Pelmanised" mind'. Many advertisers 'knocked' each other's claims, or boasted like patent-medicine men that their products had succeeded when those of rivals had failed. In 1927 a Birmingham solutionist with the slogan, 'The Handrail Up The Stairway Of Life', offered a Morris-Cowley car to any client who won a £1,500 first prize with one of his lines. Despite all this benevolence waiting to be tapped, some eighty per cent of entrants composed their own lines.

In the 1930s literary contests of this type were run not only in *John Bull* but in *Answers, Tit-Bits, Ideas* and various Sunday papers. Wits and philosophers had never had it so good, though there was plenty of heart-burning. For quips of apparently equal merit one man got a life pension, another a fiver. Most scandalously, a £5-winning 'Bullet' was later awarded £1,000 in *Tit-Bits*. To lessen such risks, a *Dictionary of Bullets* was sent to rival competition editors.

The judges of 'Bullets' were supposed to read all entries twice, slowly and carefully. All were members of the National Union of Journalists. According to R. J. Minney's biography of Lord Southwood, the Odhams chief, the choice of big winners was always made by Southwood himself. It was revealing of his social and religious sensibilities, says Minney, that so many winning entries were like these: 'Starving – Disgrace To All *Unconcerned*'; or: 'Not Only – "Please, God", *Please* God.'

Alan Brien once lamented on television that his many efforts at 'Bullets' were unsuccessful. Could they have been too barbed, too clever by half? Perhaps he would have done better to try reverent word play about the Master, the King, the Shepherd, the Great Sculptor, the Carpenter, the Cross, the Mount and the Book.

CELLULOID
The Popular Peril

It may seem perverse to cherish an affection for celluloid, but it was our first plastic and as such deserves its niche. Without it there would have been no ping-pong balls, no coloured balls dancing on water jets in fairgound rifle ranges. More to the point, there would have been no Mary Pickford or Charlie Chaplin.

This 'imitation ivory' as it was first called, was slow to find a market until manufacturers hit on the idea of celluloid collars and cuffs, for ladies and gentlemen alike. Those who could afford laundry bills sneered mightily; and, of course, their sneers eventually carried the day. Other uses for celluloid were to make knife handles (more sneers), piano keys (sneers again), pocket combs, bicycle handle grips, bicycle pumps and greetings cards (loud sneers). In 1912, in a Christmas card factory in Moor Lane, London, a boy accidentally dropped hot sealing wax on a package of celluloid cards, which caught fire, and eight girls lost their lives.

The inflammability of celluloid was one reason why the *Children's Newspaper* (see next entry) raged against it. Not only was it the vehicle of polluted entertainment from Hollywood but the reels caught fire and burned audiences to death. Every now and then campaigns were waged against celluloid dolls, which were burned by indignant parents in *autos-da-fé*. Yet there continued to flourish millions of cheap celluloid babies, with arms and legs held on by elastic passing through the body. Their cheeks would dent when experimentally pressed by the finger, but with care these hollows could be coaxed out again. Their eyes did not close or flirt, they did not contain 'Mama' voices (metal cylinders in which mysterious fittings dropped with a plaintive noise), but they had an indestructible power to harness affection just the same. And so had those delightful flotillas of celluloid ducks which, at bath-time, floated and bobbed in every bath in Britain (or, if leaking at the seams, sank).

Ah, celluloid!

CHILDREN'S NEWSPAPER
To Make Goodness News

The *Children's Newspaper* first appeared in 1919, a year after 'the darkest day ever known', 21 March 1918, when the German push for the Channel ports seemed unstoppable. It was launched with the sort of fanfarronade at which the Northcliffe press excelled. Parents who feared it would turn out to be a juvenile *Daily Mail* were disarmed by the knowledge that it was to be edited by Arthur Mee, begetter of the *Children's Encyclopaedia*, a 'child of wonder' who was convinced that only the dispersal of universal ignorance could bring peace, happiness, prosperity and 'an end to all evil things'. He was a railway fireman's son whose stint on the *Daily Mail* had left him sanguine and uncynical.

Probably the title of the paper was a mistake; children hate to be called children. Yet it was to run for more than forty years. Wary of parentally-approved reading-matter, the post-war generation gave it a cautious reception. Its news stories were about proposed tunnels under the Straits of Gibraltar, the prospect of talking films, the future of flying, the way Americans jacked up their towns and moved them on. It revelled in multi-deck headlines like: 'The Earth in the Ocean of Ether / Something Tremendous Going On / The Whole Universe Running Through the Ether at Twelve Thousand Miles a Second / First News to the World of a Surprising Discovery'. That second headline – 'Something Tremendous Going On' – was a typical Arthur Mee touch.

Alas, the outpourings of wonder were offset by dire 'pi-jaws' from that great sportsman, Commander C. B. Fry, who warned his 'dear mates' against 'discy imps', meaning discordant impulses, like too much laughing and loving; and from Ella Wheeler Wilcox, who regretted that chaperonage had gone out when young women first went into munitions. The second issue contained a 'Song for Children', complete with music, by Harold Begbie, with the words: 'If I want to be happy and quick on my toes, / I must bite my food slowly and breathe through my nose. / I must press back my shoulders and hold up my head / And not close my window on going to bed.' The second verse began: 'I must soap my bath flannel and scrub all I know . . . .'

If we wanted to know the words of 'Yes, We Have No Bananas' and 'Horsey, Keep Your Tail Up' we had to go elsewhere, as also for Hollywood gossip. If football was mentioned, it was liable to be coupled with the suggestion that the million people who paid £50,000 each week to watch a handful of men kick a ball about would do better to use the money to endow beds in cottage hospitals. However, the *Children's Newspaper* did print good adventure serials, often by T. C. Bridges.

'To make goodness news' was Mee's ambition, but the stuff was in short supply. The inescapable news was about famine, Bolshevism, reparations. There were reports from Bela Kun's Hungary, with headlines like: 'Doleful Cry of the Middle Classes / Peasants Buy Luxuries While the Old Rich Sell Their Beds'. If readers thought it no bad thing that high-born ladies should sell flowers in the street, for a change, they were given no chance to say so; the '*CN*' never published letters. A story from Russia was headlined; 'Storm-Tossed Nation of Europe / Russian People As They Really Are / Wonderful Land in Which a Prince May Put Your Bag on a Train / Simple Folk of the Land Ruined by the Czars'. The writer admitted it was difficult to discuss the Revolution and said: 'We will therefore leave the Revolution out – not to shrink a difficult task – but it is merely an episode in their lives as a nation, which will not alter their national character.'

One week we learned 'Why Britain Is Ruling Pharaoh's Land', the next that America was about to conquer the world by abandoning alcohol. We were urged to admire the great hunter Frederick Selous, who 'put 450,000 square miles on the map of Empire' and was 'one of the noblest men war ever took away'. We were taught to believe in 'the improvability of the Africans'. And, of course, to pray for the League of Nations.

On the industrial front Mee had to toe the Northcliffe-Rothermere line. An early issue described a ducal estate under which miserable miners toiled for a pittance. But men who struck against such conditions were urged to seek 'a nobler life by worthier means'. After the General Strike of 1926 the headlines ran: The Country's Nine-Day Wonder / Humpty-Dumpty Has a Great Fall / Common-Sense Beats the Bogey Man / Dauntless Spirit of the British People / Triumph of Law and Order'. A front-page picture of students working railway signals had the caption: 'Splendid were the volunteers from the

46

universities and public schools.' A signed report by Mee said there was no parallel to this event 'unless we think of the Civil War in Cromwell's days'. And the miners and trade unions? They had been misled and then betrayed.

It was rare to find firm proposals and specific courses of action set out in the leader column. The mechanics of doing things was not Mee's speciality. Easier by far to write things like: 'The *CN* will build up such a manhood and such a womanhood in this country as shall make it like the very gate of heaven.' If specific campaigns had to be run, Mee preferred a more modest objective; for example, he attacked the dove-shooting sportsmen of Monte Carlo, or the extension of bull-fighting in the south of France, or appealed for 'King Tut' to be left lying where he was found, or even urged people to be more careful how they carried umbrellas. He took on Lord Birkenhead, who had made mock of idealism ('And is God dead, Lord Birkenhead?'), and Professor Stephen Leacock of McGill University, who had jokingly announced that it was his laziest and worst-read pupils who appeared to be rising to eminence.

Not every week produced a heroine like the seventy-year-old Huddersfield charwoman who had insisted on paying back to the Board of Guardians the Poor Law relief given to her father and mother forty years earlier. She had washed out 'a family stain' and shown that we must all pull our weight in the world. She had also struck a blow for the honour of domestic service, which girls now thought beneath them. Girls were cuffed about the ears by the '*CN*' Doctor, who was given the usual four-decker headlines to denounce a growing evil: 'Dirty Powder Puff' / How To Be Ugly Though Young / Who Wants a Clean Complexion? / The Quick Way to a Wrinkled Face'.

The *Children's Newspaper* lasted until 1965, still believing in the improvability of the African and even more in the improvability of the children of Albion. But its final format would have shocked its founder. The title was in heavy coal-black type legible almost across the street and the contents were jazzed up. There was a 'Pop Spot' featuring a different singing group each week, but even this could not pull in the new problem generation, perhaps because the groups selected were the least rancid ones. A final editorial said there had been over 2,000 issues 'full of promise' and now, 'with promise fulfilled', it was time to bow out.

CHLOROFORM
'For Seasickness &c.'

In the 1970s gangs of robbers armed with chloroform nipped on and off the Simplon Orient Express between Paris and the Balkans, robbing passengers of their jewellery.

There was something delightfully old-fashioned about these reports. Chloroform was a word which used to send a cold ripple down the youthful spine. It was what sleek foreigners were thought to employ when kidnapping girls in cinemas for Rio de Janeiro. It was the resort of young wives who wanted to get rid of old husbands. It was what crooks like Raffles used against plucky youths who 'had a go' at gentlemen burglars (Raffles once stupefied a boy whom his friend Bunny had already half-strangled).

Henley wrote about 'the thick, sweet mystery of chloroform / The drunken dark, the little death in life'. As a legitimate anaesthetic, it had come a long way since moralists had denounced its use in childbirth, on the grounds that the Bible insisted 'in sorrow thou shalt bring forth children' and that no one for comfort's sake should be allowed to surrender the capacity for thought and reason. As an illegitimate anaesthetic, it had come an even longer way – if not in real crime, at least in the pages of popular fiction. 'One of the biggest mysteries of mystery-writing between 1920 and 1940,' writes Colin Watson in *Snobbery With Violence*, 'was the amount of chloroform assumed to be available to the general run of criminals.' Writers of the Raffles era had certainly sloshed the stuff about. When Holmes and Watson, searching for the vanished Lady Frances Carfax, tore off a coffin lid they reeled back at 'a stupefying and overpowering smell of chloroform' which enveloped the 'corpse' within; the rogues had first drenched Lady Frances with it and then topped up the coffin with the liquid. With the stuff in such prodigal supply, no wonder the National Vigilance Association warned girls never to sniff flowers offered by a stranger.

So where did the chloroform come from? The answer is very simple: it came from the chemist's and was sold in one form or another by the medicine departments of big stores. One of the prescribed uses was 'for seasickness &c.', which conjures up a pretty picture of a honeymoon couple taking turns to render each other unconscious in the Bay of Biscay. Under '&c.' was the cure of toothache; a piece of cotton wool soaked in chloroform was the thing to plug a carious tooth. The Army and Navy Stores sold killing bottles for moths and butterflies in which 'chloroform is dropped on the insect from the nozzle'. Killing bottles could not be supplied ready-charged, but 'buyers can always get them filled by any chemist to whom they are known'.

CHORUS GIRLS
'How Wonderful They Were!'

Siegfried Sassoon's furious poem 'Blighters', inspired by a night out in a war-time music-hall, refers to the ladies of the chorus as 'prancing ranks of harlots', surely an over-colourful description of a hard-working and cheerful body of young women.

To a sheltered adolescent, the first sight of a chorus line was a shining apocalypse. These ravishing bifurcated creatures from another world were the stuff of dreams – yet curiously innocent dreams. In *A Better Class of Person* John Osborne says he wanted to take each girl in *The Lilac Domino* out in turn to dinner at the Trocadero; but his stomach churned when 'huge chorus girls' came down from the stage at the London Hippodrome to dance with the audience and he was afraid he might be chosen. One fully understands his dread. Chorus girls were strictly for fantasy, for remote drooling. It would have been no help to see their war-paint in close-up, their vaccination marks or little bits of sticking plaster on their thighs. It would have been fatal to find they were just like any noisy, bouncy girls in the street or like other boys' sisters.

In the high days of musical comedy and the low days of variety between the wars, chorus girls were the show-stoppers and sometimes the show-savers. P. G. Wodehouse and Guy Bolton pay them a high tribute in *Bring on the Girls*, their reminiscences of life 'in the musical comedy salt mines'. But for the girls, they say, a hundred shows would never have crossed 'the thin line that divides the floperoo from the socko'. They go on: 'And how wonderful these girls always were. They did not spare themselves. You might get the impression that they were afflicted by some form of chorea, but the dullest eye could see that they were giving of their best.'

Yes, they had pep and the will to win, as these two shrewd observers say. The comedian's imitation of a drunk man clutching a lamp-post might (and often did) pall, but the chorus line made amends for all. Like the Guards they knew what they had to do and did it faultlessly, with panache. In the well-remembered bathing-dress scene in *No, No, Nanette* (the feast of flesh from which Queen Mary reputedly averted her eyes) all they had to do was stand still and look daring, joyous and emancipated, and this they did to such effect that they set town after town afire.

We all knew the form their dancing would take, but that hardly mattered. They would separate, while high-kicking, into small groups and then join up again, meshing perfectly; they would subside on to their hunkers and kick like Cossacks; they would encourage each other to perform contortions, like leaning over backwards and picking up a handkerchief with the teeth; they would somersault over each other like the tracks of a tractor; and they would finish up with an uproarious can-can, ending in that always alarming feat, the splits. They could also tap dance and do bucks, wings, struts, stomps, shuffles and coffee-grinders; but as everybody else, from comedian to soubrette, did a tap dance in those days this was really a waste of the girls' talents. The tap dance, so eloquently performed by Fred Astaire and Ginger Rogers, became the idiots' tattoo of the Munich years.

The man we had most to thank for the chorus line was John Tiller, a stage-struck cotton man in Lancashire whose business fortunately crashed, enabling him to concentrate on what became his life's work: putting discipline into the chorus. The show-girls of the Gaiety era had impressed him as a lackadaisical lot, with an air of 'I'm only doing this to get myself a peer.' Tiller picked out humble Lancashire girls and drilled them hard, while his wife attended to their welfare and morals; eventually, like all the best businesses, the Tillers had branches in London, Paris and New York. Every Sunday between the wars saw a 'general post' of chorus girls on the railways of Britain. As rail parties go they seem to have been remarkably well-behaved, proceeding unprovocatively and without any suggestion of chorea from one respectable, if dull, set of lodgings to another. Whenever Tiller girls were written up, emphasis was laid on the care with which

the parent organisation looked after them; each troupe had a 'mother' or 'captain' or some such figure, with authority to regulate behaviour and fend off pests. The public continued to believe that chorus girls had a high old time, as many of them undoubtedly did ('she never pays for a meal, yet she earns more than her father'). *Picture Post*, in the van of the new photo-journalism, was irresistibly drawn to chorus girls, as it was to artists' models and even more to women in corsets. The magazine discovered that Tiller Girls were raising up their own daughters to become Tiller Girls, in splendid defiance of Noel Coward's advice to Mrs Worthington.

Somehow, one never meets ex-chorus girls, though everybody knows the famous ones; like Dame Anna Neagle, who earned her title by her talents, not by marriage (as Marjorie Robertson she danced in West End shows like *Rose Marie* and *The Desert Song*). Jessie Matthews was a Charlot girl as well as a Cochran's Young Lady. Her memoirs show what hell and fury can rage in a chorus dressing-room when a newcomer wears her ambition too openly. Jean Rhys turned from the chorus line to novel-writing. It is not easy to picture this shy Dominican doing the splits; all too easy to see her bolting from the stage when the audience in a northern town turned nasty (for this unprofessional conduct she was sacked – see her *Smile, Please*). In a London pantomime she got on well enough with a Tiller troupe, though no Tiller girl herself. In her *Voyage in the Dark* she mentions a hostel for chorus girls in Maple Street, London, known as the 'Cats' Home', where the girls were required to attend morning prayers (period 1914). A later generation of girls risked spiritual and other attentions from the notorious Rector of Stiffkey, self-appointed protector of young stage women and waitresses. But that is another story.

Those androgynous-looking chorus boys are also another story. According to John Montgomery's *The Twenties*, in June 1919 all the chorus boys in Albert de Courville's revue at the London Hippodrome were demobilised officers and several were DSOs and MCs. Normally, DSOs went to officers of field rank; were there really majors and colonels high-kicking in front of the foot-lights? It is a mind-sapping thought. Did anyone ever cry 'Bring on the officers'?

CINEMA
(1) The Americans

In the Britain of two generations ago one could live twenty years in a country town or fifty years in a village and never see or hear an American. Our so-called cousins were known to 'flock' to Paris and the Riviera and could be found on the Scottish moors or in the West End of London. Their strange slang and speech patterns were familiar from Wild West literature, but unless one had encountered the 'Doughboys' of 1917–18 the actual sounds they made were unfamiliar.

Then, from the silent films, came light on America. To the childish eye, an incorrigibly brash and over-excited people stood revealed: people who slammed custard pies into each other's faces, drove cars over level crossings with split seconds to spare, ran to and fro along the roofs of trains and stalked each other round office blocks, colliding in wild excitement at the corners. They conversed in grimaces, the men working their eyebrows and moustaches almost to death.

Their world was a striated one, in which thin black rain was always falling. At night everything turned dark blue, except when ghosts walked and then everything turned green, or when fires raged, when all was red.

The women had waxen, doll-like faces, with heavily defined eyes as if someone had gone round them with charcoal, and they had flashing semi-circles of impossibly even teeth. Though the younger ones tended to be blank of expression, they could be seen at times to be cogitating very hard, notably when tied to railway tracks, or when faced with the foreclosure of leases. In peaks of emotion, as when being kissed, their hair would light up in a suffused glow, almost like a halo.

Their men were great back-slappers and bear-huggers who wore their hats indoors, gave each other exploding cigars, tucked burning matches in each other's boots ('the hot foot') and enjoyed scaring the wits out of simple-minded negroes. When they saw a woman they fancied they stared first at her feet and then let their eyes travel slowly and lasciviously up her body. Both men and women always kept loaded revolvers in the unlocked top drawers of bedside chests. Whenever a man slammed out of a room the woman always ran after him as far as the door, then gave up. If a woman left home she never packed more than one stocking and a silky wrap-around in her suitcase. She then drove away in a car the wheels of which initially revolved in the wrong direction, as if the vehicle itself were over-excited. Sixty years on, the wheels still behave like this.

CINEMA
(2) Came The Dawn

The Americans, it appeared from those early films, were very slow readers, or perhaps they thought people of other nations were. Titles (or captions) were left on the screen for what seemed an insultingly long time. Especially was this true of the stately prologue, which was often too long to be screened in one shot. After the first paragraphs had outstayed their welcome, and even those who read the words aloud for their companions were growing restive, the text began to move up the screen like a teleprompter for the under-stimulated, and the reading aloud was continued, with occasional cries of 'Ssh!' It has been said that a rough rule for titles was to allow one second a word, with a bonus of five seconds for slow readers. But did anyone really need eight seconds to assimilate 'Help! *Help*!! HELP!!!'? And why could the words not have been superimposed on the action, instead of on a title-board with a fancy design in one corner?

Leaving titles up too long was one thing, but showing unnecessary titles was another. This was a way of adulterating the product, since it saved the expense of shooting real scenes. Someone with a stop-watch found that in *Every Woman's Problem* the titles actually took up more time than the filmed action. As against this, one simple title could sometimes furnish twist-of-the-plot information which, in a talking film, would have had to be put over in time-wasting scenes and dialogue. Whatever their faults, the producers, unlike some of their modern successors, were punctilious in letting the audience know where they were and whether the action was in the past, present or future, or in a dream.

Some producers felt that 'Came the dawn' and 'Meanwhile, back at the ranch' needed poetic embroidery. In William S. Hart's *Hell's Hinges* (1916), 'Came the dawn' was rendered thus: 'And then from the mothering sky came the baby dawn, singing as it wreathed the gray horns of the mountains with ribbons of rose and gold' (quoted in William K. Everson's *American Silent Film*). This kind of fustian often reached its peak in the final title, on the lines of 'So the singed butterfly found peace at last in God's garden', or 'So the man whose heart was a crucible of hate perished in the red fires of Armageddon.' On a slightly higher note, Erich von Stroheim's *Greed* offered this parting thought: 'O cursed lust of gold / When, for thy sake / The fool throws up his interest in both worlds / First starved in this, then damn'd in that to come.'

The title-writers, with *Elmer Hubbard's Scrap-Book* at their elbows, were encouraged to invoke Fortune, Fame, Destiny, the Wind of Chance and other fancies. Chaplin's *A Woman of Paris* was sub-titled 'A Drama of Fate' and in a sententious opening title the audience were instructed not to condemn sinners, but to pity them. The heroine was then introduced as 'A Woman of Fate', from which it was to be assumed she had no power over her movements, especially

54

in Paris 'where Fortune is fickle and a woman gambles with life' (and where truffles are prized, the food of 'pigs and Frenchmen'). This film showed how a sub-title could be put to moral use, for when the Bible Belt objected to a woman having a good time as a rich Frenchman's mistress, an explanation was inserted saying she had received a legacy from an aunt.

Titles were often used to underline what was happening. Thus, when Dr Jekyll was turning into Mr Hyde, the words 'An Apostle of Hate' made sure there was no misunderstanding. In a war film, a shot of fighter aircraft would be underscored with 'Cavalry of the clouds' (the goodies) or 'Sharks in the high seas of Heaven' (the baddies). The titles were not above telling what was going to happen. Even Keaton, adept at letting the pictures tell the story, could slip in an unnecessary nudging title like 'Where ignorance is bliss' as the bumbling hero climbs into a diving suit.

The most relished titles in the end were the humorous ones. Indeed, there is a case for saying that the silent film was the medium through which the great American wisecrack came to be properly esteemed in Britain. The now-famous joke about the man who went to some trouble to cure his halitosis only to find that people could not stand him anyway originated (says Everson) in *Love 'Em and Leave 'Em* (1926). There were, to be sure, plenty of cheap ten-for-a-dime wisecracks, like 'Take it from me – marriage isn't a word, it's a sentence.' The Harold Lloyd films kept up a workmanlike standard with lines like 'Charley – so lazy he gets up at four o' clock every morning so he'll have a longer day to loaf.' A title which has lingered in the memory for more than half a century occurred in a flying film: '1918 – when cigars had to be made of tobacco because of the paper shortage.' At the time it seemed a truly sizzling shaft of wit, such as an apprentice humorist could never hope to emulate; and it still seems by no means a contemptible specimen of its *genre*.

In the end, however, it is the unintentionally funny titles which tend to be remembered. S. J. Perelman is strangely fond of Theda Bara's 'Kiss me, my fool', a line of dialogue he regards as 'unquestionably one of the most hallowed in dramaturgy'. Malcolm Muggeridge remembers a rather better one from a Valentino film: 'Take away the shy one. Bring me the white gazelle.'

CINEMA
(3) Came The Talkies

Those cinemagoers who had wondered what kind of sounds the Americans made when they opened their mouths learned the disconcerting truth from the talkies: the men spoke like nasal ventriloquists and their waxen-faced women sounded like buzz-saws. The crude sound reproduction was only partly to blame; it really seemed that some of the great screen heroes were unable to communicate by speech, except with their own kind. Douglas Fairbanks Sr is supposed to have said to Mary Pickford: 'Let's sell up, move to Switzerland and just get old.'

Many of the critics, having convinced themselves that 'film' was a uniquely creative art form, felt betrayed; the cinema would revert to the cheap fairground attraction it had originally been. In *Ways of Escape* Graham Greene admits he was horrified by the arrival of the talkies, 'just as later I regarded colour with justifiable suspicion'. A widespread critical view was that adding speech to film was a monstrous over-enrichment; it took away from the cinemagoer the right to free imagination; it did not recognise the eloquence of silence; it put Brooklyn accents into the mouth of the Queen of Sheba. A *New Statesman* pundit wrote: 'The average silent film drama is only bearable today because there are no words.' Speech, he said, would at once empty the cinemas of intellectuals. The non-talking film, according to an anonymous writer in *The Times*, had 'the discipline and strength of a thing which is obeying the law of its own being, not trifling with a grander but unbecoming destiny. If this eloquence, not content with itself, is to achieve the literal accents of speech, the twice-told realism of sight linked to sound, how gross and indistinguished it may prove.' Later the newspaper's dramatic critic embellished the theme. The famous actors and actresses of the silent screen had built up public images which could no longer be sustained. How could one lose one's heart to a mechanical ghost which might well be singing with somebody else's voice?

The terrible drawls and twangs, the tendency of American actors to speak with mouths closed, caused much bafflement. *Punch's* critic, the essayist E. V. Lucas, said his impression was that American male voices were apt to be more alike than English. He was irritated that titles had been high-handedly thrown out, leaving the audience to struggle with unexplained twists of plot. He observed that the freedom of action for which the cinema had been famous was now lost, as the actors had to stand still to deliver their lines, and that they were discarding subtleties of bodily and facial movement since everything was being explained in dialogue. The *Spectator's* critic, Celia Simpson, complained that 'people talk to each other with their lips almost touching, which looks very absurd, but is presumably technically necessary at the moment' (a foretaste of the absurd nose-to-nose conversations in television 'two-shots'). She also thought it bizarre to hear two persons talking in a taxi without any other sounds; but the engineers were already hard at work on plans to drown out speech with background noise.

The paying public, who never cared much what the critics said, took it all in good part and were ready to see the revolution through its early troubles. To some extent they were brain-washed into acceptance by the publicity machine. The young in particular were captivated by the strange new forms of speech. Suddenly everybody was parroting, not always in mockery, 'Says you', 'Says who?', 'Says me', 'You're telling me', 'O boy!' and even 'O baby!' The dramatic

57

critic of *The Times* said: 'Whoever is rejoicing in the coming of the talkies would do well to imagine his children and grandchildren speaking to him in the accents of Kansas and Iowa' (or perhaps to imagine the talkies bombarding his grandchildren with four-letter words in the accents of New York and California).

The transition to talkies took about a couple of years, starting with the crudities of the synchronised disc, as used in 1927 for the Al Jolson films. While cinemas were being re-wired there was a choice of silent films, half-silent films and all-talking films,leading eventually to an 'all-talking, all-singing, all-dancing' era of Broadway worship. It was a strange, exciting, often deeply disillusioning period. Why, to pick on one tiny irritation, did the Metro-Goldwyn-Mayer lion utter such a feeble roar? Audiences accustomed to stamping and jeering when the reel broke now stamped and jeered when the speech went out of synchronisation.

The change-over wiped out the need for special effects on the cinema organ. When comedians could blow half-obscene 'raspberries' at each other on the screen (there was a great epidemic of this) the organist was excused the need to improvise them, just as he no longer had to make the sounds of tearing trousers and pianos falling downstairs. Others who lost out were the musicians who had stayed at their posts to play the National Anthem, which was now tinnily recorded.

But the real losers in the talkie revolution were those who usually miss out in the march of progress: the deaf. Perhaps it served them right for boasting that they could always lip-read what the Garbos and Gilberts were really saying.

COLUMNS
A Treat For Chambermaids

A most covetable honour it seemed to a child, to have one's statue raised into the sky on a fluted column, with a lightning conductor sticking out of the top of one's cranium. And a great thrill it was to ascend the dark spiral staircase and emerge, blinking and panting, on to the viewing platform, under the hero's giant paunch, and look down on the pigmy characters and toy motor cars below.

To qualify for a statue in the sky, it emerged, one had to slay a goodly number of the King's enemies. Most of the great leaders who combined to put down Napoleon were given a tall stalk to stand on: Wellington at Liverpool, 'Daddy' Hill at Shrewsbury, the Marquess of Anglesey on the Menai Strait, Lowry-Cole at Enniskillen, the Duke of York in London's clubland and, of course, Nelson in Trafalgar Square and again in Dublin, with Nelson's Hardy raised above the Thomas Hardy country.

Then the fashion died, though they ran up a belated column in Newcastle-on-Tyne for Earl Grey, of Reform Bill fame (his head was once struck off by lightning, a reminder not to ascend columns in thunderstorms). The cost of an ascendable column, with 'suicide' gallery, some 130 feet high, was not negligible. Aesthetes began to query the sense of raising statues so high that only chambermaids in attics could see them properly. To radicals, victory columns were anathema; in 1871 the Communards in Paris, using a winch, pulled down Napoleon's column in the Place Vendôme, which brought a bill for 323,000 francs for the painter Courbet, who had abetted the wreckers in their enterprise. In Britain the triumphal columns have survived tolerably well, though in World War Two the one supporting George III on Lincoln Heath had to be shortened, to avoid endangering military aircraft. Then in 1966 the Nelson Column in Dublin was blown up and left looking like a broken tree on a battlefield, until Irish Sappers demolished the remains. Nelson's head was seized by students and later recovered in London.

In neither of the world wars were high commanders awarded columns. Would 'Monty' have relished standing, in desert garb and with hands in pockets, above Horse Guards Parade? As it is, he surveys Whitehall from a plot of grass, while Mountbatten, more recently honoured, has earned a plinth. Not even Churchill was offered a perch in the sky, though there was an American proposal, rapidly forgotten, to erect a giant statue of him on the cliffs at Dover, with a red cigar-tip glowing as a beacon to mariners.

COUÉ
Twenty Knots On A String

What a wave of credulity swept the land when Emil Coué, the French apothecary turned psychotherapist, came to Britain shortly after World War One to popularise his cult of healing by auto-suggestion.

Aches and pains could be driven away if the sufferer, with closed eyes, repeated twenty times, 'Every day in every way I'm getting better and better.' This was best done on waking up and on going to bed, preferably aided by a piece of string with twenty knots, but the recital had to be performed, like prayer, with faith and confidence. 'All of us,' the master explained, 'are the wretched puppets of our unconscious selves, of which imagination holds the strings, and we shall only cease to be puppets when the will has learned to guide the imagination.'

Women, including many with titles, rushed to Coué's London demonstrations. He was patient, gentle, unbombastic and he tried hard to convince people that he could not mend broken limbs. He laid his hands on those with rheumatism, exclaiming, '*Ça passe, ça passe*', and often the pain apparently vanished, or the patient pretended so. In repeating, 'It is going', to oneself, it was necessary to gabble the phrase, leaving no time for the opposite thought to intrude. If the trouble was mental, it helped to place one hand on the forehead.

Coué was invited to Eton College, where he asked three boys on the platform to clasp their hands together: 'While M. Coué repeated to them, "I cannot, I cannot", they appeared unable to unclasp their hands, but when they said,"I can, I can", they were able immediately to do so.' A master with rheumatism in the leg was made to shut his eyes and repeat, '*Ça passe*', after which he said he felt much better. A flogged boy with a sore behind would have made a good test case, but this was not to be. Nor did the Headmaster, Dr C. A. Alington, submit himself as guinea-pig. Similar scenes were staged among the blind soldiers at St Dunstan's, though Coué knew better than to offer to restore their sight.

In playgrounds all over the country children chanted the Coué mantra, 'Every day and in every way . . .' Vicars took it as a text for their sermons. And a wag called Charles Inge contributed the following estimate of Coué to *The Week-End Book*:

This very remarkable man
Commends a most practical plan;
You can do what you want
If you don't think you can't
'So don't think you can't think you can.

COWS
For All Purposes

Milk straight from the cow was something to look forward to on a country walk. The farmer's wife would usually sell a glass for a penny. It was even possible to get a drink from a cow, or a goat, in Hyde Park or on Hampstead Heath, though an urban school of thought held that refreshment direct from the udder was unhygienic, or even indecent. Less hygienic, it may be, were the 'Iron Cows' which used to yield milk on the insertion of a penny in a slot.

Breath straight from the cow was a less readily disposable product. The belief that cows' breath, which was notably sweeter than that of (say) hyenas, cured ailments of the lungs persisted well into this century, and there were 'spas' in Europe which provided this facility. In 1922, the ineffable Gurdjieff, in his establishment at Fountainebleau, installed the novelist Katherine Mansfield in a room above a cow byre, where she could inhale the breath and other exhalations from the beasts below. It was, he said, an old Caucasian cure for tuberculosis. She died within six weeks of taking up this pastoral residence.

Blood straight from the cow was the nastiest cure of all. According to Stuart Cloete's *A Victorian Son*, anaemic women in France queued at their local abattoir for 'elevenses' in the form of warm blood, as recommended by doctors. 'Their mouths and faces were bloody like those of vampires,' he says. If *Jack's Reference Book* is right, decent English women combated their anaemia by sucking slate pencils.

61

CRYSTAL SETS
A Licence To Twiddle

The prophet Moses smote the rock of Horeb with his staff and water gushed out. As a feat it was no more remarkable than tickling a crystal nugget with a wire and summoning up voices. That was a magic moment. What those first voices said was non-memorable (the air was infested with 'Uncles'); what mattered was being able to tune them in.

The cheapest crystal set was the 'rag and bone' type built from scrap. A silicon crystal (cost: one shilling) was packed into a borrowed thimble with the silver foil from a chocolate box; the cat's whisker was made by coiling a wisp of thin wire into a pointed spring; and a length of black-enamelled wire was wound round a cardboard roll to make a coil. The most expensive item was a pair of headphones, but a single ear-piece could be bought for seven shillings.

If one slept on a metal mattress, of the 'reticulated and decussated' type deplored by Anthony Burgess, this served as an aerial and brought in the sensual music of the Savoy Orpheans. If the bed was in the attic, reception was better. An outdoor aerial sometimes required access to the chimney stack of 'an accommodating neighbour', who might be less accommodating if he found the insulators were to consist of the necks of broken bottles. In the early days the length of aerial was limited to 100 feet. The most efficient aerials ran the full length of the garden to a mast, the higher the better; the sort of erection which, as many loudly complained, was disfiguring the face of Britain.

Amateurs had been operating crystal sets since before 1914, eavesdropping on Morse, Marconi test messages and the persiflage of engineers. In the early 1920s, when public service broadcasting began, articles on how to make simple receiving sets appeared regularly in boys' papers and journals like *Amateur Wireless* and *Popular Wireless*. Some do-it-yourself experts said there was no need to buy a crystal when a lump of iron pyrites from the coal scuttle would do, or even a well-chosen lump of coal; others described how to synthesise crystals by chemical means. However, most of us preferred to save up for a shop crystal sold under names like Zincite, Tungstalite, Hertzite and Dayzite. Where all the non-synthetic crystal came from was a riddle; if from caves or mines, their location was not advertised. We were urged to cherish our crystals, scrubbing them with a tooth-brush dipped in carbon disulphide, a substance everyone was assumed to have at his elbow. The 'live' faces of the crystal would wear away, but splitting the nugget with a hammer might yield more sensitive new ones. The best crystal units were enclosed in glass and the whisker had a screw-controlled action for fine adjustment.

Having built a 'rag and bone' set, the enthusiast was expected to pay the Post Office ten shillings a year for the privilege of possessing it. According to *Chums*, it was necessary to send the Postmaster-General his fee before starting to build a set, but the *Boy's Own Paper* thought this was nonsense and urged boys to get their sets going first. There was much strong feeling about the licensing system. For long the *Daily Express* attacked the insolence of the Postmaster-General in trying to charge for the use of the ether, which did not belong to him. Certainly it seemed an impertinence to many of us considering that (a) the only reason for listening to any station was to identify it and then move on; and (b) the Postmaster-General had no authority over the Eiffel Tower, the Hague or mysterious stations called Nauen or Poldhu. Tuning and tinkering were what mattered; or, to borrow a later saying, the medium was the message. It was our first experience of tyrannical executive power.

Because of wild freaks of reception it was possible to boast of tuning-in far-distant stations. In 1924 an enthusiast claimed to have picked up every station in Britain on his crystal set and people with one-valve sets were receiving, or so they said, Schenectady, on the Mohawk River.

Some fans could not bear to be separated from their sets. They reinforced their umbrellas to serve as aerials; they wound wire round their torsos, or inside their hats, or ran it down their trouser legs. Canoes and punts were seen with diamond-shaped frame aerials, their occupants doing battle with other craft equipped with gramophones. A schoolboy in class, with ear cupped reflectively as he gazed at his text-book, might be listening for the Derby result.

A crystal set would work reasonably well within ten or fifteen miles of a main or relay station. In mid-1925 the new high-power transmitter at Chelmsford, audible for 100 miles, gave new hope to those who were flagging. It has to be conceded that the crystal set was a real conversation killer. A slammed door, even a gently-closed door or a dog's bark could dislodge the cat's whisker from its sensitive spot, necessitating a new exploration of the rock face. A husband listening, or rather listening-in, to a symphony orchestra would make a great business of removing the ear-phones to ask his wife to repeat what she had just said, then having answered would put them on again in such a way as to indicate that the interruption had been both frivolous and mis-timed. Wives who valued their coiffure disliked ear-phones: for them there were lorgnette-style single ear-pieces, but listening like that called for great concentration.

Reception on a crystal set improved at night, or in stormy weather. Nobody knew why, or what really went on in the ether, if there was an ether. The Archbishop of Canterbury understood less than most; he is supposed to have asked whether the window needed to be open to let the wireless waves in. At least owners of crystal sets did not inflict the tuning-in nuisance of oscillation, a form of caterwauling which soured not only domestic relations but relations with neighbours. Oscillation seemed inseparable from valve sets. As inflictions go, it was far worse than that caused in the early days of television by motorists whose sparking plugs lacked suppressors. The Post Office used to send out 'frightener' vans looking for 'oscillating fiends', like those it uses to scare people into buying licences.

With a set employing two or more valves the use of a loud-speaker was at last possible, bringing a new kind of domestic distress that is still with us. Knob-twiddling rapidly became a supreme form of selfishness, akin to tinkering with a motor-cycle and for ever blipping the throttle instead of setting off for a ride. It was a male obsession; but females, as the advertisers pointed out, could always top up with nerve tonics if they did not like it.

It is no doubt deplorable that memories of what actually came over the air in those far-off days should be so sketchy. We should have been transfigured by all those talks on the appreciation of music, or taught perfect French by Monsieur Stéphan, or convulsed by the Yorkshire comedian, John Henry. What sticks absurdly in the mind is the once-maddening recital: 'Here is the news – copyright by Reuter, the Press Association, Exchange Telegraph and Central News.' Every man, woman and child could, and did, recite this roll of credits. Still, there was one other unforgettable sentence and it ran: 'The King's life is moving peacefully to its close.'

DAILY MAIL HAT
A Snub From Churchill

L ord Northcliffe's attempt to destroy the bowler hat and to replace it with something which could better express the dignity of man was good clean fun while it lasted. His campaign showed that it was one thing to topple Prime Ministers, another thing to topple headgear.

The campaign for a *Daily Mail* Hat, with an offer of £100 for the best design, opened in September 1920 and was linked to a respectful interview with the French lady who had designed such a distinctive war-time hat for Clemenceau. The artist C. R. W. Nevinson was quoted as saying that men's hats were neither useful nor beautiful and that he himself favoured the tam o' shanter type of cap worn by students in Paris. Daily the loyal but deeply embarrassed editorial staff kept the campaign going, with headlines like 'Men's Dowdy Hats', 'Hat Tyranny', 'Women's War on the Bowler', 'Sir Henry Wood's "Lifeboat" Hat' and 'Three-Cornered Hats For Men'. Meanwhile the back page featured the more outstanding designs out of the 40,000 submitted: variations on deerstalkers, balaclavas, cloches, medieval scholars' hats, slouch hats and hats like Noah's Ark. The prize went to Albert Owen Hopkins for a cross between a bowler and a topper, with a gently rounded crown. It was christened the '*Daily Mail* Sandringham Hat', possibly in the hope that it might find royal favour. Though widely attacked as ridiculous, it was fairly inoffensive to the eye and at least had nothing 'Bolshevik' or 'apache' about it. Sir William Orpen, one of the judges, thought highly enough of it to wear it for the cameras. However, 'suave reporters' were unable to persuade men-about-town to do likewise, apart from the matinee idol Owen Nares and one or two Members of Parliament. A 'free copy' was sent to Winston Churchill, well-known as a hat-fancier, but according to Tom Clarke, then news editor of the *Daily Mail*, he consigned it to his unused collection, which caused Northcliffe to take strong offence. Some members of the *Mail* staff wore it in London but kept bowler hats in which to return to their suburbs. Clarke says that Northcliffe wore a fine specimen of his hat when he boarded the boat rain for Paris at Victoria, but changed hats at Calais. In Paris, if Harry Greenwall is right, a sacked member of the *Mail* staff donned the hat and walked up and down the corridor outside Northcliffe's suite in the Ritz, hoping that this demonstration of loyalty would win him reinstatement. It did not.

DEATH RAYS
Caution: Scientists At Work

Why did car engines stop suddenly on lonely roads? Why did two or more cars sometimes come to a halt on the same stretch? Could it be that scientists up on the hillside were secretly experimenting with power rays? What a tale for the 'Ace of Spades' road-house!

The 'death ray' first made headline excitement in 1924, when the press welcomed an invention which could not only stop car or aircraft engines (at up to 58 miles), but set fire to objects, extinguish life, cure cancer and locate submarines. Two inventors were working independently on the idea, which had hitherto belonged to science fiction. One of them was Dr T. F. Wall, Lecturer in Mechanical and Electrical Research at Sheffield University, and the other, who drew most of the publicity, was H. Grindell-Matthews. It was revealed that Grindell-Matthews had been paid £25,000 during the 1914–18 war for the rights to his system of controlling a warship by a light beam, and had been promised £250,000 if he could bring down a Zeppelin by a ray of any kind. He told the Foreign Press Association, who fêted him, that he was tempted to hope his ray would make war impossible. What he needed was the chance to conduct secret experiments in the countryside.

This time the Government seemed lukewarm towards Grindell-Matthews' idea. Air Ministry experts attended a well-guarded demonstration in his laboratory, where they saw him light an electric bulb from a short distance and stop a motor-cycle engine from 15 yards. They offered him £1,000 down if he could stop a motor-cycle engine provided by Government scientists in their own test conditions. When it emerged that Grindell-Matthews was simultaneously negotiating with a French manufacturer, Members of Parliament demanded to know why the Government was allowing this invention to pass to a foreign power. Such a ray, said one Member, would be of more value to Britain's defences than 'babbling beatitudes and high moral gestures'. Another asked whether the Government would take steps to ban 'this diabolical invention'. Others, more sceptical, were anxious that no more money should be showered on this inventor. The Government remained non-committal, but the press continued to show great faith in the weapon. The *Illustrated London News* had a splendid drawing, prepared under the direction of the inventor, of an aircraft being exploded by ray in mid-air. Lord Birkenhead exercised his sardonic fancy on the subject, marvelling that a ray which could incinerate at a distance could stop a car's magneto without setting fire to the petrol, as well as having the power to kill or cure at will.

The effectiveness of the ray, the public learned, depended entirely on the amount of power made available. There was a suggestion that for £3 million Britain could be equipped with an invisible anti-aircraft defence proof against all raiders. Later that year the United States House of Representatives was informed by its own expert that 'the death ray does not exist' and that the reports of French aircraft being brought down over the Ruhr by German rays were false. But it was a good story and it took years to lie down. Many citizens were confident that the Government had just such a defence system ready for emergencies, but was saying nothing.

DICKY-BIRD CAMERAS
Waiting For The Cuckoo

'Watch for the dicky bird!' was the instruction given to small children in an attempt to get them to look straight at the camera. No dicky bird ever appeared; the shutter clicked, the photographer said 'Good boy' or 'Good girl' and that was that. It seemed just another adult confidence trick.

Yet at the turn of the century an ingenious dicky-bird camera shutter existed, trade-marked the 'Dolce'. This was the catalogue description:

It is a handsome construction of light wood, much after the style of the Swiss clocks, and fits on to the front of the camera. In the top, above the lens, is a little door in which is the figure of a bird. This is connected with a pneumatic tube of some length, and when the operator is ready he gets clear away from the camera and by pressure on the ball causes the bird to pop out from the aperture and cry 'Cuckoo'. This can be done as often as wanted, and in 99 cases out of a hundred will immediately attract the attention of the juvenile. As soon as the right expression is secure the exposure is made with a second pneumatic tube.

The description ended with an assurance that the apparatus also gave good results with grown-up sitters.

Why was this admirable device ever phased out? Surely we are the poorer for its passing.

DUNCES
A Change Of Name

Dunces are now known as under-achievers, a term thought to be inoffensive. Under-achievers are not required to stand in the corner wearing a conical cap with a 'U' on it.

As far back as 1923 a correspondent wrote to *Notes and Queries* saying that, if the dunce's cap were to be reintroduced, 'some indignant parent would probably haul a teacher before the magistrate for defaming the character of his offspring.' Later correspondence suggested that dunces' caps began to go out when the Board Schools came in, in 1870, since teachers disliked having their disciplinary methods canvassed before a public board. Teachers continued to cane children for ignorance, or for not trying harder; a punishment evidently thought less likely to traumatise a child than simply making it look silly. 'Dame' schools tended to be a law unto themselves long after the Board Schools had relegated the dunces' cap to the museum. Children's comics continued to feature conical-capped dunces, though these duffers often managed to turn the tables on the teacher. In 1983 a headline DUNCE SETS FIRE TO SCHOOL appeared in the *Daily Telegraph*. It could never have happened in the *Guardian*.

ELECTRIC HARES
Look! No Cruelty!

The Great Debate of 1926 – engulfing much of the population – was between those who thought greyhounds too sensible to chase the new-fangled electric hare and those who thought greyhounds were daft enough to pursue anything that moved. To the question 'How can they pick up the scent of an electric hare?' came the answer 'Greyhounds don't have to, they hunt by sight.'

At that time the electric hare seemed an almost macabre drollery. But was it perhaps a new refined form of cruelty to animals – deceiving them into making most strenuous exertions and then snatching the prey from their jaws? The animal welfare bodies thought the electric hare a Good Thing, as compared with the coursing of live hares. For their part the Altcar fraternity despised the new sport as a mockery of all true venery.

Those who jeered that only the Americans could have hatched such an idea overlooked the trial run held at the Welsh Harp, Hendon, in 1876, when greyhounds were induced to chase a dummy hare wound by a windlass. The 400-yards track ran in a straight line, which meant that the race always went to the fastest, not necessarily the smartest, dog. Interest soon waned. Over the years American promoters devised an oval track with an electrified lure.

The sport hung fire in America, but Britain fell for it in a big way. Rarely can a craze have boomed so fast. The first track was opened in 1926 at Belle Vue, Manchester. Attendance at the White City, London, rose from 15,000 to 100,000 in two months. It was soon all too obvious what the real attraction was. Gamblers had a new facility laid at their doorsteps, cheaper to attend than horse-racing, open two or three times a week, operating after working hours and continuing even in hours of darkness. What the animal welfare bodies had welcomed the churches now attacked with vigour. Even the animal-lovers were dismayed to find that the new sport stimulated old-fashioned coursing; indeed, Belle Vue's first season was rested to avoid clashing with the national coursing championships.

Some dogs, as was to be expected, caught the hare. Others appeared to lose interest in the bogus prey and ran back to base. But enough dogs enjoyed the competition to make the game profitable.

One inventor even sought support for an electric rat to be pursued by terriers. Brigadier-General A. C. Critchley, who founded the Greyhound Racing Association, was always looking for ways to make the sport more respectable. Explaining what a humane pastime it was, he invited C. P. Scott, editor of the *Manchester Guardian*, to offer a challenge cup, but Scott was warned by a worldly staff man what the sport was really about.

Sheer curiosity lured thousands to the new tracks. The first race at least had all the excitements of novelty: a sudden dimming of the arena lights, the flood-lighting of the green track, then the hare noisily rocketing from its lair at fifty miles an hour or so, sparking merrily. The race lasted only a few seconds, leaving plenty of time to burn one's unsuccessful tickets in one of the friendly braziers dotted about the terraces, buy a cheap mutton pie and watch the traditional bookies' mothers counting their fat rolls of notes.

The phrase 'going to the dogs' had long existed to describe the process of falling into dissipation. Among the middle classes its aptness was now reinforced.

ELECTROPHONE
For Songs And Sermons

Long before public broadcasting began it was possible to sit at home and listen in to West End shows and even West End sermons. The world has forgotten the Electrophone, which offered telephone subscribers 'Song, Mirth and Music – By Wire to Your Home' for £5 a year.

This eavesdropping facility was launched in 1895 and lasted until the 1920s. Alexander Graham Bell had shown the possibilities of music by wire when, in 1878, he delighted Queen Victoria at Osborne House with the notes of a bugle sounding Retreat at Southampton, followed by an organ recital from London. In 1883 Sir Arthur Sullivan invited the Prince of Wales to his birthday party to hear the strains of *Iolanthe*, from the Savoy Theatre, where the cast had been called together at Sullivan's expense to sing into a telephone. A single earpiece was passed around, with appropriate exclamations of wonder. Nine years later thousands of visitors to the Crystal Palace paid to hear music relayed from theatres, as Parisians had already done at their Exhibition of 1881.

The telephone companies welcomed the Electrophone as a means of stimulating business in the slack part of the day, and when the Post Office took over the networks it also encouraged the system. Most of the leading London theatres admitted the Electrophone transmitter to their footlights. In fashionable churches (among them St Martin-in-the-Fields, St Mary-le-Bow and the City Temple, but not West-minster Abbey) the transmitter was concealed in a black lead box modelled to resemble a Bible and placed in the pulpit or choir stalls.

Electrophone subscribers were given an induction coil, batteries and two receivers (or four receivers for £10). The twin-ear receiver had to be held in position by a central handle, which put a stopper on secondary indulgences like knitting. The quality of reception varied greatly; there was a stereo effect described as 'a change of sonorous intensity from one ear to the other' as singers and actors moved about.

The Electrophone began to appear in clubs and restaurants. Lord Northcliffe, a demon for progress, put the system through its paces in 1909, when a team of shorthand writers in Carmelite House took down an important hour-and-a-half speech by Lord Rosebery in Glasgow. The report was headed 'By Electrophone'.

Various stunts were organised by the Electrophone Company. In 1913 guests at its Gerrard Street salon listened to a transmission of *Faust* from the Paris Opera House, while Paris audiences, linked to the French Theatrophone, heard selections of *Tosca* from Covent Garden; but it was an evening of blocked lines and improvisations. The music-hall recruiting frenzies of 1914–15 should have given Electrophone a fillip, but by 1915 there were only 2,000 subscribers in London.

Between them radio and the gramophone killed off the system. In 1957 readers of *The Times* recalled those pioneer days. Herbert Buckmaster (of 'Buck's Fizz' fame) told how he used to sit at home listening to his wife, Gladys Cooper, performing on the stage. One night, in a 'not too serious play', an actor called out 'Are you listening tonight, Buck?', to which no reply was possible. A woman reader recalled that as a girl she listened spellbound on the school Electro-phone to Lewis Waller reciting Shakespeare and Kipling from the

Palace Theatre – 'I can still feel the thrill and majesty of the most beautiful voice I can recall.'

Nobody wrote in remembering an eloquent and inspiring sermon from a favourite divine.

EURHYTHMICS
Frightening The Cows

On the way to the water party in D. H. Lawrence's *Women in Love* Gudrun asks Ursula to 'sing while I do Dalcroze . . . sing anything you like and I will take the movement from it.' Ursula obliges with 'My love is a high-born lady' and Gudrun begins to fling herself about 'in the eurhythmic manner . . . looking as if some invisible chain weighed on her . . . pulsing and fluttering rhythmically . . . her feet all the time beating and running to the measure of the song, as if it were really some strange incantation . . .' It is no surprise when Gudrun's white figure, 'shuddering in strange little runs', stampedes a herd of cows. The reader sympathises with the wretched creatures, as with the Gadarene swine.

The Dalcroze eurhythmical cult came to Britain in the early 1920s, jostling with every kind of obsession from Couéism to Pelmanism. Young women, especially young women like Gudrun, fell for this system of constructive capering. It also appealed to the female disciples of Gurdjieff at Fontainebleau, where a theatre was built for eurhythmic exercises. The movement had been started in Saxony by Jaques Dalcroze before World War One and was originally designed to correct faults in rhythm in music pupils. Explanations tended to mysticism. What eurhythmics offered was 'increased powers of concentration, a muscular system quickly responsive to the brain and a strengthening of the automatic functions'. It was not dancing but a form of gymnastics. Teaching the muscles to contract and relax in definite time and in definite space was supposed to strengthen the feeling for metre and instinct for rhythm. Instead of forcing a boy to take piano lessons, argued Dalcroze, he should be taught to use his body musically, then music would come more easily.

Photographs of young women leaping with arms raised strike an

73

advanced note for 1920. They are wearing above-the-knee loose dresses and showing a good deal of bare thigh. Vests and shorts were more usual and were described as more seemly than the evening dresses of the day. A Queen's Hall demonstration of eurhythmics drew a bigger crowd than the auditorium could hold.

The cult of eurhythmics (still taught at the Royal Ballet School) was outshone in the 1930s by the Women's League of Health and Beauty, which also had semi-mystical origins. Rising from bed one morning the handsome Mrs Bagot Stack began dancing to a jazz record, breathing ever deeper, leaping ever higher, and discovered that, mentally and physically, she was 'bathed in gladness'. The experience was too good not to be shared. What was needed was 'A League of Women pledged . . . to *Breathe*, to *Leap* and, above all, to THINK . . . .' In 1930 the League mounted two displays in Hyde Park and another in the Albert Hall. Members wore white satin blouses and black satin pants, an eminently noticeable uniform for its day, even when unheralded by military bands. Mrs Stark died in 1934 and her daughter Prunella took over the movement. By 1939 there were 160,000 members. The League's motto, used also by Prunella Stack for the title of her autobiography, was 'Movement Is Life'. Compare the title of the Nazis' capering organisation, 'Strength Through Joy', whose uninhibited cruises caused scandal in the Mediterranean ports.

EXPLETIVES
And Ejaculations

When Shaw's Eliza Doolittle first said 'Not bloody likely' – in the summer of 1914, thus hastening the crash of the old world – respectable citizens were making do with 'Bally', 'Bother' and 'Drat', as they did for long afterwards. 'Damn' was pretty strong stuff. If people swore by anybody or anything, it was by Jove, or George, or Jingo, or Jiminy or Jehoshaphat. The nearest they got to 'Christ' was 'Christmas', 'Christopher Columbus' or 'Crikey'. Hell was 'heck' or 'blazes' or 'the everlasting bonfire'; one was not told to go there, but to 'go to Jericho'. It was not done to make light of the

Devil – he might, after all, be listening – but one could say 'What the dickens' or 'What the deuce'. A tolerable version of 'My God' was 'My goodness'. If a bested adversary had to be advised to put anything anywhere he could be urged to 'put that in your pipe and smoke it'.

In tales of the Conan Doyle era men were always exclaiming 'Capital'. Or rather, they were always ejaculating it. Today ejaculation has taken on a specialised meaning, but in 'The Story of the Naval Treaty' a character called Phelps is allowed to ejaculate three times on one page. 'Intercourse' has also fallen on evil days. A sentence like this from Baroness Orczy – 'Was there any friend to whose intercourse with Mrs Hazeldene you at any time took exception?' – raised no eyebrows then.

In popular literature foreigners said things such as *'Caramba'*, *'Sapristi'*, *'Mille tonnerres'*, *'Himmel'* and *'Donner und Blitzen'*. Frenchmen in cloak-and-dagger drama cried *'Diantre'* (the Devil) and *'Pardieu'*, *' Cordieu'* and *'Mordieu'* (which more or less explained themselves), varied by *'Parbleu'*, *'Morbleu'* and *'Sacrebleu'* (all, according to the dictionary, meaning 'Zounds' or 'Forsooth'). There were also *'Nom d'un nom'*, *'Nom d'une pipe'*, *'Nom d'un tonnerre'* and *'Nom d'un petit bon homme'*, meaning (to lexicographers) 'By Jove' or 'By George'. In *Beau Geste* Lejaune is allowed this peculiar oath: *'Sacré bon sang de bon jour de bon*

75

malheur de bon Dieu de Dieu de sort.' These quaint oaths were apt
to stick in the memory. There are said to be British tourists who
identify the great white church atop Montmartre as *'Sacrebleu'*.

EXPURGATIONS
All For A Quiet Life

An English literature lesson is in progress. Under the master's cold
eye the pupils are taking it in turn to read *Macbeth*
and those who have not yet done their stint are anxiously calculating
their chances of being saddled with one of the spicier passages.
Whoever gets Lady Macbeth's speech beginning 'I have given suck
. . .' will be the target of a campaign to make him falter; he will be
poked with a ruler, kicked from behind, bombarded with paper
pellets and whispered obscenities – anything likely to make him
break down and incur a rebuke from the master for being a filthy-
minded little beast.

Most schools used doctored texts, in which a line like 'The Devil
damn thee black, thou cream-faced loon' would appear as 'My curse
upon thee light, thou cream-faced loon'. This was not bowdler-
isation, for Dr Bowdler boasted that he did not rewrite Shakespeare
but merely left the embarrassing bits out. But editors of school texts
did not hesitate to alter the wording for the sake of a quiet life in the
classroom. The passage about Lady Macbeth's nipples usually came
through unscathed, but the witches' curse might (as in the 1925
Nelson edition) lack one notable constituent:

> Finger of birth-strangled babe
> Ditch-deliver'd by a drab.

Trouble sometimes arose when one boy lost his edited version of,
say, *The Tempest* and used the copy from the family bookshelf. As
he read out Trinculo's 'Monster, I do smell all horse-piss, at which my
nose is in great indignation' there would be a chorus of 'Sir, that's
wrong – it says pond-water here!' The teacher's explanation would
then provoke cries of 'Sir, are they allowed to muck about with
Shakespeare?' If they were studying the Nelson 1926 pond-water

edition they would not read of Caliban's frustrated hopes of violating Prospero's child and peopling the isle with little Calibans. Nor would they find Prospero's stern warning to Ferdinand as to what would happen if he untied Miranda's virgin-knot before all 'sanctimonious ceremonies' had been observed; just the sort of caution, some might think, of which school children stand urgently in need, except that in those days we were assumed to know nothing of such things.

Some editorial amendments in text-books were quite surprising. A version of Alfred de Musset's *La Nuit de Mai*, prescribed for sixth-formers, contained a passage ending;

> *Ce soir, tout va fleurir; l'immortelle nature*
> *Se remplit de parfums, d'amour, et de murmure.*

All very fine as far as it goes, but in the *Oxford Book of French Verse* there is a comma after *murmure*, followed by:

> *Comme le lit joyeux de deux jeunes époux.*

Clearly, the textbook editor had decided that joyous goings-on in bed, even by a married couple, were unfit for the contemplation of seventeen-year-olds, capable though they might be of translating French classics (see FACTS OF LIFE).

EYES
A Favourite Rumour

It was Kipling's story, 'The End of the Passage', which gave new currency to the notion that the eyes of a murdered person could preserve on the retina the image of the murderer. This was an idea which just had to be believed – and it is not yet extinct.

In Kipling's tale an engineer called Hummel is found dead with staring, terrified eyes. Dr Spurstow decided to photograph the victim's eyes with his Kodak in the bathroom, whence is heard 'the sound of something being hammered to pieces', followed by the emergence of Dr Spurstow 'looking very white indeed'. Hummel might not have been murdered, but he had seen a horrific Something. The story is Kipling at his most suggestive and least helpful.

In Richard Marsh's novel *The Beetle* (1897) the narrator, having seen something hardly less nasty, says: 'I believe that if it were possible to make a retinal print – which it some day will be – you could have a perfect picture of what I saw. Beyond doubt it was a lamellicorn,* one of the *copridae*.'

The notion of the retinal imprint is rooted in Victorian myth. Photographic magazines of the 1860s have reports of pictures in dead men's eyes from many lands, including America, Italy, Spain and Russia. It is tempting to believe that unscrupulous correspondents sent in the sort of thing they realised was marketable. The *Photographic Times* suggested that murderers would start punching out their victims' eyes after the deed – or stabbing from behind.

In 1925 a retinal print was mentioned in a *Sunday Express* report of a trial at Limburg of the criminal Fritz Angerstein, charged with eight murders: 'The police allege that a photograph of the retina of one of the victim's eyes reveals a picture of Angerstein with his raised arm gripping a hatchet.' Angerstein was convicted, but presumably not on the strength of this photograph.

Bergen Evans in his *Natural History of Nonsense* mentions a 1945 film, *Dead Man's Eyes*, which had the advertising slogan: 'Dead – but his eyes lived to condemn his killer!' He also quotes Dr LeMoyne Snyder as recording in his *Homicide Investigation* the case of a murderer who hid the clothes he had worn at the time lest the police recognise them from an image in the victim's eyes.

* A type of beetle.

FACTS OF LIFE
A Literary Quest

One does not need to have been reared in a cupboard to shy at the sight of some of the sex literature now issued to the young, with everything explained in short words, perversions included. Oh, for the days of decent obfuscation, when children grew into their teens believing that babies were born by way of the navel! Peter Quennell has disclosed that he cherished this belief even when he went up to Oxford. The navel was a puzzling organ which must have been put there for a purpose; the other body orifices could play no part in

childbirth, since they already had well-established functions of their own (yet why did men have navels?).

The real mystery was how the baby got inside the mother in the first place. Since adults withheld all information on the subject, many of us had to work from literary sources. From the Old Testament all that could be gleaned was that babies happened as a result of a man 'knowing' a woman, or 'going in to' her, or 'lying with' her. It was all far from explicit. Adam 'knew Eve, his wife', but so he should have done. How well did you have to know a woman before she gave you a child? The dictionary could have told us that a secondary meaning of 'to know' was 'to have sexual commerce with', but much good that would have been. When we did turn to dictionaries, at a surprisingly early age, we tended to look up words like rape and ravish, both of which meant 'to have carnal knowledge of a woman against her will', or virgin, which meant 'a woman who has had no sexual intercourse'. Commerce? Knowledge? Intercourse? What did it all mean?

Word went round that there were some startling bits in *Leviticus*, notably a list of forbidden 'abominations' like 'uncovering the nakedness' of one's father, mother, sister, grand-daughter, daughter-in-law, uncle or aunt. The temptation to do any such thing was easily resistible, but presumably the prohibition had some bearing on the great riddle we were trying to solve.

Those lucky enough to have access to *The Complete Works of Shakespeare* could carry out further research in the titillating stanzas of *Venus and Adonis* and *The Rape of Lucrece*. This volume was a frequent school prize, which would have horrified Dr Gordon Stables, one-time health counsellor of the *Boy's Own Paper*, who was anxious to keep boys' minds off sex, especially if it set them thinking in bed.* Shakespeare's long poems certainly contained much food for thought. *Venus and Adonis* tells of the seduction of an unwilling youth by an accomplished temptress, who seeks by kissing to kindle 'the warm effects which she in him finds missing':

> And, having felt the sweetness of the spoil,
>   With blindfold fury she begins to forage;
> Her face doth reek and smoke, her blood doth boil . . .

To a twelve-year-old who had never been kissed except in 'Postman's Knock', and then reluctantly, the thought of a furious reeking, smoking, boiling woman was daunting enough. What did *foraging* mean? What was this woman, evidently a prey to spontaneous combustion, actually doing? Was this normal behaviour when a man and woman 'lay with' or 'knew' each other?

More alarming still were the events in *The Rape of Lucrece*. Tarquin, the 'lustful lord with brain-sick rude desire', 'rolling his greedy eyeballs in his head', the possessor of a hand that smokes when laid on a female bosom, declares his intention starkly:

> Lucrece, quoth he, this night I must enjoy thee,
> If thou deny, then force must work my way,
> For, in thy bed, I purpose to destroy thee . . .

Enjoy and destroy, indeed! It was clear that something pretty wicked was happening in Lucrece's bed, something not fit to be detailed even by our greatest poet.

> For she hath lost a dearer thing than life,
> And he hath won what he would lose again;
> This forced league doth breed a further strife;
> This momentary joy breeds months of pain . . .
> Pure chastity is rifled of her store,
> And Lust, the thief, far poorer than before.

* If thinking in bed persisted, it was to be combated by a course of potassium bromide (see *The Boy's Book of Health*). Dr Stables was also against lonely walks, since these stimulated thinking too, and a boy could end up 'without nerve enough to look a tomcat in the face'.

Yes, it had been a bad business, whatever it was. The poem rolled on and on, unhelpfully, and in some dissatisfaction one returned to the Meccano set.

In the quest for the Facts we were prepared to ransack any bookshelf. The *Children's Encyclopaedia* was no help. Had we tried the *Encylopaedia Britannica* (see also LIBRARIES) we would have been completely blinded by science. Under 'Reproduction' a sub-heading 'Details of the Sexual Act' seems too good to be true, but the passage to which it refers merely says that the sexual act 'consists in the fusion of two masses of protoplasm, commonly cells, derived from two organs of the opposite sex'. Elsewhere is an admission that the reproductive system 'in some parts of its course shares structures in common with the urinary system'. The diagrams purporting to illuminate these processes are both ugly and obscurely clinical.

In every school there was an endless circulation of theories about childbirth (like the one mentioned by Dodie Smith, to the effect that babies were born flat and then inflated by a red rubber tube). More useful was the flow of dirty stories, which often contained invaluable pointers to the Facts; and it was from this source as a rule that the astonishing truth eventually emerged. It was a truth to be accepted with great reluctance, for the creative act really seemed unworthy of the Creator.

It may seem odd that the quest for the Facts was so closely confined to printed sources. Did we never see dogs pleasuring each other in the street? Indeed we did, but we were told they were just being frisky, an explanation which seemed quite acceptable. Did we receive no word-of-mouth hints from *anybody*, other than fellow schoolboys? We did not. If our parents had any views on the association of the sexes, it was that boys ought to make friends with boys and girls with girls. This was felt to be healthy in every way.

Between them, parents showed remarkable skill in hiding the imminence of a birth in the family. On a well-remembered occasion the writer, aged fifteen, lay reading on his bed when his father entered and told him he had a baby brother. He had not known his mother was pregnant, though he was aware, of course, that she had taken to her bed with some sort of woman's illness. The birth had occurred in a room across the upstairs landing, with no attendant sounds of drama. Women did not, in those days, go about with bulging frontages, in tight clothing, but took exceptional pains to

81

disguise their condition, or to pass it off, jokingly, as 'middle-aged spread'. If the above tale suggests a scarcely credible innocence, or an abysmal failure of the powers of observation, how was it that so many mistresses of households never knew their maids were pregnant until the baby was born?

FERNANDO PO
And The Lost Lands

The best-loved name in the stamp album was, of course, Fernando Po. On the stamps themselves the name was rendered as Fernando Poo, but either version was good for a snigger. Certainly either name was better than Macias Nguema Riyogo, as the island is now called (it has been absorbed into Spanish Guinea).

The world of the stamp album was one of vanished and vanishing lands. Who ever heard of Fernando Po in any other context? Who ever heard of Antioquia or Condinamarca, those mellifluously named lands which formed part of the Granada Confederation, itself unheard-of outside the pages of Stanley Gibbons? (The Confederation became Colombia.) There was once a Stellaland, which sounds as if it was named after some explorer's pretty wife but was in fact a Boer republic and is now merged in Bechuanaland. There were stamp-issuing lands called Quelimane and Inhambane, both later absorbed into Mozambique. There was an Oil Rivers Protectorate, with Victoria's head on its stamps, which became the Niger Coast Protectorate and eventually Nigeria. The good Queen even had her head on the stamps of Van Diemen's Land, since drearily renamed Tasmania.

The post-1918 years were confusing times for schoolboy philatelists. Stamps bearing portraits of Romanovs, Habsburgs and Hohenzollerns were fast becoming curiosities. Many of the issues that mocked our indigence in the shop windows bore the dramatic overprints of successful Allied Expeditionary Forces, or harsh black inscriptions like WAR TAX or WAR CHARITY, or the vengeful numerals 1918, or intimations of forthcoming plebiscites. During the war the Kaiser's stamps had been boycotted by all right-thinking

British dealers. Now it became the fashion to display German stamps which had been overprinted for Belgium, Rumania, Poland and Russia side by side with German stamps overprinted by those nations which were now occupying the Fatherland, 'gallant little Belgium' among them.

A disproportionate amount of stamp-issuing seemed to go on in Fiume, the former Habsburg port on the Adriatic which became a free port of sorts under the poet D'Annunzio and is now the Yugo-slav port of Riyeka. On the Baltic shores stamps were rushed out by forgotten 'lands' called Memel, Wenden, Courland and Lettland, which were later absorbed in Lithuania or Latvia, and we all know where they ended up.

Stamp-collecting on the exiguous pocket money of those days was a tale of frustrated hankerings, of impossible dreams. Cheap packets bought at the newsagent's were full of unexciting British Colonials, which we were supposed to esteem greatly, and endless French stamps showing that long-robed woman sowing the fields with corn. In a higher range than penny packets were the approval sheets, or folders, from which specimens might be culled and paid for. We were not encouraged to ask for approval sheets. There were dealers whose object was to 'get you in their clutches' and 'pester you to buy'. Some of these advertised in boys' papers, transparently honest men proclaiming 'no rubbish' and 'no junk sent', and offering free watermark detectors and perforation gauges to genuine applicants. We studied their lists with hopeless longing: scarce Penny Blacks, Cape Triangulars, rarities from 'Mespot', 'Bolshevik Packets', the latest lines from Shanghai and Wei-hai-wei (with English printing on them). Some advertisements were by amateurs with addresses like 'The Rectory' and 'Bide-a-Wee Cottage', claiming to be trading for recreation, not profit; a few proclaimed themselves curates or ex-regimental sergeant-majors; others thought fit to declare the respect-able source of their stamps – for example, foreign convents.

While the craze lasted we read everything that came to hand about stamp-collecting and were fascinated to learn that many issues were forged or had forged overprints. This criminal taint gave a pleasing edge to the hobby; nobody, as far as we knew, had ever bothered to forge cigarette cards. We were not to know that some stamps came from countries which had never existed, like Angelina, said to be somewhere in West Africa.

Did King George V ever get stuck with forged stamps, we wondered? We were always hearing about his zeal for the hobby. Perhaps he collected only stamps with his own portrait on them, like those British Colonials, or perhaps he favoured those of emperors he had seen off the stage. Did he pick up his stamps with tweezers as we were supposed to do? Did he have a man to stick them in his albums? Nobody seemed to know.

FIRE GRENADES
To Throw At Women

When a woman in a flimsy evening dress went up in flames, the smart thing to do was to hurl a grenade at her feet. Being made of glass, it would shatter, releasing chemical fumes which would put out the blaze, possibly helped by a second grenade. A much more gentlemanly procedure, it may be thought, than throwing oneself at the lady and rolling her screaming about the floor, trying to smother her in tiger-skin rugs. 'Harden Star' grenades, invented in Chicago, were supplied in handy carriers, the largest size holding twelve; enough to extinguish a whole group of blazing dowagers. According to a history of fire-fighting, they were 'popular but ineffective', but remained on the market for forty years after their introduction in 1883.

FIRESIDE FUN
A Whiff Of Illegality

There is already a generation which does not know how to lay a domestic fire. Homeless persons, when offered a house with fire-places, will protest complete ignorance of the procedure. How does one obtain fuel? And what happens if the chimney catches fire?

How much of life's rich experience they have missed! A chimney on fire, with flames coming out of the top and a greeny-brown pillar of smoke and smuts, was one of the unhallowed joys of childhood. Especially if it was one's own chimney.

It was, of course, disgraceful to let a chimney take alight, suggesting as it did that the family were too mean to call in the sweep. If the brigade turned up, then disgrace was black indeed, surpassed only by that of being hauled into court to pay a five-shillings fine. In the country 'burning out' a kitchen chimney might be acceptable, but deliberate firing of a flue in a city was an anti-social act. Some householders used to put devices called 'imps' into the fire, the idea being that chemical fumes would somehow remove the soot ('open the draughts,' said the instructions, 'and the work is done').

One way a chimney could catch alight was when the head of the family undertook to revive a moribund fire by using a sheet of newspaper to create a forced draught. First, he held it in position between the grate and the shutter, until sufficient suction was created for the paper to stay up unaided, thus freeing him to attend to more important matters about the house. Gradually the fire brightened behind the taut headlines, then a faint brown charring was seen, the signal for excited exclamation. As often as not the head of the household returned just as the newspaper caught alight. In the ensuing battle, waged with bare hands and poker, the blazing sheet would go up the chimney like a fire balloon. Then, after a few seconds, would be heard the urgent rumbling sound high up the flue which meant that the chimney was on fire.

It may have been from some governessy notion of the risks involved in this fire-stimulating practice that King's Regulations for the newly-created Royal Air Force, in 1919, forbade the draping of mantelpieces, a restriction otherwise hard to understand; unless it was thought that a draped mantelpiece was an undesirable affectation in a fighting service.

Mothers and aunts had a curious idea that a sluggish fire could be quickened by propping up the poker against the grate, but it rarely caused the looked-for draught. Pokers were better employed for *poking* the fire; that is, unless a world war happened to be in progress, when the officials in centrally-heated Whitehall would send out the order 'Throw away the poker!', on the grounds that its use wasted fuel. The way to 'Keep the home fires burning low' (what a slogan!) was to fill half the grate with fire-bricks and cover what fire remained with wet slack.

85

Open fires were ideal for warming male posteriors, as Holmes and Watson found in Baker Street. Women who attempted such an exercise risked setting fire to themselves; even if this did not happen they would end up with mottled legs. Children found out the hard way that direct heat was no solace for chilblains. A bright fire was, however, a useful distraction from homework, a focus for idle contemplation. Was not one supposed to see flickering pictures in the flames, or even visualise Hell in them? Against the rules, one could play with the poker, getting the tip red-hot, and look for something to bore a hole in. Or one could sit and wonder whether fire-eaters like Barnello really bit the end off a red-hot poker, even after weakening it with repeated bending, and reflect on Houdini's warning that no performer should attempt to bite off red-hot iron unless he has a good set of teeth. (The nearest most schoolboys got to fire-eating was to extinguish a burning match by closing the mouth over it.)

If substances from a home chemistry set were sprinkled into the fire, the flames would respond by burning in brilliant hues. The fire's collusive warmth also brought up messages written in invisible ink. But sitting at the fire was not all dreaming and fooling. There was real work to be done there. Beside every grate hung an ornate bronze fork for toasting bread, scones and muffins. If the fire was smoky, so was the toast, but if the coals were bright the toast tasted better than anything ejected from an electric toaster.

Other functions of a friendly fire included roasting chestnuts and marshmallows, and heating soldering irons, smoothing irons and mulling irons, to say nothing of warming the domestic water and the next day's porridge.

With a fire in the hearth, one did not strike matches. Hence the jar of spills, thin slivers of wood or paper for lighting pipes or carrying the Promethean gift of flame from room to room. Just as it was wicked to waste water, so it was wicked to waste fire.

FIREWORKS
Hardships Of A Home Industry

If the chemist had asked why we were buying sulphur and saltpetre, we should have had to reply: 'To make gunpowder.' But he did not ask, having been a boy himself. We also bought potassium chlorate and barium nitrate, which were thought to be indispensable for a good show on November the Fifth. Equally necessary was charcoal, laboriously prepared at home by smothered combustion in a syrup tin. But the greatest drudgery was making brass and copper dust, by filing away at old door bolts and the like. How did the firework manufacturers get their supplies of those precious, spark-producing powders? Was it a sweated cottage industry?

It is hard to know why we were allowed, even encouraged, to make our own fireworks. Under the Explosives Acts, as the *Boy's Own Paper* kept reminding its readers, such manufacture was illegal without a Home Office licence. However, the *BOP* did describe how to make coloured flares, which involved no more than screwing up the mixture in an old newspaper and igniting it on the ground. Fortunately there were encyclopedias which saw no reason why their readers should not have the information necessary to blow themselves up. The luckiest boys were those who could get hold of an old copy of the *Boy's Own Book* (no relation of the *BOP*), which even Guy Fawkes might have found helpful. It described how gunpowder was to be 'mealed' into 'an impalpable powder' and then carefully set aside in a dry, safe place. In order of diminishing excitement, the names of the principal compositions ran thus: Strong Black Charge, Ordinary Black Charge, Dark Gray Charge, Light Gray Charge, White Charge and Whitest Charge. When rammed into containers these mixtures would give 'a gradual and lengthened burst of sparks or flame more or less bright', which sounded a little disappointing. There were various ways of imparting colour, but these called for a wide range of exotic substances, from resin, camphor, powdered flint glass and iron sand to arsenic, bismuth and dust of lycopodium (club moss).

Containers for powder were made by taking leaves of old copybooks, winding them round and round a rod and then pasting the paper down. For jumping crackers, of the kind regrettably popped through letter-boxes, a narrow paper tube had to be bent backwards and forwards and the powder trail within it reinforced at each corner. Touch-paper was made by soaking blotting-paper in saltpetre. Needless to say, home-made jumping crackers never jumped.

Occasional warnings about danger punctuated the instructions. When brewing up the wherewithal for crimson fire in a gallipot over a gridiron it was important to avoid the poisonous fumes. Puffing at touch-paper which seemed reluctant to ignite was not recommended, 'or you will probably get a sudden and violent blow in the face'. Squibs and crackers could be held in the hand and fired, 'but they must be thrown into the air before they finish'. Only 'very small rockets' were to be held in the hand.

When Guy Fawkes Night came, the home-made fireworks varied from 'more or less bright' to a few dubious sputters. Certainly there were no crystal waterfalls, no peacocks' tails, no Bruce's Spangles, no flights of jewel-headed cobras. In adjacent gardens the sizzling products of Brock and Pain showed what we could have done if our manufacturing enterprise had not been seriously under-capitalised, or if we had had more time to pursue lampblack and seek out pure resins. Anyway, we had done our best and next year would be different.

The *Boy's Own Book* described, a little imprecisely, how to make emerald-green fires for incantation scenes in pantomimes, or flaming red swords and fire-forks for waving by demons in melodrama. The compiler had a favourite firework of his own, 'a most wonderful chemical and philosophical toy' called Pharaoh's Serpents, as supposedly used to bamboozle the simple-minded by priests in Biblical times. All one needed was a quantity of sulpho-cyanide of mercury mixed with nitre, enclosed in a cone of tinfoil. When lit at the apex it disgorged a serpent-like coil, brittle and dirty-white, which twisted and turned in all directions. If mixed with 'thin gum water' it would 'burn with astonishing fierceness', producing a snake many yards long. Since the fumes were hurtful (a considerable under-statement) the philosophical demonstration was to be staged in the fireplace of a well-ventilated room.

Less alarming versions of Pharaoh's Serpents used to form part of indoor firework sets, the other items of which included: paper balloons which ascended when lit, burning out before reaching the ceiling; Bengal lights; sparklers like fairy wands; and touch-paper pictures in which a spark burned along a set trail, creating a picture and exploding a percussion cap at the end.

FIRST DIVISION
Ample Meals In Gaol

Until 1947 there was a 'cushy' form of imprisonment, in theory intended for the gently nurtured who depended on servants and whose crime involved no real moral turpitude. This was known as imprisonment in the First Division, where the prisoner could send out for meals and hire a servant from the riffraff in the Third Division.

The two best-known beneficiaries of this system were both members of the House of Russell. In 1901 the second Earl Russell was sentenced to three months in Holloway, in the First Division, after pleading guilty, before his peers, to a charge of bigamy. Bigamy may involve a high degree of turpitude, but this was a misunderstanding about the validity of the laws of Nevada, where the Earl had married 'one Mollie Cooke', and the Lord High Steward, passing sentence, took notice of the 'extreme torture' Russell had long suffered at the hands of his legal wife.

The day after he entered Holloway (not yet an all-woman gaol) Russell had his own clothes, his own writing desk with unlimited stationery, his own wash-stand, bed and armchair. 'More than ample meals were brought in by a caterer from outside and served by magnificent attendants in the King's uniform. A debtor prisoner was assigned to me to clean my cell at wages more exiguous than any charwoman would have looked at' (*My Life and Adventures*). The prisoner was allowed a morning paper, any number of books and visitors three times a week. His light was left on an hour later than regulations specified. In spite of all this, and in spite of tea parties in his cell with the governor and deputy governor, he was 'stunned and embittered beyond all bearing'.

The Earl's fellow prisoners in the First Division included men who had flouted court orders against the infringement of patents, an 'unspeakable ruffian' of a doctor held as a witness on a coroner's warrant and a feeble-minded youthful coal-stealer.

In 1918 Earl Russell's more famous brother, Bertrand Russell, was sentenced to six months' gaol for publishing an article saying that American troops in Britain would be used as strike-breakers, a role for which they were trained in their own country. The Bow Street magistrate ruled, originally, that the philosopher should be confined in the Second Division (less privileged than the First, more privileged than the Third) but Russell expressed fears that his mind would lose its competence. 'I should regret this,' he told Gilbert Murray, 'as I still have a lot of philosophy that I wish to do.' He mentioned the names of law lords who might be able to get him into the First Division, and also Asquith and Grey. Somehow the trick was done, possibly with the aid of Balfour, and while the conscientious objectors whom Russell had encouraged to defy the call-up were subjected to extreme rigours, he was able to hire a servant at sixpence a day, surround himself with books, receive visits from other men's wives, accept flowers and soap and settle down to a regimen of four hours writing, four hours of philosophical reading and four hours of general reading. He admitted that First Division treatment had a class flavour about it, but saw no reason why he should not take advantage of the rules, try to extend them and even flout them, as by smuggling letters out.

Membership of the peerage did not automatically qualify an offender for First Division privileges. The shipowner Lord Kylsant, found guilty of commercial offences in the 'Royal Mail' case in 1931, served his sentence in the Second Division. Members of Parliament sometimes enquired what were the privileges to be expected in the Second Division, but received only the thinnest dribble of information. It appeared that Second Division prisoners wore dress of another colour, were segregated as far as possible and were allowed more frequent letters and visitors than ordinary prisoners. On the Labour benches were several 'old lags' who had served gaol terms during or after the 1914–18 war and should have known the answers to these questions without asking. James Maxton twitted a fellow Member with being the type who, if gaoled, would try to wangle himself into the First Division as a political offender. According to F. W. Pethick-Lawrence there was 'a very small number of super-intellectual people whose peculiar idiosyncrasy is an extreme individualism' which led them to carry their principles to extremes, and they obviously deserved a different type of treatment from that given to other offenders. However, it was made clear by Sir John Simon, when Home Secretary, that there was no special category for political offenders and never had been.

Quite substantial numbers of offenders qualified for the Second Division between the wars. Examples were: an erring motorist from a 'good' background, a war hero fighting drugs and an eighteen-year-old of doubtful sanity who had lain down in the path of an express train.

During World War Two the luxurious gaol conditions supposedly enjoyed by Sir Oswald and Lady Mosley, who were internees and not convicted prisoners, had the Sunday papers in a frenzy. Sir Oswald was represented as living a life of bridge and champagne, with a prisoner valet to bring in his silk underwear laundered in Mayfair; but life in 'F' Wing at Brixton, though it had its privileges, did not reach these gracious standards. Indeed, the wing appears to have been run-down and bug-ridden. Lady Mosley was interned at Holloway, where her husband eventually joined her in 'Lady Mosley's suite'. Whether or not the Mosleys were entitled to a daily bath was discussed at the highest Government level.

The idea of class distinctions in prison found little favour with the Attlee Government and in 1947 the system of three divisions was swept away. With it went hard labour and penal servitude. The *Solicitors' Journal* said that in practice the distinction between the three divisions of imprisonment had long ceased to exist.

FLYING
(1) Trail Of The Rope

It is odd that in the early days of flying there was no loud and universal outcry against the assumed right of aviators to levitate heavy dangerous objects over the heads and hearths of others and bring them down, without a by-your-leave, on anybody's meadow, crop fields or paddock.

Balloonists had cheerfully assumed this right. Part of the fun of this sport was 'trailing', according to an article in the *Pall Mall Gazette* in 1906. Trailing meant that 'a rope 250 feet long is let down and allowed to drag over the face of the country. If it diminishes the pace, it gives one an idea of the rate one is travelling, and a sense of motion absent under other conditions . . . Over trees, houses, haystacks, everything, glides, twists and winds the rope. It causes consternation in the poultry yard and a sensation among grazing cattle . . .'

However, Major Hermann W. L. Moedebeck in his admirable *Pocket Book of Aeronautics* seems to recognise the nuisance of trailing, though his landing instructions in general show a no-nonsense attitude towards groundlings.

Descend until the trail rope is on the ground. Prevent the rope going over houses on account of the damage thus caused, and the danger to persons below, and prevent it passing over railway tracks for your own sake, and over telegraph wires and trees.

Diminish the buoyancy as desirable by opening the valve for short periods. Prevent the velocity of descent becoming too great . . . by an energetic discharge of ballast (shake out, but do not throw out whole bags) . . .

Tear the envelope open as soon as favourable landing con-

ditions occur, some fifteen to twenty metres above the ground or after the first bump. Hold fast to the car on the trail rope side; bend the legs before a bump occurs to reduce the shock to the system. If a dragging voyage begins, which only occurs when the tearing arrangements do not act or when the wind forms a sail of the empty balloon, one protects oneself by holding on to the grips inside the car and by taking precautions against a sudden loss of balance and against being thrown out by the car turning over.

It is the duty of every conductor in critical moments to set an example of coolness and cold-bloodedness to the passengers. . .

After landing. Determine the time and place; keep at a distance persons with cigars, pipes &c. Seek out persons who are willing to offer assistance (*for instructions in foreign languages see V. Tschudi, Instruktion für die Ballonführer, Berlin, 1905*). Unfasten the car and hoop. When sufficient intelligent helpers are at hand fold the balloon carefully gore by gore. Bind everything firmly together with the car ropes; order waggons; write out consignments; instruct the carrier as to the handling of the balloon; do not put the car on top of the envelope; all instructions and charts should be carried by the aeronaut himself.

Enquire about damage to fields and compensation. Obtain at once a written statement.

Reward the people assisting, obtaining receipts.

Pay for the carriage of the materials to the station.

Forward telegrams as to the success of the voyage.

The policy was 'coolness and cold-bloodedness' to all, not merely to the passengers. Note the importance of recruiting only intelligent helpers, not the first wave of bumpkins. Note the insistence on making angry farmers and landowners write down their claims, instead of jabbering and shaking their fists at foreigners. Presumably the Major demanded receipts from his helpers to stop them holding out their hands a second time. Perhaps he should have had an ink-pad and a stamp to mark the backs of their hands. According to the *Pall Mall Gazette* article, the total expenditure on groundlings was fairly trivial – 'five shillings for ascent' and 'six shillings-and-sixpence for descent'.

FLYING
(2) The Circus Is Coming

Between the world wars hundreds of thousands of people had their first taste of flying in a 'five-shilling flip'. Sometimes the thrill was offered by rather raffish young heroes whose stock-in-trade might be no more than an old biplane, a windsock and a tent. The aircraft was possibly one of those spared from the post-war orgy of destruction when the Royal Air Force found itself with 20,000 unwanted aircraft, and women at Farnborough, Henlow and elsewhere were set to work on these machines with saws, hatchets and hammers, and householders lit their fires with the wreckage of brand-new Bristol and de Havilland fighters.

The 'five-shilling flip' was an incredible bargain and it is hard to know how the operators ever made a profit from it. Even though the flight was not much more than round the field, the concentration of excitement was unforgettable. First, the swinging of the propeller, performed by a mechanic trained to avoid decapitation; then the flattening of the grass as the engine roared, the savouring of all those virile hot smells, the now-or-never whoosh forward over bumpy terrain, the excitement of the landscape tilting on its axis, the fierce battering wind, the grab for support at a handy pipe which turned out to be damnably hot, the beads of oil blown back from the engine, the antics of the air-speed indicator, and, all too soon, the sudden hushed moment before the bump of landing.

The pilots were often ex-war flyers of the 'go anywhere, do any-thing' breed, desperate for a job that would keep them in the air. The only opportunities were barnstorming, flying errands for newspapers, or performing the odd taxi mission like rushing those two anxious husbands, Harold Nicholson and Denys Trefusis, from London to Amiens to catch up with their runaway wives who had eloped to-gether (surely one of the historic flights of 1920).

Among the first to buy an Avro from the Aircraft Disposal Board, which saved many aircraft from the hatchet, was Alan Cobham. It cost him £450, early in 1919, and he had it converted to a three-seater. By the end of the year he had given 500 flights and his Berkshire Aviation Company ran the first really successful 'road show'. The air circus nomads were a high-spirited lot, but very different from the brash hooligans seen in *Sergeant Pepper's Flying Circus*, a film which gives the impression that barnstorming in America was an advanced exercise in hysteria, braggadocio and the death-wish. If one of Pepper's wing-walkers panicked and fell to earth, it was a fate no more to be noticed than that of someone who died going over Niagara in a barrel.

Some of the barnstormers were seduced into sky-writing, intro-duced in 1922 by Captain J. C. Savage, who inscribed 'Daily Mail' above the Derby crowds; this called for the ability to execute legible handwriting on a flat plane, even to the dotting of i's and the crossing of t's. Others gradually found their way into commercial flying (Im-perial Airways was founded in 1924), or went, as did Cobham, into long-distance record-breaking. Every year the Boat Race inspired its own aerial pageant, with as many as forty aircraft executing the prescribed left-hand circuit above the Thames. But the air circuses kept going and in the 1930s Cobham launched the really big display. For four years his heterogeneous formations streamed across the skies, like a private air force, giving very nearly a million joy rides. His craft ran the gamut from a Clive bomber converted to an air liner to a Drone powered by a motor-cycle engine, with a Cierva Autogyro thrown in for novelty. As a feat of organisation it was prodigious. The field-screeners and poster men travelled and slept in trucks; the engineers had their own tented mess, with 'batmen'; and the pilots, for whom sound sleep was essential, stayed in hotels. Wherever this corps of daredevils rested, small boys clamoured for odd jobs which would get them into the display for nothing.

The Cobham circus performed all the now-customary stunts, from loops and bunts (inverted loops) to wing-walking and picking up handkerchiefs with a hook on the wing tip (Cobham has confessed in *A Time to Fly* that the shooting of balloons on the ground by a pilot with a revolver was a fake – they were exploded by a hidden accomplice). One clowning act involved a 'volunteer' falling from the aircraft he was trying to master, but the 'body' was a bouncing rubber figure.

In 1933 Cobham, now operating two fleets, arranged for them to make a noon rendezvous over London at 4,000 feet, no mean exercise for a showman to stage above a capital city. But there were bad days. One of them was at Leeds, where an alighting aircraft, coming in low over spectators in gusty weather, struck and killed two boys (pilot exonerated); another at Blackpool, involving four deaths in a mid-air collision.

Many other circuses ranged the skies. One of them called itself the British Hospitals Pageant, but in 1933 was preparing a change of name to 'The Sky Devils Air Circus'. The Crimson Fleet was known to its shareholders as Modern Airways. Long-distance flyers like Captain C. D. Barnard and Captain C. W. A. Scott had their own displays, performing at home and abroad. The problem was finding sites; almost every farmer with twenty-five acres of flat land was approached. Somehow there was always room for a determined newcomer. Pauline Gower, who was to command the women flyers in the Air Transport Auxiliary in World War Two, began in the traditional manner – hiring a Moth, then hanging round a field trying to charm passers-by into the cockpit. Later she was a stuntswoman for the Crimson Fleet. These were the pilots who did so much to make us air-minded; more, perhaps, than that curious breed of hearty titled women who racketed round the world, with or without male co-pilots, breaking records but breaking no hearts.

Pilots who had been seduced into sky-writing, which depended over-much on clear skies, now learned the new trade of banner-towing. This feat delighted the young, but their elders showed resentment as the noisy aircraft with their incitement to consume bile beans flew low and intrusively. In 1962 all forms of aerial advertising were made illegal in Britain. Anyone who has seen aircraft in formation over New York 'sky-typing' in puffs of smoke a message about World Cup baseball – all done by computer, apparently – must wonder whether our young are being unfairly deprived of a chance to marvel at the many-sided audacity of man.

FOG
It Had Its Moments

How could one feel nostalgia for 'pea soup' fog – Eliot's 'yellow smoke that rubs its muzzle on the window panes'? The fog which assailed all five senses at once – blocking sight, muffling sound, corrupting taste and smell and leaving objects filthy to the touch? The fog which entitled cinema-goers to their money back? The kind which left only the top of the control tower at Croydon Airport visible, a real shaker for the incoming pilot flying by the seat of his pants from Paris? The kind which, as advertising men complained, prevented the public from seeing posters? The 'London Particular' which, billowing into the Law Courts, served (as Dickens explained) to symbolise the perennial legal fog endemic to the Court of Chancery? The kind which filled the cemeteries with the old and left the young sneezing black horrors into their handkerchiefs?

Ah, yes, but it could be exciting too: the bus conductors, armed with torches, marching six paces ahead of their vehicles, not at all sure they were on the right route; the crunch underfoot of broken glass from motor cars; the crackle of detonators on the railway lines and the hoot of foghorns; the street lamps glowing eerily like rotten mackerel; and collisions with frightened masked housemaids, lost on their way home from the pillar-box.

In London it could be very freakish. Big Ben might be lost to sight from the street, but visible from the third or fourth floor of an office

building, serene above the flocculence. Commuters could ride in by train from a sunny countryside and find themselves in a terminus where they could not see the platform as they alighted and then could not find the ticket barrier.

The fog varied in colour from off-white to sepia. When the sun became visible it was likely to be as a crimson disc behind a thread-bare Army blanket. As the fog eventually lifted, and the pigeons which had gone to roost at noon began to circulate again, the sight of tall buildings swimming half-defined in the haze and great bridges reaching out into dreamy oblivion was something not to be for-gotten. Monet, we are told, came over to London especially for the half-lights of winter. As he told René Gimpel: 'Without the fog, London would not be a beautiful city. It is the fog which gives it its marvellous amplitude. Its regular, massive blocks become grandiose in this mysterious cloak.' Monet, however, would have found it difficult to get his effects in a real 'London Particular'; a half-fog was more his style.

98

In a 'pea-souper' the really happy man was the thriller writer who, having stocked up his sitting-room fire (thus contributing a little further to the gloom), sat down at his typewriter to rattle out a tale called 'Murder in the Fog'.

FORE-EDGE PAINTING
A Game For Ladies

The book looked like any other book, but when it was opened – hey, presto! – the fanned-out fore-edge revealed a delicate water-colour of the Lakes of Killarney. When closed and reopened from the back another picture appeared along the fore-edge: Giant's Causeway.

Binders had indulged in this form of embellishment in the seventeenth century. The fore-edge, when the book was closed, was often masked by gilt. In the nineteenth century fore-edge painting was the hobby of ladies who never quite knew what to be at, the sort of ladies who had probably never made a pot of tea in their lives but wanted to do something creative. It was an eminently harmless hobby, unless practised on valuable books, and the results could be quite charming. All one needed was a clamp to hold the pages fanned and a box of water-colours, which had to be applied thinly (oil paint was unsuitable). Serious bibliophiles shake their heads at these latter-day dabblings, but are keen enough to collect early examples.

Was a secret message ever transmitted on a book's fore-edge? The answer must be yes.

FORMICARIUMS
A City Under Glass

A formicarium for Christmas! This irresistible gift, from Gamages as like as not, consisted of a 'Lilliputian city' of streets, bridges and tunnels, populated by ants – and with a queen ant in residence. The city was glass-topped and there was an optional magnifying glass the better to study the teeming life of the metropolis. Only the boy next door was likely to get a formicarium; one's own parents were too nervous of ants vacating their city and taking over the house.

There is much one would like to know about the vanished formicarium industry. Where were they made, and by whom? How were the ants induced to take up residence? How were they nourished? How long was it before the Lilliputian city became a City of the Dead, and was consigned to a garden hut, along with the sordid relics of the previous year's silkworm enterprise?

FORMING FOURS
And 'Puff Visage'

It was that restless meddler Leslie Hore-Belisha who, on the eve of World War Two, abolished forming fours and replaced it by forming threes.

There was something very satisfying about forming fours. It was an exercise carried out not only on Army parade-grounds but in school playgrounds, for formal occasions. The ritual began when all fell in shoulder to shoulder, in two orderly ranks, and then numbered off as often as was necessary to get the sequence correct, stumble-free and as rapid as machine-gun fire. Then, on the order 'Form fours', the even numbers took a rearward pace of thirty inches with the left foot and a sideways pace of twenty-seven inches with the right foot, thus creating four ranks. The manoeuvre was rarely achieved to perfection the first time, and there was usually trouble over something called a blank file, but we did not mind repeating it; anything to postpone whatever might next be in store. Unless memory errs, there was none of that shuffling which disfigured the three-ranks drill, with every man extending an arm and a clenched fist, pushing his neighbour off and holding him at bay.

Fortunately Hore-Belisha did not mess about with the noble position of Attention, which involves balancing the head evenly on the neck, carrying the body evenly over the thighs, letting the arms hang easily from the shoulders (and from nowhere else), and allowing no part of the body to be drawn in or pushed out.

A leader-writer in *The Times* once professed to remember a command 'Puff Visage'. What a sight it must have been: a battalion swelling and gradually reddening, followed, on the command 'As you were', by a sudden deflation and paling, along with a puncture-like hiss. In bayonet drill recruits were expected to look suitably fierce, but there was never, so far as one remembers, an order 'Contort Visage'.

FROST
Keeping The Pot Boiling

'Ice formed on the butler's upper slopes' runs one of P. G. Wodehouse's happiest images. But surely ice, real ice, did form on our upper slopes in the winters of childhood? Ears tingled abominably and seemed to become brittle to the touch; noses grew unimaginably gelid. In Siberia, one gathers, people tap each other on the shoulder when their noses look like splitting in the frost and advise going indoors. Well, it wasn't quite as bad as that, nor were birds frozen to death in flight, but it was *cold*.

Ice formed on iron railings and fingers could freeze to them. And not only fingers. Were there not small boys who licked frozen railings and found themselves captive? It is hard to recall how they were freed; presumably with the aid of a warm cloth, though it may well have been a job for the fire brigade, as when a boy got his head wedged between railings.

The great thing about frost was that it paved the way for slides, those polished slippery tracks along which citizens of all degrees

101

whizzed in a standing position, making wild balletic gestures. Some slides, one suspects, were helped to form with the aid of buckets of water. They were to be found in school play-grounds, marvellously long and treacherous affairs on which small boys were liable to be swept off their feet by big boys hurtling behind them. At the far end might be a spiked railing, but no matter. The great thing was to 'keep the pot boiling', that is, to have as many people whizzing over the ice as possible.

Some slides were established on pavements (an illegal proceeding) and wrathful householders often strewed ashes or salt on them. The best of all were worked up, or 'cut out', on frozen ponds and some were of a daunting length. On one such pond Sam Weller displayed 'that beautiful feat of fancy-sliding which is currently denominated "knocking at the cobbler's door", and which is achieved by skimming over the ice on one foot, and occasionally giving a postman's knock upon it with the other.' Mr Pickwick did not attempt this gasconade, but went 'slowly and gravely' down the slide, with his feet just over a yard apart; until, with a loud crack, he disappeared through the ice.

FROTH-BLOWERS
Immune From Arrest?

The more we are together, together, together,
The more we are together
The merrier we'll be.
For your friends are my friends,
And my friends are your friends,
And the more we are together
The merrier we'll be.

Drinking songs are rarely sophisticated and this all-pervasive 'Froth-Blowers' Anthem' of the late 1920s was the least sophisticated of all. Those who roared it out had the excuse that they were roistering in a good cause.

The Ancient Order of Froth-Blowers existed 'to foster the gentle art and healthy pastime of Froth Blowing amongst gentlemen of

leisure and ex-soldiers'. For a subscription of five shillings, members received a card entitling them to blow froth off any member's beer, 'and occasionally off non-members' beer, provided they are not looking or are of a peaceful disposition'. For what it was worth, they received this assurance: 'The Metropolitan Police have been requested not to arrest, annoy or apprehend any member under or over the influence of Froth, should the same member be wearing the AOFB cuff-links at the time of the debauch.'

The Order's motto, 'Moderation in Lubrication', had to be squared with instructions like 'three gulps to the pint, fourteen to the gallon are customary'. It could have resulted in much tiresome horseplay by hearties, but one never seemed to read about Froth-Blower disturbances, such as might have impelled a judge to ask, 'What is a Froth-Blower?'

The official organ of the Order was the notorious *Sporting Times*, or 'Pink 'Un'. All annoucements were relentlessly waggish, in the saloon-bar manner – 'We insure your dog against rabies, your cook against babies, yourself against scabies.' There was a suitable range of titles for those who distinguished themselves in recruiting members: Blower (one member), Blaster (25), Tornado (100) and so on up to Grand Typhoon (1,000). Failure to wear the Order's cuff-links could not only jeopardise one's supposed immunity from the law but make one liable for a round of drinks. There were many other accessories, including powder compacts for Froth-Blowers' girl friends, if any.

From 1926 onwards the Order owed almost everything to Sir Alfred Fripp, a benign and distinguished surgeon who stumped the country founding 'Vats' (or gatherings) until 1930, when he died. By 1929 the Ancient Order had endowed forty hospital cots and helped thousands of needy children to attend camps. That year it erected a roof garden for mothers and children on the Marylebone Housing Association's first block of slum-clearance flats and was described by the Lord Chancellor (Lord Hailsham) as 'a great charitable organisation'. By the time of Fripp's death there were 700,000 members.

The printed list of 'Vats' shows that Froth-Blowers flourished in the military stations of India, the commercial banks of Chile and the Argentine and outposts like the Dynamite Factory Club at Modderfontein. The anthem continued to be chanted at outings and re-unions long after the Order was forgotten. A reference to the cult survives in Betjeman's poem. 'The Varsity Student's Rag' – 'I started a rag in Putney at our Froth-Blowers' branch down there'. One may also read of an induction into the Froth-Blowers in 'Sapper's' *The Female of the Species*. It was very much the sort of ceremony to appeal to Bulldog Drummond and his mates.

GADGETS
For Easier Living

Egg-Decapitators
The humorist D. B. Wyndham-Lewis alleged that a typical *Punch* article of his day began: ' "I say," said Cecilia, as she decapitated her breakfast egg . . . .' That word 'decapitated' was not necessarily a literary flourish. People like Cecilia probably used egg-decapitators, as their parents had done, rather than descend to the vulgarity of slitting off the top with a knife. Egg-decapitators came in various forms, the commonest of which resembled a pair of scissors with curved, spiked blades which closed on top of the egg. With a soft-boiled egg the result could be less than admirable.

Table Blowpipes

These were for extinguishing the lights under chafing dishes. Only the completely insensitive would blow with the naked mouth across the table at the flickering flames. Sir Compton Mackenzie remembers as 'an absurd trifle' how the novelist Rhoda Broughton, with whom he was taking polite tea in 1903, blew out a spirit lamp 'with a sort of pea-shooter'.

Lazy Tongs

A lady comfortably seated in an armchair, or an invalid propped up in bed, would have to hand a pair of silver lazy tongs, defined as 'a series of diagonal levers pivoted together at the middle and ends, capable of being extended by a movement of the scissors-like handles so as to pick up objects at a distance' (*Chambers*). The claws of the tongs were suitable for recovering dropped handkerchiefs or *billets doux* but not for anything heavier or breakable. If the desired object was out of range, the lady had no option but to ring for a maid from the basement to pass it to her.

Port Tongs

If a bottle of port had a suspect cork, the way to open it was to heat the jaws of the long-handled port tongs until they were nearly red-hot, grip the bottle with them about the neck, saw back and to slightly, remove the jaws, then flick the hot surface of the glass with a cloth or feather soaked in cold water – and off came the neck, clean. Why not pick up a pair of port tongs in a junk shop and amaze your friends?

Bottle Locks

'For instantly snapping over the neck of a bottle to prevent inter-ference with contents', this device was supplied with a warded lock 'suitable for ordinary wine bottles', or a superior Bramah lock. It was intended to deter servants rather than wives and had more justifi-cation than, say, a Bible-carrier with a lock to discourage access to the Scriptures.

Possibly the inspiration for the bottle lock was the Tantalus, the cage for enclosing two or three ornamental liquor bottles in such a way that the stoppers could not be removed until the lock was opened. In *Summoned by Bells* Sir John Betjeman recalls, as a boy, visiting the family factory in Islington and seeing '. . . stockrooms heavy with the Tantalus / On which the family fortunes had been made'.

Ceiling Clocks
With the aid of a battery, a magnified version of the clock face at one's bedside was projected on to the ceiling. Ideal for the man determined not to sleep in, yet one could search a thousand books of memoirs for a reference to this useful device.

Toe-Straighteners
These miniature metal dumb-bells were worn between the toes, presumably only at night . . . along with, perhaps, a nose-straightener (strapped round the head) and a set of anti-rheumatic rings, one on each finger.

Railway Keys
Costing less than a shilling, this elementary instrument enabled the rail traveller to open compartment doors which had been locked so that the staff could solicit tips by unlocking them (or for some more creditable reason). Once inside, the traveller could lock out other travellers, to save himself the fatigue of pretending to be a lunatic. The most respectable motive for carrying a railway key was to save oneself from being burned alive in an accident.

GASLIGHT
Mind That Mantle!

One does not read far in Betjeman without finding evocations of gaslight: the poet likening the surge of his spiritual aspiration to the hiss of the Low Church gas-jets; the ritual turning down of the gas in the hall in 'Death In Leamington'.

We who did our homework by gaslight do not wish to be told that gas was noisy, dirty, unhygienic and dangerous. The light from incandescent mantles was both bright and soft, quite good enough to illuminate logarithm tables. On landings or in passages a bat's-wing burner threw exciting shadows, like those cast in earlier years by wax night-lights, or 'burglars' horrors'.

To be allowed to light the gas was a notable step in growing up. Gas mantles were outrageously fragile and any clumsiness with a match could bring disaster. It has to be said that Count Auer von Welsbach's gas mantle was, in every sense, a brilliant invention. It gave the gas industry a much-needed boost just when electricity was getting ideas above itself; and like the pen nib and the safety razor blade it fulfilled the manufacturer's dream of a low-priced, short-lived artefact which everybody needed and had to keep replacing, but which could be advertised as well-nigh immortal. A famous poster showed two workmen in a wrecked building surveying a gas mantle miraculously intact on its bracket. 'Lumme!' says one to the other, 'it must be a Veritas!' (The Veritas Incandescent Mantle Company still appears in the London telephone book.)

Shoppers handled mantles as gingerly as eggs. There were two main kinds: the upright cylindrical model and the small cup-shaped one which shed its radiance downwards. When first installed they had to be 'burned off', which meant that most of the basic cotton of which they were made disappeared, leaving a mesh of chemical filaments which became incandescent at low temperature. A light bump on the bracket, a foray by a clumsy bluebottle could reduce the mantle to white powder; so could turning up the gas too hard at the moment of lighting. Every child had to touch a gas mantle once with a finger, just to see what happened.

The pressure of the gas was supposed to be regulated so that the flame 'fitted' the mantle exactly; a harder pressure meant waste and smelliness. Even well-regulated jets raised the temperature of a room, which was why some families resisted electricity. Others opposed electricity because its light was hard and unflattering. Sensibly, Ellen Terry insisted on gas lighting at the Lyceum.

Which is a reminder that gas inspired a wonderfully creepy murder play: Patrick Hamilton's *Gaslight*, in which the lowering of the light informs a frightened wife that her husband has returned to the room above and is up to no good. For most of us the dimming of the gas meant that another coin had to be put into the meter.

GRAMOPHONES
Should We Have Waited?

'I sound my barbaric yawp over the roofs of the world,' cried Walt Whitman, as if speaking for the early gramophone. The tinny screech of this green-horned monster, re-played today, is as potent a memory-stirrer as a whiff of old-time coal gas, and has about the same aesthetic appeal. The sound itself does not evoke affection, but it is the background to the sound that counts. To a much-dwindled few it may summon up a rather neurotic party, of the kind known as a 'jolly', during the Kaiser's war; to others it may recall once-peaceful quads and quiet backwaters resonant with ragtime stridor; to others again it will recall home foxtrot lessons – or advanced tango lessons from a blonde instructress in a studio, with an anonymous eye peering between the wall mirrors to see that standards of propriety are being maintained.

The Victorians made do with all sorts of mechanical music-makers, forerunners of the juke-box. Edison's phonograph, with its fragile cylindrical records, did not produce an adequate volume of sound, but its successor, the disc gramophone, which swept ahead in the Edwardian years, was soon being reviled for its stentorian attack, allied with a tooth-loosening timbre. Indeed, there is much to be said for the view that this was just another invention put on the market too soon. It built up for itself such an excess of ill-will that landlords and house agents began writing into their leases a clause forbidding the use of a gramophone. But raucous ragtime was no hardship to those brought up on hurdy-gurdies and fairground music.

The 1914-18 war was the first in which the Forces carried their own music with them. Every unit had its portable Decca and those at home were urged to send out all the records they could lay their hands on. The 1915 range of titles included 'When the Angelus is Ringing', 'Nearer, My God, to Thee', 'A Little Drop of Scotch', 'They All Do the Charlie Chaplin Walk', 'I'm Glad My Boy Grew Up to be a Soldier', 'Which Switch is the Switch, Miss, for Ipswich?' and 'You Can't Get Many Pimples on a Pound of Pickled Pork'. If we go by Robert Graves's *Good-Bye To All That*, the choice of records could cause severe dissension in the officers' mess. A captain puts on a frivolous record, the lieutenant-colonel angrily orders it to be replaced by some 'real music', namely 'The Angelus', and the colonel, next to enter, demands that the 'wretched Angelus' be replaced by 'something cheery for a change'.

That was the mess of the Royal Welch Fusiliers. Its repertoire of records is unlikely to have contained any of the non-musical records of that year, which included 'Mr Bottomley, John Bull', 'Beaconsfield's Famous Historical Speech, "Peace Only With Honour"', 'Gladstone's Eulogy on the Bravery and Loyalty of Irish Soldiers', 'General Buller's Farewell Speech to His Men on Leaving South Africa' and 'General Gordon's Soliloquy on His Last Stand'.

The too-loud gramophone was a real problem. As the century came in the manufacturers had been at pains to boast of the volume of sound available. Claims included 'as loud as a man sings', 'loud enough for dancing' and 'SIXTEEN TIMES louder than any other'. The editor of a short-lived gramophone paper published in 1915 faced up to this problem. He thought that muffling devices like 'tone-control shutters' were unsuitable; the effect was as if every instrument was being played with a mute. One remedy was to put the gramophone in an adjoining room, when 'all the beauty of the record will be heard with considerably less volume and all surface noise will be eliminated.' Most singers, it appeared, came over too loud to be heard in the same room and band records were nearly insupportable. 'Loud band records, to be heard to the best advantage, should be played outdoors in the garden, or upon the water for instance.' Then as now, the right to impose music on others was unhesitatingly assumed. Possibly the expression 'Put a sock in it' (that is, into the trumpet of the gramophone) was coined at this period.

The gramophone makers of the day did not regard the provision of entertainment as their sole *raison d'être*. They also turned out models for teaching languages. In the Pathegraphe a roll of paper with printed words accompanied the recording and a pointer indicated the exact position reached by the speaker. The manufacturers also stressed the opportunity offered by the gramophone to 'record and repeat the sweet utterances of the family' (just as the manufacturers of cameras were saying 'Capture their smiles for ever!'). The writer Richard le Gallienne went one better by suggesting that a young man could carry his loved one's voice around with him – 'She can still go on speaking to you, if you have the urge to listen, from beyond the grave.' ('His Mistress's Voice' would have made a touching trade-mark.) T. S. Eliot took a less sentimental approach to the gramophone. Rewriting Goldsmith's stanza which begins 'When lovely woman stoops to folly', he came up with:

> When lovely woman stoops to folly and
> Paces about her room again, alone,
> She smoothes her hair with automatic hand
> And puts a record on the gramophone.

The struggle to improve the quality of reproduction was intense, for there were prodigious markets to be won. Piano notes came over with the pank, pank of a banjo; piccolos were indecently shrill; the human voice could be an adenoidal disaster. Yet Caruso and Galli-Gurci risked their reputations in the studios. In 1921 Sir Edward Elgar announced that the gramophone was no longer a toy or a 'scratch' form of entertainment. The cultured classes, he said, were taking it up and every school would soon have to install one. As he was opening the new headquarters of the Gramophone Company he could hardly have said otherwise.

In 1923 Compton Mackenzie, then living on the Channel isle of Herm, founded the magazine *The Gramophone*, which appraised records seriously. Mackenzie had found that he worked better to a background of music and this new enterprise at least ensured him a

110

generous supply of records. Frequently, in the early issues, he said that *The Gramophone* would have nothing to do with 'the wireless', but in 1924 he had become, as he claims, the BBC's first disc jockey, at Savoy Hill, a chore later taken over by his brother-in-law, Christopher Stone. This was about the time when the cry went up that the gramophone was finished, doomed to extinction by the wireless loud-speaker. The cheap tinny version died hard; and the sound of a jazz band suddenly slowing, as if overcome by agonised torpor, until restored to normality by a rapid winding of the handle, survived into the age of high-fidelity and golden discs.

GRAND GUIGNOL
A Waste Of Sybil?

A *guignol* is a Punch and Judy show and a *grand guignol* is a Punch and Judy show for adults. The city of Paris kept a horrific Grand Guignol theatre going for generations. Failure to establish the cult in Britain can be attributed to many factors, but it cannot be blamed on Dame Sybil Thorndike.

The impresario José Levy was all set to introduce the theatre of horror to Britain in the summer of 1914, but a major outbreak of *grand guignol* in Europe compelled a postponement. In 1922 he took over the Little Theatre in the Adelphi, London, hired nurses to tend the expected casualties and smartened up the foyer to accommodate those who could not take it. Aubrey Hammond devised a splendid poster showing petrified couples clutching each other in the stalls and strong men draped in a state of collapse over the edge of the dress circle.

Sybil Thorndike headed the cast and her husband Lewis Casson produced. Not all the plays were gruesome; some were light, others satirical. But it was obvious that 'grue' was to be the main attraction. In the first run was a French import called *The Hand of Death*, in which the inventor of an electrical machine for reviving the dead is awaiting a body from the executioner. Instead he receives the body of his daughter killed in a car crash. Amid groans from her distraught lover and the frenzy of a stage storm he tries to revive her, without

111

avail. Then, in the throes of *rigor mortis*, her hand (the hand of Sybil Thorndike) rises, grips him by the throat and strangles him.

In *Private Room No. 6* Miss Thorndike played a *décolleté* Nihilist forced to suffer the caresses and bites of a Czarist ogre, who is doomed to be strangled by one of her gloves. In another play, for a change, she was herself strangled. She was crushed to death by a hydraulic press masquerading as a ceiling. As a street-walker hiding from the police in a waxworks chamber of horrors she frightened to death a man spending the night there for a bet.

It was the play called *The Old Women* which created the biggest stir. Sneaked past the Lord Chamberlain by Lewis Casson, who said it was to be produced for villagers at Wrotham, it featured a convent for the mad in which a girl (Sybil again) had her eyes put out with knitting needles by three apparently harmless old women. One man in the stalls cried 'This is monstrous!', rushed out and was sick in the foyer. 'The actors,' says John Casson, 'were all delighted at the effect of their artistry.' The drama critic of *The Times* thought the play too disgusting to describe and said it should be taken off at once. Presumably this was A. B. Walkley, who had already written about the Guignol cult and talked of 'the immense fun of theatrical experiment, of seeing how far you can go, what shocks the public can stand and

112

what it cannot, the joy of adventurously exploring the unknown and the *inédit*'.

In *The Kill* a lover was thrown to the wolves by a jealous husband. Two fine wolfhounds were paraded on stage and it was assumed by an RSPCA inspector (who may have been put up to it) that their hideous off-stage howls must have been produced by cruelty. He was shown the sounds being produced by blowing into lamp glasses.

One play which *The Times* thought had 'its moments' was *The Regiment* (as usual, from the French), in which a Uhlan medical staff prepares to inoculate a regiment against smallpox. When a Polish anarchist switches the serum tubes to a deadlier mixture, the troops go barking mad and are shot down like dogs.

On the whole *The Times* thought Miss Thorndike was wasted on such stuff. The critic St John Ervine believed the Thorndikes were catering for debased tastes; James Agate found his own reasons for defending the plays. The future Dame confessed that she went into *grand guignol* with much gusto, found that it cured her nightmares by a form of release, and said afterwards that it had all been 'absolute bliss'. Possibly her nightmares were merely passed on to others. In 1922 the season ended. If it had been proved that there was a British audience for a Theatre of Cruelty, no other producer seemed eager to rush in and satisfy it.

Today anything goes in the theatre, but *grand guignol* is scoring quite exceptional triumphs in the blood-and-sex shows staged in Japanese music-halls (*see* Paul Theroux's unsparing account in *The Great Railway Bazaar*).

GROCERS
Was G.K.C. Unfair?

Why the 'wicked grocer' should have been so heartily, if enter-tainingly, reviled by G. K. Chesterton is a real puzzle. 'He keeps a lady in a cage / Most cruelly all day, / And makes her count and calls her 'Miss' / Until she fades away . . .' But were there not thousands of numerate ladies only too keen to be kept in the grocer's cage? Were there not also thousands of 'pert lads' longing for the chance to 'bang about and do his wicked trade'? Especially when this involved performing acrobatics in the street on their delivery cycles? Chesterton does not mention another familiar figure on the grocer's payroll – the 'grocer's man' who used to tour street after street to take down the busy housewife's weekly order, sitting with her at her fireside, writing to her dictation with a copying-ink pencil and making sure she forgot no staple food. To children he was a clamorously received visitor, a source of cigarette cards and sweets, and a go-between thought to have the power of interceding with his master to ensure that the next consignment of candied peel would have even more lavish encrustations of that wonderful, jade-coloured sugar. (Did not Lord Willis once go out of his way to enthuse about this delicacy?)

Poor grocer! A few villains may have put 'sand of Araby' in the sugar and sold dust as salt (in fact, salt came in huge hard blocks, for crushing at home). If the honest grocer gave short weight it was because pride, and pride alone, induced him to polish away at his splendid brass weights, making them fractionally lighter than they should have been; and the Weights and Measures inspectors were always there to add bits of lead as needed and warn on the perils of bullshine. The grocer was always ready to pluck from his open sacks – with their odorous and colourful contents, a sight now only to be seen in *souks* – titbits for customers to taste. And in his doorway he put bran tubs in which children could grope for packets of transfers and tin whistles.

The public did not properly appreciate the grocer. Because he very civilly kept his shop open late in the evening many of his customers most incivilly left their shopping until the last half-hour. After finally pulling down the shutters the grocer and his wife then had to spend their few minutes of leisure rolling sheets of paper into conical pokes so that he could sell small quantities of unpackaged sugar and currants to the needy. Yet he was in the shop early next morning refreshed and whacking away at the butter with his ping-pong bats as if he had no cares, an apostle of goodwill to all respectable women, a pillar of the community and a potential father of prime ministers.

Evidently Chesterton was annoyed with the grocer for supplying footmen with wines and spirits which were carried off to duchesses and 'drunk in dressing-rooms', instead of being consumed 'frankly and in fellowship' in public-houses, where people got drunk openly and decently. Perhaps G.K.C. should have directed his blast at the wicked draper, who bombarded his lady in a cage with whizzing overhead missiles, or projectiles blasted through tubes, and who reputedly kept his exhausted staff sleeping under the counter at night. What a poem that would have made!

GUINEAS
Once Good For You

A once-prized status symbol has all but vanished, flushed away in the torrent of decimalisation. The last guinea was coined in 1817 and governments tried hard to extinguish its memory; but the harder they tried the more fiercely the barristers, the doctors and the auctioneer hung on to it. For barristers it was one of the things that set them above solicitors (though some solicitors also charged guineas). Harley Street doctors expected to have guinea fees left on their mantelpieces; in the 1890s there were complaints that some specialists were charging a guinea a mile for visits in the London area and 35 guineas for a visit to Brighton. The Lord Chamberlain used to demand guineas for reading a dirty play, which showed that even Great Officers of State cherished the few pennies over the score which were supposed to be the entitlement of a professional man. Only the higher tradesmen, like tailors and bootmakers, charged in guineas; the fishmonger was content with pounds, even when selling ptarmigan and salmon. Newspapers and magazines often paid their free-lance contributors in guineas and half-guineas, a surprising gesture to a breed who were supposed to know their place. Learned societies invited subscriptions in guineas; the unlearned societies did the same for the sake of prestige, as did superior professors of phrenology.

After decimalisation came in there was nothing to stop people writing cheques for £1.05 or £19.95, but there was little cachet about getting a cheque for a broken sum like that. Soon, perhaps, the guinea will be remembered only in those two classic horse races: the One Thousand Guineas and the Two Thousand Guineas, sums unlikely ever to be rounded off.

HEATERS
Bonfires For The Body

Did clerks really sit at their stools with miniature bonfires burning away in their pockets? Did a faint whiff of hot tinder rise from worshippers in their pews on the First Sunday after Epiphany? Well, somebody must have bought and used those assiduously advertised pocket stoves, fuelled by charcoal or spirit. Leading the field was the 'Patent Instra', advertised as 'the only practical means by which slow-burning fuel has been made available for warming the human body in a safe and cleanly manner'. As good a place as any for it was the hip pocket, but ladies had to make their own arrangements. With ingenuity and motivation, it could be suspended against any part of the body where hypothermia threatened.

Ladies had muffs to keep their hands warm, but first the muff needed to be heated with the aid of a little cylindrical muff-warmer. There were portable heaters 'for desk, table or carriage', in which 'non-explosive' spirit was absorbed in spongy tissue and would burn for twelve hours without renewal. The head of the family might have a pair of boot-warmers, resembling hollow lasts, filled with hot water. The servant who filled the lasts would also pour hot water into any ottoman foot-warmers which were likely to be in use, and any oval stomach-warmers which invalids might wish to clutch to their persons.

At night, beds could be warmed by hot coals, water, bricks, charcoal or spirit, or even by the interaction of chemicals, if the sleeper did not mind acids working away in his bed. Gladstone, a frugal soul, is supposed to have filled his stone hot-water-bottle with his morning tea, which was still reasonably hot after a sleep of four hours. Carlyle's idea of an efficient bed-warmer was a healthy chambermaid, ordered to lie between the sheets for an hour or two before bed-time; but it was an idea better attuned to the eighteenth century than to the late Victorian age.

HOME DISCIPLINE
Braces And Bitter Aloes

A splendidly simple cure for lying, swearing and blaspheming was to wash out the offender's mouth with soap, preferably a nasty, strong brand. It was, however, a cure more often threatened than administered. In the Boy Scouts the punishment for dirty talk used to be a jug of cold water poured down the culprit's sleeve by the members of his patrol. The Chief Scout, Sir Robert Baden-Powell, got this idea from Captain John Smith, the fastidious coloniser of Virginia.

The Prayer Book forbade the use of hands for 'picking and stealing'. No adult ever explained exactly what 'picking' meant, but in most homes it was held to include picking the titbits from a plate, picking at one's food, picking the nose and picking at scabs.

A tendency towards round-shouldered posture or lower-class slouching was met by 'If you're going to go about like that you'll have to wear a brace.' The shoulder brace was no meaningless threat. Advertised as 'invisible under any garment', suitable for man, woman or child, this ingenious strait-jacket held the head erect, the shoulders back and expanded the chest, 'thereby allowing the wearer to breathe correctly'.

Nail-biting and thumb-sucking were cured by an application of bitter aloes, tying cloth bags over the hands or by a reading from *Struwwelpeter* (see STRUWWELPETER). A famous joke postcard showed a mother directing her son's attention to a statue of the Venus de Milo, with the caption: 'Now you see what'll happen if you go on biting your nails.'

Almost every house had a rule that children must eat two, or even three, slices of plain buttered bread before being allowed to reach for the jam-pot, or to eat cake. Food rejected at one meal was liable to be produced in a congealed form at the next meal; the despised dishes tended to be ground rice, semolina, sago and tapioca ('Ugh! Frogspawn!').

117

Hot drinks were not to be poured from cups into saucers for cooling, or slurped direct from the saucer, though unregenerate adult males, like fathers, uncles and grandfathers, were allowed this liberty. The Duchess of Gloucester (Princess Alice) says her father, the Duke of Buccleuch, used to cool his tea in his saucer on formal occasions, 'no doubt quietly amused by the horrified expressions as people agonised over whether to follow the ducal example'.

In some homes there were rules against cutting string on parcels. All knots were to be untied, even on Christmas and birthday gifts. Girl Guides were (and still are) encouraged to tie knots with their toes, but there is no mention of untying knots this way.

Members of the family leaving home to stay overnight with friends or relatives were required to send postcards saying 'arrived safely'. This applied most stringently to daughters. Sons setting off on cycle tours were expected to send a card from each nightly stopping-place; there was no objection to these being written and stamped beforehand so long as they arrived with appropriate postmarks. It is all hard to credit in a day when parents may never hear from wandering sons or daughters until they fall foul of the Turkish Customs.

HOME HEROICS
Ready? Steady! Slam!

The simplest method of extracting loose teeth has now fallen into disrepute. One end of a piece of thread was tied round the tooth, the other to a door-knob and the door was then slammed. This was a humane variation of the hot-coal method described in *The Adventures of Tom Sawyer*. 'The old lady made one end of the silk thread fast to Tom's tooth with a loop and tied the other to the bed-post. Then she seized the chunk of fire and suddenly thrust it almost into the boy's face. The tooth hung dangling by the bedpost, now.' Another variation was to tie the tooth to the bumper of a car. Such extractions qualified for a substantial addition to the week's pocket money, as a recognition of fortitude; a bonus much more worth having than a coin left under a pillow by a fairy.

Parents whose children were swotting for examinations would sometimes ask, half-jocularly, half-seriously, 'Would you like a cold towel round your head?' Sir Victor Pritchett, in *A Cab at the Door*, says that when he was a boy in Dulwich a next-door neighbour, the hearty Mrs O'Dwyer, stood over her sons while they studied, refreshed them with beer and made cold compresses for 'the clever one' who hoped to go to university. It was not all hard work and hydropathy, however; sometimes she gave her sons boxing lessons in the garden.

American cartoonists show men with ice-packs on their heads, but they are less likely to be studying than recovering from hangovers.

Tonsils were often removed in a rough-and-ready operation on the kitchen table – 'just lie still and sniff this . . .' (yes, we are back to chloroform). The tonsils of poor children were snipped out in hospitals, after which the victims walked home excitedly, spitting blood as they went.

HYMNS
For Workers And Others

The edition of *Hymns Ancient and Modern* current in the early twenties contained a hymn 'For A Service of Working Men'. It begins:

> Sons of Labour, dear to Jesus,
>   To your homes and work again;
> Go with brave hearts back to duty,
>   Face the peril, bear the pain.

This was not intended as an exhortation to strikers to return to work; it was composed for a fibre-stiffening service to make the toiler more contented with his lot. If he was unhappy about his housing conditions, Hymn 586 had this thought for him:

> Be your dwelling ne'er so lowly,
>   Yet remember, by your bed,
> That the Son of God most Holy
>   Had not where to lay his head.

119

And, if his work seemed unbearably menial:

> Think how, in the sacred story,
>   Jesus took a humble grade,
> And the Lord of Love and Glory
>   Work'd with Joseph at his trade.

The need for humility was stressed in other hymns, with sentiments designed in particular to prevent servants grumbling: 'The task Thy wisdom hath assigned / O let me cheerfully fulfil', and so on.

In this old edition of the *A. and M.* the browser will find appeals to the Almighty to let bygones be bygones and forgive the Jews, who have purged their guilt by good conduct ('These are not aliens, but Thy sons of yore'). But the *A. and M.* never took the impatient line with the Almighty that is found in (say) *A Democratic Hymn-Book* (1849);

> How long, O Lord, wilt Thou permit
> The poor to lie at Moloch's feet?

or in Ebenezer Elliott's famous rebuke:

> When wilt Thou save the people?
>   Oh, God of Mercy, when?
> The people, Lord, the people!
>   Not thrones and crowns, but men!

Among hymns no longer in the revised *A. and M.* are those to mark the occasion of Christ's circumcision. The writer treads a difficult path delicately:

> Scarce enter'd on this life of woe,
> His infant blood begins to flow:
> A foretaste of His death he feels,
> An earnest of His Love reveals.

Yet, even in this context, a play on words is permissible:

> Lord, circumcise our hearts, we pray,
> And take what is not Thine away;
> Write Thine own Name within our hearts,
> Thy law upon our inmost parts.

How would the flat-footed hymn-writers of today have tackled this one?

INDIAN ROPE TRICK
And A Few Others

The Maskelyne family of magicians offered £2,000 to anyone who could perform the Indian rope trick in the open air. Old John Nevil Maskelyne, the scourge of Victorian mediums, once sent a man round India dangling the bait; his grandson Jasper, who became a camouflage expert in World War Two, let the world know that the money was always there for anyone who could earn it. (At one time Lord Lonsdale, the 'Yellow Earl', offered £10,000.)

The Maskelynes did not ask the utterly impossible. All they insisted on was that a rope should be made to stand up vertically and that a boy should shin up it and vanish. The full Indian rope trick, as known to so many who had not actually seen it but knew someone who had, called for a second stage in which the magician climbed the rope after the vanished boy and slashed furiously in the air with a knife, until dismembered pieces of the boy tumbled to the ground;

these were then tied up in a sack, from which later the reassembled victim emerged grinning.

The Maskelynes stipulated that the trick had to be performed out of doors. In theatres a humbugging version was sometimes staged by hauling up a rope with an unseen thread into the 'flies'; the boy would then ascend it and vanish, not into thin air, but into friendly cover.

In fact, variations of this trick were even performed at the Maskelyne Theatre of Mysteries, whither the luckiest children in the land were taken for their Christmas treat (the rest of us considered ourselves singularly lucky if a needy conjuror turned up for our entertainment). The Maskelyne Theatre flourished at St George's Hall, London, where the great attraction was a play called 'Will, the Witch and the Watchman', in which humans were turned into animals and vice versa. In 1933 the BBC took over St George's Hall for its own dull purposes and the West End children's party which had lasted for nearly thirty years was over. A whole jolly family of Maskelynes, having cleared the basement workshop of all their secrets, disappeared – temporarily – up their several ropes.

Those of us who knew of Maskelynes only by repute sighed frustratedly over books with titles like *One-Hundred-and-One Tricks Anyone Can Do* (meaning, in practice, 'One-Hundred-and-One Tricks Anyone Can Spot'), and more advanced manuals if we could get them. Naturally, the feats which made most appeal, after the Indian Rope Trick, were those which involved bisecting, decapitating or levitating women, or at least making them vanish inside sofas, which unfortunately called for a prohibitive outlay on pistons, pulleys, steel harnesses, mirrors and trapdoors, not to mention the services of pliant (and pliable) women. So we settled for plucking pennies from the air, paper-tearing and attempting to remove each other's waistcoats without taking off the jacket. Some of the catalogues which came our way offered tricks which required 'no palming', had 'nothing to go wrong' (not even in a string of self-locking sausages), 'no threads, no elastic' and required 'no skill whatever'. Others called for some slight dexterity, with comforting assurances like 'In the excitement your audience will never notice that you have an extra finger on your right hand' (an extra finger from which to extract the flags of all nations). We brooded also over books of ready-made patter, but it was clear that conjuring was going to be hard enough without trying to remember other men's puns.

There was never any prospect of owning a sophisticated conjuror's suit, or the kind which was then thought sophisticated. However, nothing was more delightful than to contemplate a diagrammatic picture of this rig, with dotted lines indicating *profondes* in the tails, *pochettes* at the back of the legs, and two rather special breast pockets, one for rabbits and the other for doves; all this plus an open-ended sheath in one trouser-leg for sliding watches down through a tiny trap-door to an accomplice. That was only the suit. Under the shirt would be a system of wires, pulleys and spring-loaded pulls of great intricacy, designed for the rapid transference of bunches of chrysanthemums and live canaries.

The professors of magic warned that many hostesses were reluctant to have live game and poultry at large in their drawing-rooms, especially if the family pet was to be in attendance. Other hostesses worried over the welfare of vanishing doves and canaries, or did not like to see the conjuror hurling 'harmless' flash paper into the air to distract, by a burst of flame, from whatever legerdemain he was attempting. (Flash paper was ignited by crushing into it a tiny tube containing acid.)

One of the best-loved manuals was *The Art of Conjuring and Drawing-Room Entertainment* published without author's name or date by Ward Lock. It described how to produce a flaming bowl from the pocket which normally harboured livestock. It told how to run a sword through a person's body (insert the tip of the weapon into a curved tube extending round one side of the victim, piercing a bag of red ink on the way). Among 'advanced' tricks it described how to fire a bullet into an assistant's mouth. This was easy enough, largely a matter of well-timed palming, but the book warned of 'a case on record where a performer shot his wife when performing this trick, which is undoubtedly dangerous'. The most famous mishap of this sort was the one which befell the American, William Elsworth Robinson, calling himself Chung Ling Soo, who fell dead on the stage of the Wood Green Empire in March 1918, having failed to catch a live bullet on a plate. The rifle had, in effect, two barrels; in one of these the bullet was held by a clip while the explosion took place in the other, but a faulty breech plug had allowed the force of the charge to send the bullet on its way. (Across the Channel that night, tens of thousands were also facing live bullets.)

This Ward Lock book gave the low-down on the controversial vanishing-canary-in-the-cage trick: 'the bird goes into a little compartment in the centre of the collapsed cage, which is drawn up the right sleeve by means of the pull.' But did that always happen? In 1921 there was a Parliamentary enquiry into the training of performing animals and a conjuror was called on to vanish a canary, as he claimed to have done already before Edward VII and George V. It had been darkly hinted that the bird was killed in the course of the trick, but this was disproved, though the committee seemed unhappy about the abruptness with which the canary was transferred from one spot to another. The performer maintained that when his birds died it was from asthma or a common cold.

The ideal conjuror did not spare his personal appearance. He coated his face with pearl white which would turn black when he sniffed the appropriate fumes, 'a very startling effect'. Or he would smear his features with a phosphorus-and-olive-oil mixture, avoiding the eyes, so that when the lights were extinguished he would present a horrifying supernatural aspect, appearing to be covered with blue flame, the eyes and mouth remaining dark.

Was this the paste which was used to touch up the Hound of the Baskervilles? Dr Watson's description of the 'enormous coal-black hound' which burst from the fog on the Grimpen Mire runs as follows: 'Fire burst from its open mouth, its eyes glowed with a smouldering glare, its muzzle and hackles and dewlap were outlined in flickering flame.' After Holmes had shot the beast, Watson put his hand on the muzzle and his fingers gleamed in the darkness. 'Phosphorus,' he said, and Holmes added, 'A cunning preparation of it.' Exegetists of the Sherlock Holmes texts have argued about how the dread appearance of the Hound was produced. With a good conjuror's handbook anything was possible.

IRISH SWEEP
'Are you "Fifth Time Lucky"?'

In the Depression years one of the most popular events in the newspaper calendar was the draw for the Irish Sweep. Every year scores of national and provincial reporters were invited to Dublin to watch pretty nurses drawing tickets from the giant drum in the Plaza Cinema. While they enjoyed prodigal hospitality, the front pages back home were given over to interviews with local residents whose names came up in the draw. 'Good morning! Are you "Fifth Time Lucky"?' – 'What are you talking about?' – 'Did you sign your Irish Sweep counterfoil "Fifth Time Lucky"?' – 'What if I did?' – 'Well, you may be getting £30,000 . . .' Sometimes the good news from Dublin had the same effect as bad, causing collapse (at the draw for the last State lottery in London in 1826, hard-up surgeons haunted the Guildhall ready to bleed anyone overcome by good fortune).

Then in 1934 came the Act of Parliament forbidding the British press to publicise sweepstakes. Its chief object was to staunch the flow of £10 million a year from England and Scotland into De Valera's coffers, though it was aimed also at other overseas sweeps. The Act could have been branded a gross interference with the freedom of the press, though one recalls no outcry at the time. Sir John Gilmour, Home Secretary, assured the Commons that 'the provisions of the Bill have been welcomed by nearly every section of the press in this country.' Isaac Foot said it had taken two pages of *The Times* to give the names of winners, but the roll-call of losers would have filled twenty-four pages for 100 issues. The Clydeside Member, John McGovern, warned that in Glasgow there would be no difficulty in buying tickets in defiance of the Act, a prophesy amply fulfilled, for the city was soon overrun by surreptitious collectors and couriers. Many Members wanted to know why football pools were to be allowed to court publicity when hospital sweepstakes were banned. Indeed, those who, in later years, remembered the excitement over the Irish Sweep draws, felt it was pretty odd for papers to be able to print pictures of £500,000 winners being kissed by actresses for clever work in sticking a pin into a list of names, when it was illegal to mention that a washerwoman who had drawn a lucky ticket in the Irish Sweep had won £5,000, or even £500.

JACK'S
The Gospel According To

According to *Jack's Reference Book*, a well of wisdom much tapped in the earlier years of this century, 'the peevish child, the nagging woman, the irritable man, the morbidly religious and the would-be suicide have one thing in common, they are all constipated.'

Should the would-be suicide really be included in this *galère*? 'It has been said with no little truth,' continues *Jack's*, 'that no man ever committed suicide after a full meal, a sound night's sleep or a free action of the bowels.'

What, then, of peevish children, who are not normally a prey to suicidal thoughts? Castor oil is the answer. Indeed, says *Jack's*, 'castor oil is in fact very often the wisest form of punishment for a child.' There must have been parents who took the hint, for tales abounded of naughty children who had incurred this penalty, though no physical details were ever divulged; we assumed that the punishment lay simply in being forced to swallow something outstandingly nasty. Castor oil was to attract lasting disgrace when Mussolini and Hitler dosed their opponents with it.

The medical staff of *Jack's* knew all the tedious tricks played by children: trying to sleep with their heads under the bedclothes; stuffing slate pencils and other foreign bodies up their noses, which caused the breath to smell offensively; speaking with a lisp, which 'persists in adult life and is from some strange whim regarded as good style by some people'; and hysteria, a complaint to which the Latin races were more susceptible than the Anglo-Saxons. Tiresome though children were, there was no case for oppressing them unreasonably. 'To laugh, romp, make weird noises and get spotted with dirt are essential to health and to normal growth of body and mind.' A child should be taken for a run in the country like a dog and be allowed to poke about and find objects of amusement. Always within reason, of course; implicit obedience should be insisted on and should be habitual at three years of age.

At this rate one would have expected *Jack's* to be in favour of a jolly seaside holiday, if only to get children away from those slate pencils, but its advice is decidedly discouraging. To start with, sea air encourages constipation, which we are so anxious to avoid. Water-cress and shellfish may carry typhoid contamination. Paddling in the hot sun is dangerous. There is a tendency to eat too many large meals. As for the holiday lodgings, there is always the risk that they have just been vacated by a family with the measles, 'and such people are often present in shelters on the sea front.' The rooms are likely to be too small and too infrequently aired, and the sanitary and cooking arrangements may be poor. It is necessary to check whether the cistern has a lid, whether the window sashes are fixed to save the curtains and whether the chimney register is shut to protect the fireplace decorations.

Jack's did not overlook the health problems brought about by drink, notably in women, 'the grocer's licence being largely respon-sible for this'. It condemned the habit of resorting to the bottle to cure 'that sinking feeling', which Bovril was trying to remedy by topping up people with beef extract (the mysterious sinking feeling, according to *Jack's*, was merely indigestion). Just how *delirium tremens* took people was graphically described. 'The chief symptoms are fear, tremor and restlessness; the patient always makes for his trousers to get up and do some imaginary business round the corner.' He sees 'imaginary objects, usually black and crawling . . . the miner just back from the Cape picks up diamonds all day, the soldier back from the war sees Boers and shouts for help, the potman incessantly polishes imaginary glasses, the cab driver sees horses on the ceiling which he directs with stentorian tones, whilst two men, who both saw imagin-ary rats, and were confined in the same ward, spent all night looking for the man who had put the rats there and finally picked their mattress to pieces to see if he was inside.'

As well as craving drink, certain women – anaemic ones in particu-lar – developed an unhealthy craving for slate pencils. Did they suck them, crunch them or, like children, put them up their noses? Alas, *Jack's* does not say.

JELLYGRAPHS
For Satirists And Others

When a child decided to astound family and friends by producing a magazine, often scurrilous in intent, the answer to the printing problem was a jellygraph, or hectograph. It was in essence a shallow metal tray filled with gelatine, smooth and firm enough to take the impression of a purple-inked sheet of paper. Other sheets could then be rubbed lightly on its surface and would take a reasonably legible copy.

Many an 'alternative' school magazine was produced in this manner. So were reports of semi-learned, reforming or hobbyist bodies. Small firms operating on a shoestring sometimes jellygraphed their lists of bargains.

When Claud Cockburn planned his in-the-know organ, *The Week*, in the days of the Dictators, he had to choose a form of printing apparatus which would not be worth seizing to defray libel damages. A jellygraph would have fulfilled this requirement, but Cockburn flew a little higher and hire-purchased a mimeographic equipment, which called for the ability to type and cut stencils. The object was to produce something noticeable rather than neat, so *The Week* appeared in dark brown ink on buff foolscap. Says Cockburn with pride: 'It was not merely noticeable, it was unquestionably the nastiest-looking bit of work that ever dropped on a breakfast table' (*Cockburn Sums Up*).

JEW'S HARPS
Well Played, Eulenstein!

The advertisements in *The Hotspur* called it a Jaw's Harp, not from any sense of delicacy towards Jews, but because that is what millions have always called it. It was never a Jewish instrument, but may have been popularised by Jewish pedlars.

The Jew's harp is a lyre-shaped device designed to be played against the teeth by twitching a metal tongue with the finger. It was warranted to irritate parents, though not as much as a nose-flute (also advertised in comics) played with nose and mouth simultaneously ('no knowledge of music required'). Made in Birmingham by the sort of firm which turns out mirrors for budgerigars, the Jew's harp came in various finishes, the most expensive being chromiumplated, with gilt tongue, 'as used in Henry Hall's Band'. The *Dictionary of Music* devotes an astonishing amount of space to the Jew's harp, and mentions one Eulenstein who ruined his teeth by rapid playing of sixteen harps fitted together in a frame, producing 'fairy music'. His dentist prepared for him a glutinous compound to protect his teeth, but apparently to no avail. A real schoolboy's hero, Eulenstein.

Then there was the kazoo, a hollow metal instrument shaped like a submarine, containing a strip of catgut which resonated to the human voice. The best that can be said of the kazoo is that its manufacture, like that of itching powder, kept people off the dole.

JOURNALISM
(1) Cliché Days

How backward, how mealy-mouthed, how cliché-ridden and yet how endearing were the newspapers of between the world wars. The secret of the identity of Santa Claus was never wantonly disclosed in their pages. The crime of rape was rarely mentioned, certainly not in giant headlines, and no readers felt fobbed off on reading that persons had been sent down at the assizes for 'offences of an unsavoury nature'. A plucky postmistress who routed assailants was not mocked as 'Battling Lil (71)' and no pricetags were put on people's houses, love-nests or motor cars.

As for clichés, the worst of the older ones had been weeded out. Some of them had been dreamed up by the penny-a-liners, whose version of 'A doctor was called, but the man was already dead' was 'A medical practitioner was summoned in haste to the scene of the tragic occurrence, where a small crowd had gathered, and after a careful examination of the victim pronounced life to be extinct.' What Fowler calls 'elegant variations' were in retreat. A church had more or less ceased to be a sacred edifice and an oyster was no longer a succulent bivalve, but those who sat in what was still called the editorial sanctum tolerated much they should have rooted out. Women still tended to be the fair sex and tobacco was the fragrant weed or My Lady Nicotine. Births were happy, or blessed, events and deaths still called for floral tributes. The sun, especially in the sports pages, often figured as King Sol and sports fans – in Glasgow, anyway – seemed to understand what was meant by 'Jup. Pluv. Stops Play' (Jupiter Pluvius was an associate of the Clerk of the Weather).

The sports pages gathered clichés as a cat gathers fleas. For a start, they were crawling with genial managers. The test of a sub-editor was whether, faced with a grand assemblage of clichés purporting to be a report of a football match, he could dash off a headline which should be peppy and eye-catching. It was no job (as H. G. Wells would have confirmed: see page 37) for a university man, whose only function on a newspaper was to write leaders urging the Dictators to look before they leaped. If the reader thinks writing sports headlines is no problem, let him exercise his brains and invent a headline of approximately twenty-six letters describing a match between Saints and Rangers, in which play at the outset ranged from end to end, until the Holy Boys crowded on sail and Thompson rattled the upright, following it with a pile-driver past the custodian, who never stood a chance, whereupon Rangers, nettled by this reverse, took up the running and slammed home two sizzlers, both by Owen, after which the fat was in the fire, tempers became frayed and Saints, seeing the writing on the wall, adopted tousy tactics in a vain bid to wrest the equaliser, only to be again humiliated by Owen, who thereby scored his second hat-trick of the season. A sub-editor whose mind had not been cluttered by learning simply glanced through this copy, struck out any phrases which particularly offended him, and then scribbled a headline reading GLORY GOALS ROCK TOUSY SAINTS or DANDY OWEN SEALS RANGERS' JOY-DAY. The chief sub-editor might reject both of them and substitute RANGERS' JIG-TIME PACE HAD SAINTS COCK-EYED. (How splendid if concert reports in the stuffier papers could have been headlined in the same spirited vein: DANDY SOLOIST SEALS BERLIOZ JOY-NIGHT or ZIPPY FLAUTIST IN TEARAWAY FINISH.)

The sub-editors of those days prided themselves on their ruthless pencils, but in fact they left in much dead wood and muckage. The tendency was to exclaim at the news, or to prepare the reader for it. There was a traffic in amazing statements, astonishing outbursts, sensational revelations, shocking scenes, extraordinary allegations, dramatic sequels, poignant echoes, baffling riddles, sinister developments and the like. It was all part of the tradition of an earlier day. *The Times* used to have headlines like DREADFUL DISCOVERY IN A BARREL AT DIJON and MOST SHOCKING AFFAIR AT SMYRNA (such items were helpfully indexed under 'D' for Dreadful and 'M' for Most in Palmer's Index to *The Times*).

Part of the trouble was that headlines often had to be three-deckers. All that was needed was MAN THROWS CHAIR AT JUDGE but this had to be preceded by AMAZING SCENE IN COURT and followed by COUNSEL DIVES FOR COVER. Mercifully, World War Two came along and the ensuing shortage of newsprint helped to tighten up headline writing. Today's sub-editors, though revelling in their own clichés – paper tigers, blackboard jungles, concrete jungles, whiz-kids, boffins, dream tickets, Steptoes (for dustmen) and Mrs Mops (for cleaners) – do at least hit the reader over the head direct.

JOURNALISM
(2) Real News Bills

Those who wrote the headlines also wrote the newsbills. Before the war these were always printed from wood type in concussive sans-serif letters, unlike the newsbills of today which give the air of having been dashed off in a hurry by a none-too-literate fellow with a burnt stick. It was very satisfactory to ride home on a tramcar and see one's bills displayed along the mean streets: PEER'S NIECE SENSATION (they were a lively lot, peers' nieces) or TORSO RIDDLE: A LEG FOUND. There were tricks and temptations in this trade. Hardened readers might suspect that PRINCESS CANCELS ENGAGEMENTS meant merely that the lady had the 'flu, not that she was pregnant, and they would be right. But would they guess that PRINCE OF WALES'S PLANE IN CRASH referred to an aircraft once owned by the Prince? Almost everybody knew that DEATH OF FAMOUS STAR, especially if it was a first edition newsbill of an evening paper, meant somebody who had once

131

played a walk-on part in an obscure Buster Keaton comedy. (It was an old game: in 1820 Princess Lieven wrote to Prince Metternich saying that London newsvendors were displaying announcements saying DEATH OF THE KING, with 'of Abyssinia' added in small letters.)

To what extent the newsbills sent up the sales of aspirin and bromides in the late 1930s will never be known. Members of Parliament complained that one could drive for hundreds of miles through an England blazoned with nothing but HITLER SPEAKS. Well it was Hitler who finally put paid to our newsbills, which were abolished during the war to save paper, though newsvendors often scribbled their own witty (and misleading, and libellous) headlines on anything handy. Newsbills did not return until 1953, when a Labour Member, Marcus Lipton, was kind enough to say they had been 'a happy feature of the London scene before the war' (he was thinking, perhaps, of PHEW, WHAT A SCORCHER!). The revived bills were in hand-written form because of some union dispute still, apparently, incapable of resolution.

JOURNALISM
(3) Pigeon Post

The final Saturday afternoon edition of the evening paper is about to go to press. All the results of the big football matches are in except one, that of an important semi-final. The pigeon carrying the result has evidently been delayed. On the newspaper roof the pigeon-handlers scan the sky anxiously. At last the bird appears, but shows no sense of urgency; it alights teasingly on an adjacent roof and, with head cocked, surveys the frantic scene beside the pigeon-house. Meanwhile the sub-editors are going demented; the machine-room men are making threatening noises. Then, when all seems lost, the bird coolly flies in, is collared and deprived of the vital sheet of flimsy.

That's how it happened in many a city before telephone lines were run to all the football grounds. There's a picture of the old pigeon loft used early this century by the *Sheffield Telegraph* group in Guy Schofield's *The Men That Carry The News*; it was preserved until 1960. Alas, the book tells us nothing about those roof-top dramas, which were much talked about by ancient sports writers. There were tales like that of the reporter at the football ground who took a chance, tied to the bird the report giving what looked like being the final score and sent it off, just before a last-minute goal was netted. 'Tell them Hibs scored the equaliser!' he shouted after the vanishing bird.

Newspaper reliance on pigeons was, of course, an old tradition. *Bell's Life* used birds in pre-telegraph days to bring in the horse-racing results from Ascot, Newbury and Goodwood; and *The Times* had a Paris-Boulogne pigeon service to carry the European market prices.

In quite recent times the photographers from the New York papers, boarding incoming vessels at Quarantine, would photograph celebrities and attach the films to pigeons. When the liner docked the stage folk would find their pictures already in the papers.

133

KANGAROOS
With The Gloves On

Readers of comics like *The Wizard* and *The Hotspur* were brought up on boxing kangaroos, which were portrayed putting on the gloves to do battle not only with humans but with apes and other animals. In real life the heyday of the boxing kangaroo was probably in the 1890s at the Royal Aquarium in Tothill Street, London, where the advertised acts included not only 'Boxing Animals' but Wrestling Bears, Dancing Elephants, Performing Bulls and the Missing Link (played by a gorilla).

The Aquarium's first boxing kangaroo, introduced by 'Professor' Landerman from Australia, greatly excited the Bostock brothers, who toured the main zoos of Europe buying up saucy male kangaroos and then sending them out on circuit, along with bruisers hired to box them. One animal, bought from London Zoo, was a great success at the Trocadero, but died of lockjaw. Sparring with a kangaroo was a useful trade for a broken-down boxer; he would be under orders never to strike below the belt and never to hit the animal unnecessarily. If it looked like being bested in a bout the kangaroo was liable to retire in a sulk. It would have gloves on its fore paws and another on its tail, which was popularly supposed to be its most potent weapon, though its rear feet needed careful watching.

When the House of Commons, in 1934, debated the Protection of Animals Bill, designed to prevent the cruelties practised at rodeos, the clause which prohibited 'wrestling, fighting or struggling with any animal' provoked misgivings. According to T. F. Groves, it directly threatened the future of the boxing kangaroo, 'a turn which has interested thousands of people in this country . . . a perfectly simple and amusing turn that involves no cruelty'. Lt-Col. R. V. K. Applin reassured him by saying that the Bill did not impose a ban on boxing – 'fighting is an illegal amusement, whereas boxing is legal . . . In struggling with an animal you must catch hold of it. The whole point of a boxing kangaroo is that you do not touch him, except to hit him on the nose.'

Has anyone boxed with a kangaroo lately?

LEAD SOLDIERS
Dashing But Distressed

BRITAINS 17TH LANCERS, at full gallop (*one with head and arm missing, another with leg missing*).
BRITAINS 21ST LANCERS (Active Service Order), at full gallop, (7) (*only one piece not damaged*) together with bugler (2).
BRITAINS FUSILIERS, oval-based, marching at slope (11) (*nine bayonets missing*), with officers (2) (*one head repaired*) and goat (*one horn broken*), together with mounted figures (11) (*mainly damaged*).
BIKANIR CAMEL CORPS with riders (3) (*three riders damaged, one camel damaged*), RASC supply wagon (*distressed*) and three tents with flags.

So it went on, for page after page, in Sotheby's 1980 catalogue of lead soldiers up for auction. And how poignantly those descriptions recall one's own collection of lead soldiers, which suffered such dismaying losses of limbs, swords, lances, bayonets, plumes and other fragile military accoutrements. Heads could be restored, after a fashion, by jamming a piece of matchstick inside skull and torso. A father skilled in the use of a soldering iron could sometimes replace horses' forelegs and tails, but restoring a whole array of bayonets was a tall order. Sometimes it seemed better to accept the casualties as illustrative of the carnage of battle. How very fitting for the 21st Lancers to continue at full gallop with only one rider not damaged!

In the entries quoted, 'Britains' refers to the famous manufacturer of lead soldiers, William Britain, who in the 1890s invented a method of making hollow-cast figures lighter and cheaper than the solid models hitherto on the market. His firm made metal soldiers until 1965 and then went over to plastic.

The Sotheby's list shows that William Britain was no narrow chauvinist. He turned out boxes of Cossacks, Carabinieri, Bulgarian infantry, Argentine cavalry, French legionaries, Swedish life guards, American Federal infantry, Capetown Highlanders, Venezuelan cadets and even more exotic lines. No doubt he was attacked from time to time for encouraging militarism in the young, but he could always point to his splendid range of 'British Civilians'. One lot for auction was described as: '. . . including chauffeur carrying lamp, yachtsman, brown-suited gentleman with tropical hat and red sash, two other gentlemen in brown suits and bowler hats, one carrying a pipe and the other a paper, *dated 1908*, and two ladies dressed in red with full-length dresses.'

These were a rather superior range of civilian, but William Britain could also provide a policeman, a pastor, a shepherd with crook, a girl with feeding bucket and an old woman sitting. The catalogue shows that these civilians had escaped the ravages of shot and shell; the shepherd's crook was evidently intact and nobody was distressed, not even the old woman sitting.

Who buys these mutilated lots of soldiers? The grave gentlemen who play at war games prefer their own model (not toy) soldiers, immaculately turned out. And for that matter, who bids for those old Noah's Arks, with three-legged oxen and, sadly, many incomplete pairs?

LEECHES
Not Yet Obsolete

Instructions on how to pack leeches for transmission by post appeared in the *Post Office Guide* in the years between the wars, as if to challenge any notion that medicine had advanced into the twentieth century. At this writing, there is a report that they are still employed to suck away coagulated blood during skin-graft operations.

It is true that in the post-Victorian years plethoric male relatives were rarely to be seen with swollen leeches pasturing on their brows or ankles. It is equally true that chemists no longer displayed these creatures in a jar. A Wordsworth might have had difficulty in finding a leech-gatherer ('employment hazardous and wearisome') in the Lakes, but Europe was still very much in the blood-sucking business. In 1915 the Master of Christ's College, Cambridge, Sir Arthur Shipley, wrote to *The Times* complaining that 'General Joffre, General von Kluck, General von Hindenburg and the Grand Duke Nicholas persist in fighting over some of the best leech areas in Europe, possibly unwittingly.' London, he said, had only a few dozen leeches left and they were second-hand (see *The First Cuckoo*, ed. Kenneth Gregory).

Leeches were kept in porous-topped glass jars and were deliberately starved, though not so seriously as to drive them to cannibalism. From time to time they were washed and then rubbed down, several at a time, to remove the slime. If a leech was to be laid on a particularly sensitive spot (never over a vein) it was first dipped in warm water; and if it was temperamental it might have to be pointed two or three times to the required spot, or confined there by means of an upturned test-tube till it gripped. When its work was done – it was expected to remove half an ounce of blood – it was allowed to drop off naturally, not pulled off; but if reluctant to disengage, a pinch of salt would change its mind. The charge per leech to the patient was about sixpence and the creature was not supposed to be used a second time, but in wartime London, as is clear from that letter, standards were of necessity relaxed and sacrifices were expected of all.

137

LIBRARIES
(1) Clean Hands And Minds

Today anyone trying to take out an unchecked book from a public library is likely to set off a shrill *peep, peep, peep* from an electronic device, like a terrorist attempting to smuggle a gun on to an aircraft.

Sixty or so years ago no anti-theft device was necessary, for the public were not let loose among the shelves to pick out their books. In, for example, Shrewsbury Public Library, the procedure was to look in an index for the title of the wanted book, obtain its number and then consult a large indicator board filling one side of the room. If the desired number was displayed in red, as it usually was, the book was out; if it was displayed in blue the book was in and could be applied for at a counter. The Shrewsbury system was in widespread use; according to Dorothy Scannell's *Mother Knew Best* it was to be found in the East End of London. It was a fine authoritarian set-up strongly defended by the old guard of librarians, who did not want potential book thieves, rowdies and idle browsers to roam among the shelves, squabbling over wanted books or picking volumes out and putting them back in the wrong place, or bringing their children with them for a scamper. Another system of control allowed the would-be borrower to see the spines of the books through a wire mesh and push with a finger at the volume he wished to borrow. The librarian would then extract it from the other side.

Libraries have changed prodigiously. It is some time since signs exhorting SILENCE were displayed. These were discontinued partly in accordance with the principle that if nobody obeys an order it may as well be withdrawn and partly to conform with the decision of librarians that libraries are 'no longer to be regarded as quiet academic places'. That was the pronouncement in 1981 of John Saunders, Chief Librarian of Surrey, when he sought to justify placing 'Space Invaders' machines in the foyers of his larger libraries. Boys were liable to make rather a noise with them, he admitted to a critical headmistress, 'but that is better than ripping up the books'. In some libraries, 'Space Invaders' machines are excused on the grounds that they provide revenue.

Even before the Surrey experiment, the interior of the public library had begun to resemble an amusement arcade. What appears to be a cross between a 'Space Invaders' game and a colour television set is the Prestel 'data view' apparatus, a gaily-coloured but pathetically under-programmed service which, unlike Mulhall's *Statistics* in an earlier day, cannot even give the weight of a Scotsman's brains or say how much the philosopher Seneca was worth (£3,500,000). If Mulhall were still going today he would certainly record that the income of the average librarian is three times that of the author whose book he stamps and whose right to receive more he still disputes. Do not expect to find information like that in Prestel.

In the reference department people turn away at handwheels of peepshow machines, for all the world as if they were on a seaside pier, or in a Sexorama. They are in fact consulting old Bernard Levin articles in *The Times*, recorded on microfilm. And there is a very busy coin-in-the-slot machine used by schoolmasters, choirmasters and the like to pirate books and music.

It is all very different from, for example, the reference library at Partick, Glasgow during the Depression years. In this building a bold

139

sign said COME WITH CLEAN HANDS, but it was ignored by those who arrived to consult volume REF-SAI of the *Encyclopaedia Britannica* (see FACTS OF LIFE). The entry on 'Reproduction' had clearly been studied by hundreds, nay thousands, of apprentice welders and boilermakers. The pages were glisteningly grubby and beginning to disintegrate, a really repulsive sight. In other libraries, in other cities, the same phenomenon could be discovered, though Clydeside's volumes were surely blackest of all.

At Partick the zeal for knowledge in other fields was such that it had to be officially suppressed, as for instance in the Reading Room. When the new editions of the newspapers were put up, each locked down under a shiny brass bar, a lady librarian ran an inked roller up and down the racing columns. Under the black smear the words 'Obliterated By Order Of The Council' could sometimes be deciphered. The workless who thronged the library would jostle round and try to read the starting prices before they were obnubilated. They never protested; people knew their place in those days. The rather shaky pretext for this censorship was that non-punters had a right to read the newspapers too and were not to be deprived of more serious reading, like reports of torsos found in left-luggage offices. One now learns from Roger Millington's *The Strange World of the Crossword* that, when the crossword craze first hit Britain in the mid-1920s, Dulwich Public Library blacked out crosswords in newspapers, while other libraries had to ration the use of dictionaries.

One table in the Partick reading room was set apart for ladies. At the other tables tramps fell asleep over *The Tatler* and *The Sketch*, never over *The Unitarian* or *The Veterinary Record*. If one tried to pull *The Tatler* away the sleeper awoke and began scrutinising afresh the pictures of the smart set at Le Touquet. Nowadays, depending on the area, a nap in a library can cost up to £20.

In those days libraries existed simply for lending or consulting books, not for supplying black plastic bags to ratepayers during dustmen's strikes (still, that sort of thing does bring a new class of people into the library). Libraries did not set themselves up as community centres, catering for all those cultural and political groups for which the proper place, as some of us think, is the swimming baths. One likes to speculate how a poet-in-residence would have got on at Partick, encouraging the punters to make up little poems about lady librarians with inky rollers.

Those who used reference libraries tended to keep up puzzled conversations, *sotto voce*, with themselves, as if the ingestion of knowledge was a taxing process. Today such persons, still mumbling away, are finding themselves increasingly flummoxed by electronic data banks, microfiches and microfilms. Who can be expected to understand such things, except ten-year-olds?

LIBRARIES
(2) Crash Of The Giants

The higher bourgeoisie were never seen in the public libraries, which had, in their eyes, a dispensary or workhouse image; though they were occasionally seen in the reference department, where they made known their requirements in firm, resonant tones. Some undoubtedly shared the view of Ruskin: 'We call ourselves a rich nation, and we are filthy and foolish enough to thumb each other's books out of circulating libraries.' Of the private libraries to which Ruskin referred, the one with the least polluting wares, both physically and morally, was Mudies, which serviced the carriage trade of borrowers. Charles Mudie started his library in 1842 and made a tremendous success of it; the arrival of his boxes of books at rectories and spa hotels was tinglingly awaited. At one time he bought more three-volume novels than did the booksellers. But the twentieth century brought its peculiar problems and in 1937 the library was closed by court order, shortly after it had given up its famous headquarters in New Oxford Street, London.

By that times Mudies' two main rivals, Smiths and Boots, were greatly prospering. They had fought shoulder-to-shoulder with Mudies in the battles over whether to stock books like *Jude The Obscure, Esther Waters* and *Sinister Street* (Sir Compton Mackenzie has described the *Sinister Street* rumpus at some length). Of these two giants, the 'Booklovers' Library' of Boots was the pace-setter. It was founded in 1899 by Mrs Jesse Boot (Lady Trent), partly to please the firm's more literate customers, partly to stimulate impulse-buying by borrowers as they moved to and from the back of the shop. By the mid-thirties Boots had 450 branches with almost half a

141

million subscribers and by 1945 nearly a million. Between them the two chains subsidised the publishing industry to an extraordinary degree.

But there was now fierce competition, especially from the no-deposit 'Tuppeny Libraries', specialising in crime, romance and cowboy fiction. These libraries, which had mushroomed in the thirties, were often less furtive than they looked and some of them even leased High Street shops. The public libraries were fast shaking off their dispensary image and greatly improving their standards. Then came the paperback revolution. On top of it all, television inspired, if not a flight from literacy, a reluctance by millions to be seen struggling with a book. In 1961 Smiths announced the closing of their 286 libraries, after 103 years of service. Some of their subscribers were passed on to Boots. A year later the Times Book Club, a lesser operator, was absorbed into Harrods' Library. Then, incredibly, in 1966 all Boots libraries closed. Private libraries survived only in scattered stores and bookshops. The 'Tuppeny Libraries' declined because the rising cost of hardbacks made them uneconomic to operate.

It was a melancholy business. A great cry went up from elderly women borrowers who had been accustomed to read three or four light novels a week. Some public libraries were reluctant to keep lightweight fare; they would lend books to people whose hobbies were flower-arranging or making rabbit hutches, but they disapproved of people whose hobby was merely reading. From authors, too, came cries of tribulation. For all their periodic complaints about 'censorship', they had depended on the library orders for about a third of their sales. The libraries' order could make or break a novel. And just occasionally there had been moments of great joy. To know that people with 'on demand' subscriptions were clamouring for one's book and that stacks of copies were being rushed about in taxis was a fortifying experience. It was the collapse of the two giants which did much to stimulate the campaign for public lending rights.

By an irony, the public libraries, supported by the ratepayers, were now left with the task of censoring novels. In the headlong rush to a permissive society they soon gave up the struggle.

LIFE PRESERVERS
And Sharper Weapons

In tales of the Sherlock Holmes era people in tight corners laid about themselves with life preservers. These could be simple weighted sticks or, on a more sophisticated level, springy clubs rather like the devices clutched by strap-hangers in the London Underground. A life preserver of this type shown in the Army and Navy Stores catalogue for 1915 cost one shilling-and-ninepence, or, in 'superior quality, leather-covered, with spring, very effective', five shillings. That same year the advertising pages of *Punch* offered 'Loaded Sticks for Officers', strong pigskin-covered canes with weighted knobs. It was not explained why officers should need such things.

Other defensive weapons could be bought in umbrella shops. One of them was a Night Companion, a heavy walking-stick with a rugged, knobbly top. More lethal was the sword-stick, a species of flick-knife for gentlemen, consisting of a cane from which a sharp blade could be extruded by pressing a button. Sword-sticks seem to have been favoured by authors, a naturally quarrelsome and exhibitionistic breed, G. K. Chesterton carried one to go with his cloak and wide-brimmed hat. According to his brother, he always hoped some wild untoward happening in the streets would impel him to use it. Sometimes the blade fell accidentally from its sheath, clattering on the pavement, as he hurried to a pub. Dennis Wheatley, who had his moments of fantasy, boasted of his sword-stick that 'one swift jab . . . aimed upwards to pierce beneath the chin would promptly have settled any man's business.' Fortunately for himself he never had occasion to spit anybody. Evelyn Waugh records that he carried a sword-stick on his visit to Abyssinia in 1930 for the coronation of the Emperor; he seems unlikely to have flourished it in later years, defending his home at Combe Florey against invaders.

At Thomas Hardy's home at Max Gate heavier armaments were apparently held in reserve. In 1913 (according to *The Second Mrs Hardy*, by Robert Gittings and Jo Manton) the novelist's secretary-companion, Florence Dugdale, was left in solitary residence while he went off on a sentimental pilgrimage to the place where he met his first wife. Florence, later to be the second Mrs Hardy, wrote to a friend: 'It is very quiet here and I keep a loaded revolver in my bedroom . . .' She was in a state of depression at the time. Had she fired the weapon, at an intruder, or at herself, or at Hardy, what a headline that would have made!

In 1921 Katherine Mansfield, in an ultra-respectable hotel above Montreux, kept on her bed at night 'a copy of Shakespeare, a copy of Chaucer, an automatic pistol and a black muslin fan'. What right she had to carry this weapon is hard to see; but pistols weighing only just over one pound, and suitable for the handbag, could be bought for about £2. Purchasers were expected to produce a gun licence or a police authorisation. To obtain the latter it was necessary to show an intention to be abroad for not less than six months; which almost sounds as if it was designed to discourage duelling at Dieppe.

LIFTS
Living Dangerously

In very old office blocks there used to be ornate lifts which were set in motion by the operator pulling on a weathered-looking rope in one corner. Take-off was never quite instantaneous; there was a moment of mechanical grunting up aloft, as if opposition was being overcome. Meanwhile the operator, who looked like one who had marched with Lord Roberts from Kabul to Kandahar, glared defiantly at his passengers, as if daring them to pass comment.

Some of these rope-activated lifts were worked by water pressure in a long, stout cylinder. A more primitive kind which survived into this century was operated by the delightfully simple principle of allowing water to flow into a large bucket until it outweighed the car with its passengers. If the car was at the bottom, the operator's tug on the rope opened a valve which let water into the bucket. At the top of the shaft, when ready to descend, the operator would pull the rope and open a valve in the bottom of the bucket to let the water out, until it became lighter than the car. The ride, which could be quite rapid, was controlled by the operator with a brake. If this brake failed, or was tardily applied, the results could be mitigated if the passengers remembered to bend their knees as the car reached the bumper at the base, or shield their heads when it hit the top of the shaft. Defective valves could cause a car to creep when it was supposed to be stationary, or to judder when coming to rest.

Some lifts operated in tight-fitting shafts where, if the brakes failed, the pressure of air cushioned the drop. One of the thrills of the Chicago Exposition of 1880 was to enter a lift at the top of a shaft in the knowledge that the rope was going to be cut – and that the descent, though initially swift, would not be fatal.

It was always a delightful surprise to find oneself in a building with a 'Paternoster' lift system – a series of small, open-fronted cars continually ascending on one side of the shaft and descending on the other. The selected car had to be entered smartly, without dithering. The curious would ride to the top to see what happened; but all that happened was that the car side-stepped and came down again. A lift of this type was still operating in the Four Seasons Hotel in Hamburg in 1945 when most of the city lay flat.

LIQUORICE
Pleasures Of Pontefract

This splendid substance, pliable, malleable, ductile, impressionable and, above all, edible was chewed by the Romans, though not in the shape of bootlaces, braces, belts, garters, ribbon, braid, diamond twist, nail-rod, skipping ropes, clothes lines, lassos, bell-wire, tennis rackets, medallions, pistols, babies' dummies and old boots. Liquorice plants were grown near Pontefract ('In the liquorice fields of Pontefract / My love and I did meet' – Betjeman) and Monday morning in the creative departments of the liquorice factories must have been a taxing time: 'Why don't we do liquorice shaving kits?' – 'Because we've already done them.' Liquorice allsorts, however, were not the inspiration of a creative team. Legend says that a young woman bumped into a traveller called Charlie Thompson and spilled his samples of liquorice sweets all over the potential buyer's carpet. 'Hold it,' said the buyer, 'send me some of those, just as they are.'

The sherbet sucker, known as a quencher, owed a modest debt to liquorice. A black pipe was inserted into a triangular bag of crystals and the idea was to ingurgitate them by this means. It was an imperfect system in that the tube was liable to clog. Dissatisfied customers could always turn to sherbet dabs and pick up the crystals with a blob of toffee on a stick. It is surprising that liquorice pipes or dabs were not supplied to assist the intake of the recently-invented 'Space Dust', a sweet powder which explodes riotously on the tongue and has been falsely represented by children to their parents as a stimulant and mind-expander.

'Liquorice Imps' could have given liquorice a bad name. They were tiny black pellets fiendishly strong to the taste, sold in a penny box with the assurance 'Keep You Cosy'. They were akin to those dubious cachous scented with violet, lavender and musk which heavy smokers and drinkers kept about their persons, or those hard white ultra-strong peppermints handed out to accompanied children by elderly floor-walkers in drapery shops.

In its lowest form liquorice was bought as fibre, which (like ducks' feet in China) had to be sucked very hard to extract any taste. It was to be had in the shops which stocked the equally cheap 'locusts', hideous objects resembling dried and blackened banana skins, which the more innocent supposed to be the shrivelled insects consumed in the desert by John the Baptist. They were, in fact, locust beans, as once used by the British Army in Mediterranean lands for horse fodder (see SWEETS).

'LOBBY LUD'
The Man Worth Finding

It takes a national newspaper to run a treasure-hunt. One of the most enduring – and endearing – of these quests was that for Lobby Lud, which brought much-needed zest to seaside resorts from 1927 onwards (and caused less havoc than the *Weekly Dispatch's* 1904 stunt which had half the population digging up public places in a search for buried medallions).

Though started by the *Westminster Gazette*, the Lobby Lud stunt is chiefly associated with the *Daily News*, which gobbled up that paper in 1928. Every summer morning the mystery man with £50 to give away described how he ran the ambushes set for him by holiday-makers. A photograph of Lobby Lud, his Irish-looking features shaded by the brim of his trilby, was published daily along with his physical description; his likeness also appeared on posters and vans all over the chosen town. To make a successful challenge the holiday-maker had to carry a copy of that day's newspaper and say 'You are Mr Lobby Lud. I claim the *Daily News* prize.' Any variation on this rendered the challenge invalid. Every day the newspaper described where its man would be at certain times: on the pier, in Dreamland or lunching in a popular restaurant. To show that he had made the scheduled visits, he reported next day exchanges he had had with identifiable people – perhaps a fortune-teller, or a band leader he had asked to play 'The Londonderry Air'.

Fifty pounds in those days was quite worth picking up and compared well with the sort of bait other newspapers were offering, like £500 for a Fatal Accident at Work. Hordes of day-trippers would arrive for the hunt, picketing railway stations and piers, cordoning off the likeliest restaurants. Some determined trackers followed their quarry from one resort to another and he had much quiet fun baiting them. When faced with an imminent challenge he would himself challenge, even pester, someone else. Searchers assumed he would be a loner, so he tagged on to parties, especially when going through pier turnstiles, or walked with a girl on his arm or helped push a bath-chair, enjoying the sight of crowds besetting innocent holiday-makers or penning suspects in bathing huts. One of his pranks was to slip IOUs for ten shillings into the pockets or under the collars of his most persistent hunters. Surprisingly few of the challenges he received were correctly worded and he would carry his £50 for days on end. Meanwhile other resorts clamoured to be put on Lobby Lud's visiting list.

The stunt went on with variations year after year, even after the *Daily News* absorbed the *Daily Chronicle*. Came World War Two and the piers where Lobby Lud had strolled were cut in two to frustrate enemy landings and the beaches he patrolled were strewn with label-less tins of food from shipwrecks. But with peace again Lobby Lud made spasmodic reappearances, as did mystery men from rival newspapers. In 1983 the original Lobby Lud, now aged 93, was interviewed under his real name, Willie Chinn, by Miles Kington on BBC radio. That same year visitors to London were trying desperately to win £100 by accosting strangers with the formula: 'I identify you as the *Standard* Man, and claim my prize.'

MARBLES
Alleys In The Alleys

It was once an offence (and possibly still is) for undergraduates at Oxford to play marbles on the steps of the Bodleian Library. There are thought to be wives who would like to make it an offence for grown men to play in marbles tournaments.

Losing one's marbles has come to mean losing one's wits, though it is hard to know why. In childhood the loss of a bag-full of marbles, whether by bad playing or bad guessing ('How many marbles in this hand?'), was a grievous matter, though not quite the end of the world. In those days one just did not like losing zealously hoarded possessions. To forfeit clay marbles mattered less than forfeiting blood alleys (alley: 'a choice taw or large marble') or those glass ones with bright spiral filaments.

The game tended to be played, not on the steps of libraries, but in alleys and gutters, with grids as an unwelcome hazard. Strictly speaking, a marble had to be flipped with the thumb from the forefinger, with the hand close to the ground. There were innumerable sorts of marble games (all laboriously described in works of reference) but the general idea was that if a player hit the other man's marble it was his and *vice versa*. Marbles mattered a great deal for a few weeks, then not at all.

If anyone ever made money out of marbles it must have been the man who found out how to use them as stoppers in fizzy drinks bottles, a feat of technology as admirable in its way as the invention of the self-wiping cat's-eye on the highway. The inventor was Hiram Codd, of Camberwell. Provided with each bottle was a wooden device for depressing the marble, which was held by gas pressure against a rubber neck-ring. All too often this admirable bottle was smashed open for the sake of the marble.

MECCANO
A Force For Uplift

Those elder citizens who, instinctively, find the idea of factory 'sit-ins' repugnant were thrown into a fine confusion by the report in 1979 that 900 employees of Meccano, in Liverpool, had occupied their plant in protest against a closure notice. Surely, for once, strikers were inspired by the noblest of instincts. It was unthinkable that this holy fount of angle brackets, pawls, trunnions, boss bell cranks, architraves and contrate wheels should ever be allowed to dry up. (Contrate wheels are the ones with cogs parallel to the axis and are unpleasant to sit on.)

Puzzlingly, the British Library keeps its old Meccano handbooks in the notorious Cupboard, where pornography is stored. The only justification for this must be that Meccano undoubtedly inflamed the imagination of youth and set it coursing in fanciful channels. But the two Meccano boys portrayed on catalogues and box-lids looked healthy-minded enough; they were probably the sons of those jolly rubicund Tommies in the 1914–18 advertisements, downing their Sanatogen in no-man's-land.

In its heyday Meccano had a second factory in Elizabeth, New Jersey, and agents everywhere from Constantinople to Iquitos. It claimed to be much more than a toy. Its ability 'to duplicate any and every movement known to mechanism' gave it a wide edge over inferior imitations. It was used, not only by engineers, architects and inventors, but by professors in their demonstrations. It was even employed, in World War Two, by the War Office Selection Boards seeking 'officer material' for the Royal Electrical and Mechanical Engineers. Candidates were confronted by a Meccano working model and invited to assemble a similar one from loose parts. Those who had frittered away their youth building candy-pullers, oilcake-choppers and luffing jib cranes now found themselves half way to a commission.

What a delight to see again pictures of all those improbable models which the lack of a couple of bush wheels and an angle girder had prevented one from completing: the pile-driver, derricking grab, flax cleaner, snow plough and manure distributing cart (later called a fertiliser distributing cart); and the telferage system, akin to that designed by H. G. Wells to supply the front line in Flanders at reduced cost in men and horses.* There were contraptions with names never encountered before or since: the lurry (a sort of trailer); the aeroplage (a sort of land yacht); the cake-walk (for shaking up revellers); the opisometer (for measuring curved lines); the devil wall (a wheeled affair possibly for storming citadels); and the twin-elliptic harmonograph (for tracing fancy designs).

Meccano could be a cruel hobby. The dealer's window would show a fully functioning model of a grandfather clock, or a mighty Forth Bridge or Runcorn Transporter Bridge or Eiffel Tower (complete with electric lift), whereas the No. 1 Outfit received at Christmas had only parts enough to make a tea trolley, a ducking chair or a primitive railway signal. Additional parts were not cheap. Nuts and bolts were sixpence a dozen, which could mean two weeks' wages for a budding Brunel. For the sons of the affluent there were Presentation Sets costing £5 and £6, with a lock for deterring younger brothers.

The handbooks could get fairly technical and they even incited boys to make vehicles with clutch, differential and three-speed gears. But sometimes they unbent enough to show how to make a 'drop the nigger' device or how to blow up a battleship (if the missile hit the

---

* Working versions of Wells's system were set up on Clapham Common and in Richmond Park, but the Staff, 'those fine, handsome, well-groomed, neighing gentlemen', rejected the idea.

right spot amidships, the percussion cap attached to Flat Trunnion 8 would explode and a lever would cause the superstructure of the warship to leap upwards). A French boy was awarded a prize for a model of a diplodocus which had no mechanical merit, but everyone realised that the occasional sop had to be thrown to the French.

The *Meccano Magazine* existed 'to help Meccano boys to have more fun than any other boys'. It carried news of the Meccano Guild, which existed 'to foster clean-mindedness, truthfulness, ambition and initiative' and sounded like a serious challenge to the Boy Scout movement. Run by earnest pastors and masters, who evidently believed that the spirit of engineering was not in itself uplifting enough, it organised lectures, concerts, exhibitions, visits to factories and cross-country runs. There were competitions for the best motto, resulting in entries like 'Live long, speak true, right wrong and honour the King.' Readers submitted poems, expressing sentiments like this:

> Who invents the Sprocket Chain?
> And then the Hornby clockwork train?
> He must have a tremendous brain,
>   Frank Hornby!

The magazine warned: 'Any boy who fails to join the Guild is withholding his friendship and help from the best and brainiest boys in the kingdom and is also depriving himself of their help and companionship.' Some of us are still living with the shame of it, like those who, at a later date, swigged Ovaltine and failed to become Ovaltineys.

The decline in Meccano began, surely, when it took the first step into colour, in 1927. Red and green, the firm proclaimed, were 'real engineering colours', as used to protect girders against rust. Later came blue and gold, which were hardly engineering colours. 'The Meccano boy of today will design the air liners of tomorrow,' cried the advertisements, but what were these air liners going to look like? It was all a disaster comparable with the coming of colour television, with its unspeakably florid and sometimes green-eared newscasters. There is much to be said in this life for decent monochrome.

MILESTONES
Casualties: Enormous

Milestones are now an anachronism from the days when labourers wore smocks in the field, and acorns strewed the woodlands, and tramps sat at the road-sides breaking stones to pay for their night's lodging, and flocks of sheep moved with a tinkling of bells. They were a real solace for the footsore traveller. Some of them set out the distance to the next town not only in miles but in furlongs and yards. Others bore pointing hands to ensure that the stranger did not walk in the wrong direction. They ranged from solid stone posts of the kind Dick Whittington sat on ('London V Miles') to the three-faced, white-painted cast-iron ones, useful for supporting the tired rump.

There are said to be about sixty Roman milestones left, in or out of museums. These were usually stone posts designed as much to remind the natives who was master as to record the distance to the next town, which was revealed only after a recital of the Emperor's titles, dignities and conquests. Other Roman stones took the form of stepped mounting-blocks. Milestones began to appear again at the direction of the Turnpike Trusts, first along the Dover Road and then the Great North Road.

Then came the motor age, with the 'scorching' driver making his little joke about the milestones flashing past so fast he thought he was in a cemetery. The road engineers followed, trimming away corners, by-passing towns, piercing cliffs and making nonsense of the old mileage calculations. World War Two brought its own peculiar upsets, for, in order to baffle invaders, milestones (along with signposts) were hauled out of the ground like so many bad teeth. Some were buried a short distance away, to await resurrection, others were put into storage. A few were defaced with chisels, contrary to Government instructions. Some had detachable indication plates which were unscrewed and filed away. After the war the restoration of milestones was not the highest of priorities. Today the motorway designers' idea of a milestone is a huge illuminated sign comparable in size to the pre-war hoardings which proclaimed 'Blackpool Only 100 Miles'.

MOTORING
(1) Road Hogs

In *The Chauffeur's Companion*, published in 1909, appears this stirring advice to the motorist on what to do in an emergency:

If . . . on a fairly broad and slippery road you have the alternative of going on and killing someone, or stopping, and you find you cannot stop, there is one desperate remedy which may or may not come off, and that is to try and swing the car round with the bonnet pointing to where the back was. To do this (and I only advise it in cases of absolutely dire necessity) swing your steering wheel hard round and at the same time open your throttle and jam in your clutch with a jerk. This should skid the car round and when you are round you must get the wheel over on the other lock, and send her straight along the road again. The impetus of the car forcing her in the original direction and the engine pushing her the reverse way (when you have got her round) will neutralise each other and she should stop almost dead.

The early motorist was made of stern stuff. He was accused of being a road hog, of indulging in every form of arrogance, and of driving decent people into the embrace of socialism, but if he could perform feats like the one described (juggling with up to six driving controls) he was a man to inspire confidence and pride. As children we looked on so-called road hogs as an enviable race of supermen. It would never have occurred to us, as it did to *The Times*, to view them as 'masked highwaymen', or to assert that their facial disguise of helmets, goggles and veils was evidence of evil intentions, namely, to break speed limits without being recognised; though if it had we should probably have commended such enterprise.

It was the dust cloud he created that earned the early motorist the name of road hog (a term often applied today to a motorist who drives too slowly, impeding others). Rural dwellers objected to being suffocated by 'persons whom we do not even know by sight'. Housewives complained that they could no longer hang out the washing; their menfolk were unable to sit in their gardens.

To a great extent the dust problem was bound up with roadmanship. The man with a cheap, under-powered car was eager to get the maximum speed out of it at any given moment rather than let the cars of richer men overtake him and deluge him with dust. Scorching through villages was necessary in order to get a flying start on other drivers in open country. By dint of dangerous overtaking a determined driver could eventually break away into clean air.

By late Edwardian times much of the dust problem had abated. Also, horses had largely ceased to be frightened of mechanical monsters. But it had been an ugly fight at times. For every motorist who offered carrots to timid horses or strewed corn on the car bonnet to encourage them to eat (with the engine first switched off, and then switched on), or stroked their noses from the seat of his throbbing machine, there were dozens who drove past without slackening speed, arguing that, the shorter the period the horse was frightened, the better for all parties (and the less likely the motorist was to be lashed with a whip, whether by a coster or a clergyman). Motorists were supposed to stop when a drover held up his hand, but this signal was widely disregarded as an impertinence. In the fullness of time, owners of horses were able to advertise them as 'perfectly safe with motors' and promised that they would 'pass all road nuisances'.

Intermittently, there was debate on the ethics of horn-sounding. Was an Englishman entitled to make another Englishman leap out of the way by blasting him with crude noise? In 1905 the Bow Street magistrate had refused to uphold this right, setting back the cause of motoring by at least five minutes. *The Times* had campaigned against the motor horn, wondering (in 1907) whether road hogs might not be abolished by prohibiting the practice of hooting: 'It is the business of everybody not to run into what is in front of him and it is the privilege of everybody not to have to concern himself about what is behind him.' Yet motor horns were advertised as 'road-clearers', warranted to empty the highway for a couple of miles ahead. The most hated of the road-clearers was the Klaxon, which survived into fairly recent times (a miniature version was available for cyclists). Its memory still sets the teeth on edge. The device was operated by depressing a plunger, and the resulting sound – like that of a massed choir of robots gargling – was created by the fast vibration of a ratchet against a diaphragm. For all one knows, this hideous sound saved many a life. In contrast, the 'clear sweet tone' of the Gabriel horn, advertised as a welcome herald of Spring in the countryside, may have failed to save lives because it was too mellifluous.

John Masefield, a devoted early motorist, described in a letter how he sounded 'soul-animating strains' (on his Gabriel horn?) as he sped over the Downs in his Overland, and boasted playfully that 'children were crushed into pulp, wives were left widows and husbands widowers.' It is unlikely that he was a real road hog, but his fellow poet, Kipling, has come under strong suspicion. To be sure, Kipling was not the sort to sit hooting outside a public house until the peasants came out to give him directions; but, in his motoring tales, village policemen are boobies, fit to be kidnapped by motorists when too meddlesome, and magistrates who try to impose the law on drivers are cramping the free spirit of man. Kipling's motoring career began with an exceedingly unreliable steam car, a yellow Loco-mobile, which 'reduced us to the limits of fatigue'. He then graduated to the first of several Lanchesters, which 'sang like a six-inch shell across the Sussex Downs', eventually turning to Rolls-Royces. He did not drive himself but, like many a militant motorist, preferred a back seat.

If only the two speed-drunk poets could have indulged in advanced roadmanship at each other's expense on a narrow dusty road, hurling at each other those fierce imprecations they were so much condemned for using in print!

155

MOTORING
(2) Names Of Glory

We all know what happened after the Austrian archduke was shot dead in his car at Sarajevo in 1914. Some of us know his name, which was Francis Ferdinand; some of us can even name his assassin, Gavrilo Princep. Yes, yes, but what was the name of the car?

It was a Gräf und Stift, the Habsburgs' favourite limousine; and it was in a Gräf und Stift that the last Emperor went into exile. This 'Austrian Rolls-Royce', as it became known, would have made a welcome addition to one's spotter's log in those days, but alas, it was a rare bird.

The excitement of car-spotting was fuelled by the rich variety of makes, shapes and styles, not to mention smells and noises. Some cars chugged, some whirred, some throbbed, some thrummed, a very few purred; the La Buire, made in Stockport, claimed to be silent – 'when we say SILENT we don't mean almost silent but ABSOLUTELY SILENT' (and into absolute silence it vanished). These cars were built not by computer-controlled robots but by inspired designers who were not afraid of the jeers of posterity. They were lucky, too, in their purchasers: men who polished the serpent horns as lovingly as attendants used to polish the brasswork in public conveniences; owners who did not cover their new model with slogans, or pennants saying 'We have seen the Cheddar Caves', or 'decals' of shamrocks and star-bursts; men who did not allow the suppliers of their cars to advertise on the rear (why modern drivers leave their dealers' stickers in the back window for years on end is an impenetrable mystery).

There were cars from the small nations as well as the big: from Scotland, the Argyll, the Albion, the Arrol-Johnston and the Beardmore; from Wales, the Gwalia; from Belgium, the Minerva and the Metallurgique; from Holland, the Spyker. (Now, these countries, if they turn out cars at all, turn out those of other nations.) The best cars, like the best people, had hyphenated names: Alfa-Romeo, Angus-Sanderson, Armstrong-Siddeley, Chenard-Walcker, Delaunay-Belleville, Hispano-Suiza, Isotta-Fraschini, Lorraine-Dietrich (a perfect name for a screen star), Panhard-Levassor, Pierce-

Arrow, Rolls-Royce, Ruston-Hornsby, Sizaire-Berwick, Straker-Squire, Talbot-Darracq, Willys-Knight, even Willys-Overland-Crossley. What a superb roll-call!

Car-spotting brought out an unpatriotic snobbery. A De Dion Bouton was worth more than a mere Singer or Standard; a long rakish Delage or an Amilcar (the car that was to strangle Isadora Duncan in her scarf) outclassed any number of Beans, Clynos and Rileys. A few of the foreign names seemed rather ill-chosen, like Hurtu (said to be a great climber), Mors and Dodge. There was a Blériot Whippet, obviously meant to be a real flyer. There was a Palladium, a name better suited to a picture-house or a nib point. There were not only Sunbeams, but Moons and Stars and Meteorites. There were Kings, Queens, Princes and Princesses. There were names like those of characters in space fiction: Vandy, Zedel and Sigma. Some cars aspired to win fame on the strength of their initials alone, which included ABC, AC, BSA, FN, GN, NAG, SCAT and SPA (Fiat and Simca began as initials). One short-lived American car was depressingly called the Average Man's Runabout.

America's chief contributions were the Model T Ford and the Overland, with a few Cadillacs, Hupmobiles and Oldsmobiles. Despite its record on farm and battle-front, it was hard to take the Model T seriously, perhaps because it was the car doomed to be humiliated in the Keystone film-comedies, falling to bits as it was pursued, squashed flat between street cars, annihilated on level crossings. The 'Tin Lizzie' jokes seemed fairly terrible at the time and they have hardly improved with age ('Two Ford cars pass each other, what time is it? – Tin past tin.').

Among the 'heavies' to be logged was the Sentinel Steam Wagon, a real Puffing Billy, with its wisp of white smoke from the funnel and glow of red-hot coke under the engine; it kept the tradition of steam going long after the Locomobiles had given up. Another willing work-horse, somewhat despised, was the hard-tyred Trojan. The name Leyland was associated with brute strength, in the form of heavy lorries or charabancs; we were not to know the execration it would one day inspire.

Both during and after the 1914–18 war the game of car-spotting was supported by the publishers of cigarette cards. One of the most covetable issues was 'Military Motors', which featured not only auto-cannons and machine-gun batteries, but motor pigeon-cotes (former

Paris buses with the upper deck replaced by an array of bird cages), motor sheep-buses (former Paris buses again, this time with the lower deck carrying live sheep for *poilus'* rations), motor wire-cutters (open touring cars festooned overhead with sharp blades to slash through entanglements), motor ambulances disguised to look like Another Part of the Forest, motor horse-ambulances and motors adapted to haul freight on railway lines. What a marvellous war it was in which such mechanical wonders abounded! But the only military motors we ever saw were the open Vauxhall, which was the favourite car of the Staff, the car in which Allenby rode into Constantinople; and the open Crossley, which lent distinction to the Royal Flying Corps. Eventually, however, the war brought us the remarkable sight of cars, lorries and buses converted to use coal gas, contained in giant billowing bags installed overhead. These were refilled from stand pipes or, in emergency, from domestic gas taps.

The early 1920s were the car-spotter's heyday. All too soon the multitude of car manufacturers – they could be numbered in hundreds – began to go to the wall and the day of the ubiquitous Morris and Austin small cars had arrived. Even the small sports cars with their bonnet straps and knock-on wire wheels had a stereotyped look. Yet some of the finest cars ever seen dominated the 1930s. They included the long Lagondas and Delages, the sports Bugattis with a sound like that of a mainsail splitting or a plague of hornets, the monster eight-cylinder Duesenbergs, the rumbling Bentleys ('the fastest lorry in the world,' according to Ettore Bugatti). They were the backbone of the *concours d'élégance*, that fashionable event of the day, held in the unlikeliest places, not just at Le Touquet or Cannes. The Jaguar was not yet ripe for spotting, except in its early version, the long-bonneted, under-powered SS (said by some to stand for Sexual Six).

The 1930s saw the fast decline of the open car. For the fresh-air fiend there remained the 'dickey seat' (in America, 'rumble seat'), an exposed rear perch where the thrust of the wind was augmented by the rain water swilling back from the roof. A Rover 'limousine coupé' designed for winter sports was advertised as snug, warm and draught-proof, with a large dickey for two passengers exposed to the worst that winter could bring. What sort of people were they who drove their friends to St Moritz in this barbarous manner? What sort of people were they who went along for this sort of ride?

MOTORING
(3) The Dreadful Charabanc

Charabanc: 'a long open vehicle with rows of transverse seats'. It was all that and much more. It was the noisy triumphal chariot of the Age of Emancipation and it made road hogs out of the proletariat. The charabanc and Donald McGill were made for each other.

In its horse-drawn form the charabanc came from France. No one could think of an English name for it, but 'sharrabang' had a robust, vulgar charm. The vehicle was used, like the brake and the waggonette, for race meetings, football matches and weddings. The first motor charabancs appeared before 1914; in 1912 one of them ran away on a hill near Durham and killed ten members of a co-operative choir, a big death-roll for those days. But it was not until the early 1920s that the charabanc set the nation by the ears.

These rumbling juggernauts turned out by Commer, Bristol, Thornycroft, Tilling-Stevens and Leyland brought a new tumult to Bank Holidays. By popular agreement the women were worse than the men. Vaguely, as children, we knew that women in Britain had been going through a difficult time. We had never seen such unbuttoned, raucous females. Where had these tribes of Amazons come from? They were a real fascination to watch. When would we

159

be able to go on a charabanc outing? And why was it wrong to scramble for pennies thrown by these unruly but plainly generous people?

Ever alert for news of road hogs, *The Times* in 1920 printed blast upon blast against these self-propelled pubs, these mobile bear gardens, excoriating the drunken rabble who threw bottles, bellowed bawdy songs and waved everything from wooden rattles to articles of women's underwear.

The charabanc 'explosion' had been made possible by the spare capacity in the war factories. Scenting a boom in mass transit, needy operators rushed into the new trade, sometimes making only minimal conversions to trucks and troop transports. Some so-called charabancs were simply lorries with wooden chairs or deckchairs and stacked crates of ale. Signs like 'Owned and run by Ex-Servicemen' began to appear. Soon the 'toast-rack' type of charabanc gave way to plumped-out monsters with names like 'Pride of the North' and 'Queen of the South'. In some there was room for dancing between the seats, a sight well-calculated to inflame other road users.

A charabanc expedition would replenish its stocks of ale as the day proceeded, hurling its empties on to the highway. On a midsummer weekend in 1920, reported *The Times*, fourteen roads out of London were paved with broken glass from charabancs. This did not impede the juggernauts' own progress, since they had solid tyres.

High-perched above the road, the occupants of charabancs were well-placed to catcall others, especially those trying to overtake – a difficult feat, since the monsters cruised in close convoy. Aware without being told that the occupants of private cars looked on them as witless riffraff, the charabanc riders felt they might as well behave accordingly. It was naked class war. Had these trippers stood baying outside a grand hotel in Eastbourne, the police would have dispersed them soon enough, but on the new King's Highway insults could be hurled with impunity.

In Brighton and Blackpool hundreds of charabancs arrived with their occupants already deep in liquor. Some publicans put up signs reading 'No Charas'; others sold the operators enough portable liquor to enable them to move on. Drivers were supposed to stop only at designated inns, but rowdy passengers, sighting an attractive pub, would fling their caps, or each other's caps, from the vehicle, telling the driver they had blown off; if he wanted to receive a whip-round later he would stop while the caps were recovered and their owners nipped into the pub.

As indignation mounted against the charabanc, attempts were made to impose discipline. A 'charaphone' at the rear of the vehicle was supposed to transmit the honking of frustrated motorists to the driver's ear. The driver was also encouraged to interest his passengers in the passing scene. One method was to issue cards with numbered descriptions of sights along the route; then, at the right moment, the driver would ring a bell and call the number. Alternatively, a conductor would describe the scene through a megaphone.

A charabanc outing could be a gruelling ordeal, as the railway companies did not fail to point out. In 1921 the legal maximum speed was 12 miles an hour, which meant that a law-abiding journey from London to the coast would be full of *longueurs*. Only a few passengers benefited from the windscreen. In rain squalls some did what they could with umbrellas and parasols. Putting up the hood was like erecting a small marquee in a gale and was delayed as long as possible. The pretence that a charabanc was a limousine with twenty-four comfortable seats was a poetic fiction. But at least, unlike a train, it waited for you and saw you home; and you might even be given a souvenir photograph of the party setting out.

The postcards of Donald McGill show charabancs overflowing with red-nosed roisterers. One of them has a crimson juggernaut balancing on the edge of a cliff – 'We're stopping here, for the present.' The comic papers of the day rang all the changes on the subject. A popular word-of-mouth story concerned the hospital visitor who learned that nine women in the maternity ward were expecting on 1 March. When she said to the tenth, 'And I suppose yours is due on March the first too?' the others cried 'Oh, no, she wasn't in our charabanc!' (The Medical Officer of Health for Chelsea, Dr Louis Parkes, told the Royal Commission on Divorce, which reported in 1912: 'One frequently sees a number of births returned within about nine months after the Bank Holidays'.)

It was possible, watching the procession of Royal Blues and Royal Reds going down to the sea, or massing symmetrically in parks like the mobile divisons of an army, to rejoice that the common man was at last entering on his heritage. Resorts like Llandudno might complain that, thanks to the charabanc, miners and cotton workers were reducing the resort to the level of Rhyl, but might not some of

161

Llandudno's polish be absorbed by these coarse invaders? The *Commercial Motor*, an interested party, said in 1920: 'The beauty spots themselves should have a refining influence which, eventually, should eliminate the vulgarities that are at present so evident.'

There was, undoubtedly, a sober and respectable side to the charabanc boom. On superior excursions the driver made no intermediate stops but headed straight to the night's hotel. Employers with reputations to lose saw to it that their workers did not get too carried away on the summer outing. Indeed, old photographs of charabanc parties tend to show grave, cloth-capped men sitting in orderly rows, or sober-hatted matrons who look like ranks of worshippers in chapel. For every uproarious works outing or printers' wayzgoose, there were dozens of blameless 'mystery tours' and 'moonlight cruises'.

By the 1930s the charabancs were turning into roofed coaches, which made the hurling of bottles that much harder. But not all publicans were happy; they merely changed the sign 'No Charas' to read 'No Coaches'.

MOTORING
(4) A Slight Miscalculation

It was about 1930 that the cross-roads of Britain began to be sprinkled with 'Robots', the name then given to traffic lights (how much more graphic is the French description: *feux tricolores*). In North America automatic signals had been working successfully and to everybody's surprise the system worked in Britain too.

What did not work was the idea tried out by Morris Motors, in the autumn of 1932, of equipping new models with their own double set of miniature traffic lights, one on each side of the car, to serve as direction indicators. These red-amber-green lights were operated by the driver from a switchboard and other road users were supposed to work out for themselves the driver's intentions.

The system, which the makers claimed to be as near foolproof as possible, worked as follows. When the driver wished to make a right turn he first showed an amber light, indicating to the driver behind that he was contemplating a change in direction. The amber was then followed by red, which meant no overtaking on that side. On the left side of the car he would simultaneously show a green light, meaning that overtaking was safe. Neither red nor green could be displayed until amber was shown.

Far from being foolproof, these 'Christmas tree' signals caused confusion and bafflement to drivers and pedestrians alike. Sir Malcolm Campbell, the racing driver, attacked the innovation in the *Daily Mail*. Very soon the Ministry of Transport issued its own regulations for direction indicators, which were to be simple illuminated amber signs, with no flashing or occulting lights. Vehicles without a suitable electric system were to have a semaphore device in the shape of a hand painted white. Morris got the message and replaced their twinkling light-sets free of charge, at no small cost. Some of the unwanted sets were sold as novelties to Gamages.

NOTICES
Attention to Hat-Pins

THE POSTMASTER IS NEITHER BOUND TO GIVE
CHANGE NOR AUTHORISED TO DEMAND IT

This notice, once prominently displayed in every Post Office, was widely criticised for its Olympian unhelpfulness, but much commended as a well-balanced English sentence, reflecting great credit on its unknown author

BEWARE OF THE BULL

This famous aunt-frightener was found beside country footpaths but could just as sensibly have been placed outside Marks and Spencer's or the Scotch Wool Shop in every market town. 'Bad-tempered, slavering bulls, with rings in their noses, were led, flogged and otherwise manhandled through busy shopping streets by bad-tempered, slavering drovers, causing women and children to cower in doorways. From time to time a beast escaped and the prospect of a bull in a china shop ceased to be a far-fetched fancy.

And angry bulls were only half the story. On market days whole

herds of jostling cattle were chivvied along High Streets – even along the High, in Oxford – bruising cars and leaving roads steaming with dung. Small boys sometimes earned pennies by 'helping' to control the herds. It was no use complaining; farmers saw it as their right to turn any sleepy town into Pamplona without warning.

THE ATTENTION OF LADY PASSENGERS IS DRAWN TO
THE DANGER TO OTHER PASSENGERS AND THE COUNCIL'S
SERVANTS THROUGH THE PRACTICE OF WEARING HAT-PINS
WITH UNPROTECTED POINTS

Signed by the Chief Officer of London Tramways, this notice first appeared in tramcars in 1913, the year when men finally rose up against the hat-pin menace. Paris had 'decreed' smaller hats, which meant that greater lengths of cold steel were free to do their fell work in jerkily-driven vehicles and on crowded pavements. London, Berlin, Paris and New York all took action against hat-pins, but many women declined to fit corks or other protectors. At Worthing County Court, Judge MacEarness said to a woman: 'If you walk about with a hat-pin sticking out like that you will be up for murder some day. Follow my advice and take it out.' The reply was: 'Well, I must keep my cap on somehow.' A report in the *Daily News* for 14 January 1913 describes how nineteen women and girls were prosecuted in the State Children's Court at Adelaide for wearing unprotected hat-pins. One defendant said she had walked in the roadway to avoid mutilating pedestrians. Magistrate: 'It seems to me that the hat-pin you are wearing now is a very long one. Is it used for any other purpose?' – Defendant (angrily): 'No, but it might be.' Which is a reminder of the secondary purpose of hat-pins: to protect ladies against cinema pests.

> WILL THOSE WHO HAVE SEEN THE PROGRAMME KINDLY
> VACATE THEIR SEATS IN FAVOUR OF PATRONS WAITING
> *Thank you*   *The Management*

If the cinema manager was a wag, the notice might read: 'Will those who have seen the programme twice . . .' Whichever version was shown, there was never any rush of guilty departures.

The concept of 'Continuous Performance' (dating from the birth of the cinema) now seems extraordinary. People entered in the middle of the big picture, saw how it finished, then waited through a string of supporting films and another big picture for the beginning. It was like reading the last six chapters of a novel before turning to the start. However, not everybody cared about the big picture. Motives for cinema-going included: to get the weight off one's feet while shopping; to escape from a noisy or measles-infected home; to get some warmth; to snatch a nap; to listen to lively music; to cuddle a companion; and to make a pick-up.

ODOURS
Dangerous . . . And Delicious

Some of us can remember when the odours of geranium, mustard, pear drops and musty hay were, if not especially allur-ing, at least innocent. By 1939 these had become the 'signature smells' of various poison gases, one whiff of which was calculated to send an overwrought citizen to his respirator in 'an ecstasy of fumb-ling'. Another lethal odour was said to be that of Portuguese laurel, but nobody knew what Portuguese laurel smelled like anyway. There was a story, no doubt mischievous, about six evacuated children, in 1939, who pulled on their gas masks at a High Church service, mistaking the odour of incense for that of musty hay (phosgene). In R. C. Sherriff's *Journey's End* there is a reference to soldiers on the Western Front putting on their respirators to protect themselves from a sudden whiff of may blossom.

To those who lived beside gasometers, or near tanneries, or in Warrington or Widnes (rivals for the title of farthest-smelling town) the likelihood of being able to detect the scent of geranium on the breeze was probably slight. We forget in what fearful stenches so many lived. Perhaps we also forget how children were sent to the gas works for a good sniff of gas to cure their colds.

The odour of new-mown hay, as distinct from musty hay, was once sold in phials (and perhaps still is). As children we may well have sniffed it on one dressing-table or another, along with frangipani, patchouli, chypre, Ylang-Ylang and Phul-Nana (or were those too *demi-mondaine* to have come our way?). Women's furs and muffs, even the dead foxes they hung round their necks, smelled quite delightful, in happy contrast to the reek of naphthalene or camphor from mothballs in forbidden clothes drawers. Did the smell of mothballs really overhang smart public gatherings, or did we imagine that?

The lost smells of childhood are an alternation of sweet and sour: the witching smell from even the dingiest bakery; the ante-room-of-Paradise smell of a really high-class chocolate shop; the musty smell of front parlours, rather like that of an old parish church; the pungent stink of carbide and the acetylene gas derived from dripping water on it, as in cycle lamps (a stink which sometimes rose from school inkwells); the hot, dusty, metallic smell, impossible to analyse, of electric tram-cars; the aromatic attack of camphorated oil, as rubbed on the chest; the greasy smell of dubbin, as rubbed into football boots; the tell-tale reek of carbolic; the cleanly smell of starch; the stale-sweet smell of the cinema, not unlike that of a busy phone-box in Brighton; the sickly smell of a book from a damp room; the horrific smell of the occasional bad egg at breakfast (surely a vanished hazard now?); and the reek left by incontinent horses (as still encountered in full strength at spots where carriages await the patronage of sightseers).

Byron complained that the English miss always smelled of bread and butter. As one recalls, this tea-time aura attached itself to girls and boys alike. At least garlic was no great hazard in those times. Fish took a more powerful revenge on the human race than today, when the 'wet fish' shop is becoming a rarity. Parson Kilvert quoted the Vicar of St Ives as saying that the smell of fish in that resort was sometimes strong enough to stop the church clock.

More fortunate resorts were supposed to smell of ozone, which is cynically defined in *Chambers' Dictionary* as 'an imagined constituent in the air of any place that one wishes to commend'. Had these resorts really been charged with 'pure ozone' (or with the degree of radioactivity that some of them claimed), the populations would have been extinguished as efficiently as by poison gas. What our elders thought was the smell of ozone was presumably that of salt, seaweed or drains. Genuine ozone, an allotropic form of oxygen, reaches us only in minute quantities, unromantically, in air-fresheners.

PAINT-BOXES
What, No Nymph's Thigh?

Crimson Lake, Prussian Blue, Burnt Umber, Raw Sienna, Burnt Sienna, Vandyke Brown, Cobalt, Chinese White ... these are the well-remembered names from one's first paint-box. Was there (we wondered) a far-off crimson lake into which emissaries of the paint trade dipped their buckets? And why did white have to be *Chinese*? (The name now suggests that of an old Chinese hand, as Rose Madder conjures up a Hardy heroine.) To a child beginning to love polysyllables, some paint-box names had a very fine ring: Viridian, Vermilion, Indigo and Ultramarine. Yet poets never seemed to use these names, preferring feeble combinations like rose-red and pea-green. The paint-box colours were as rarefied as the heralds' gules, argent and sanguine.

It was a long time before we heard there were colours with names like Nymph's Thigh, Bath Crimson (the crimson of the Order, not of Marat's bath) and Isabella (a drab off-white supposedly named after the daughter of Philip II, who swore not to change her linen until after Ostend fell, which took three years). Henry Ford, having long proclaimed that 'You can have a Ford in any colour so long as it's black', suddenly astounded the world by offering models in Arabian Sand, Niagara Blue, Gun-Metal Blue and Dawn Grey. For Henry this was wild imaginative stuff, but he was hopelessly and perennially outshone by the rag trade, with names like Dragon's Blood, Pigeon's Blood, Ghost and Elephant's Breath.

PALAIS DE DANSE
A Partner For Sixpence

If one had never been in a *palais de danse*, and was fearful of what lay in store, one could pay to enter a spectators' gallery. It was a shilling well spent. Below lay a packed and throbbing vivarium, drenched in strong and ever-changing colours, in which young men and girls, hugging each other closely, circulated all in the same direction, except for a wilful exhibitionist few who tried to obstruct the flow. From time to time fell a flurry of giant snow-flakes, these being patches of light cast by a revolving glitter-ball up in the roof.

It was a revelation akin to that of seeing one's first chorus line; a world unrealised, a realm of the senses in which it seemed unlikely one would ever be able to move with confidence or distinction. Where had this throng learned their fancy footwork? How had one missed out in this rich experience? Closer inspection showed that some males were merely striding round the floor chatting to females who were content to walk backwards in their path. That should not be too hard to master . . . Even the waltz seemed to call only for half-revolutions.

The *palais de danse* came not from France but from America. The first to be opened in Britain was the Hammersmith Palais, in 1919: an old tram-shed fitted up with a sprung-maple floor and Chinese lighting, and billed as 'the largest and most luxurious dancing palace in Europe'. There had been, and still were, skating rinks which offered limited body contact to music. There had been a rage for the *thé-dansant*, very popular with young officers on leave from the Front. Before the dancing teas there had been dances in assembly

NO SMOOCHING

rooms, or in theatres which cost huge sums to hire and adapt. Now, in the relaxed post-war mood, dancing had become the obsession of the masses (wiseacres talked of a wave of 'tarantism'). With minimal ceremony, shopgirls were passed from clerk to clerk, in the condition lip-smackingly described by Byron:

Hot from the hands promiscuously applied
Round the slight waist, or down the glowing side . . .

No good would come of it, in the view of the nation's elders; and their fears were not lessened when the Hammersmith Palais held a famous Birth Control Ball, the subject of a merry limerick or two. But very soon most of the Locarnos and Plazas and Ritzes turned out to be hotbeds of respectability, especially when the' middle classes moved in with their white ties and tails. It was at the Hammersmith Palais, the *Oxford English Dictionary* helpfully informs us, that Mrs Mary Whitehouse met her future husband.

The opening band at Hammersmith was 'The Original Dixieland Jazz Band', a blow for those who despised 'nigger music' (though the players were white). Like the other dance-halls which now sprang

169

up, it offered tea-time sessions as well as evening sessions. Strangely, it boasted 'a most luxurious promenade' for non-dancers and dancers alike, promising 'sheer irresponsible merriment' (London's music-hall promenades had been shut down in disgrace during the war). What fascinated many was the system of pens containing professional partners, male and female, available for sixpence a dance. An American songwriter later tried to invest with pathos the girl hired for 'ten cents a dance'; but the lot of the male partner, provided in principle for 'the lonely flapper' but more obviously for the middle-aged lady, must have had its poignancies too (the song 'Only a Gigolo', if memory serves, dealt with a higher-flying type).

The 'sixpenny dip' system, which to the worldly invited comparison with the choosing of a partner in a brothel, called for tact on the customer's part. To buy a single ticket looked cheap; to buy half a dozen meant spending the price of a good meal; to hire a girl for the evening, buying her refreshments and giving her a £1 tip, was the act of a rich voluptuary. In *Punch* in 1922, A. P. Herbert described a visit to a dance-hall where he bought half a dozen sixpenny tickets and waited 'sheepishly with some other desperadoes' near the pen, until the music started. It was not done to eye the partners too closely, but one could stealthily form some notion of the more desirable. They all wore 'neat uniform'. When the music started the desperadoes quickly pounced on the best-looking girls. A.P.H.'s partners, by his account, were stilted conversationalists, returning what seemed like standardised responses to his small talk. Even his suggestion that the fern-fringed block of ice in mid-floor would look better with a salmon on top raised only a maybe-it-would, maybe-it-wouldn't reply. In this dance-hall, male partners cost ninepence, an unexplained injustice. When Herbert's friend George performed an acrobatic dance with his partner he was tapped on the shoulder by a man in evening dress who said: 'Sorry, sir, we don't allow that here. This is not the West End . . .'

The floor supervisors, later to be dubbed bouncers, broke up 'smoochers', turned out under-age girls and pounced on those who smuggled in liquor (notices in cloakrooms warned against this). What did not help *palais* decorum was the song 'Dancing Cheek to Cheek', with couples taking it as authority to clamp their faces together in the Astaire-Rogers manner. The managers were reduced to shrugging; soon enough they would be up against jitterbugging, the palais glide and 'Knees up, Mother Brown'.

Some of the big dance-halls, having survived the Charleston in 1925, became ice-rinks in the Depression years, the Hammersmith Palais among them. About 1930, competitive ballroom dancing began (as featured in the BBC's 'Come Dancing' from the Nottingham Palais, recently closed). Jazz went one way, ballroom dancing another, but there were always big bands to provide every style of music. As the standard of dancing improved in the *palais*, so it degenerated in hotels and night-clubs, where the floors shrank to handkerchief size and couples engaged in 'crush' dancing, clinging together and swaying gently, which often was all they wanted to do.

Born of one world war, the Hammersmith Palais was born again after another. But the old *palais* routine was dying – dying from lack of variety, from respectability, from too much grace and style. The new dancers no longer wanted to touch each other, except to throw each other about.

PAPER CHASES
For Boys And Gentlemen

Paper chasing would now appear to be illegal under the 1958 Litter Act. The implications of this measure were much debated at the time, but no public voices seem to have been raised in defence of paper chasing, perhaps because the sport in its literal sense had virtually died out. One or two MPs were worried about how the Act would affect confetti throwing.

Many elder citizens can remember, as boys, panting over the fields after 'scent' in the form of shredded *Daily Mails*, strewn from satchels by a couple of 'hares', who were usually given ten minutes 'law'. The character-forming aspect of the exercise was presumably thought to outweigh any offence caused to the environment. *Tom Brown's Schooldays* reveals how earnestly paper-chasing was taken at Rugby School, where tearing up 'scent' was a task for the fags. The notion that what was good for schoolboys must be good for men animated such bodies as the Thames Rowing Club, whose gentlemen-amateurs were anxious to avoid putting on weight in winter; and in the late Victorian years hundreds of so-called paper-chasing clubs flourished on the London outskirts. They tended to be based on public houses, like the Thames Hare and Hounds, which met at the King's Head at Roehampton, and the South London Harriers, pride of the Greyhound at Streatham. In military country, packs of soldiers could be seen following up paper as zealously as the Staff pursued it indoors. Gradually the larkier aspects of the sport – laying false scents, leading the pack through deep slimy brooks – faded out and inter-club cross-country running on the modern pattern took over. If any resemblance to hunting persisted, it did so only in school runs.

The French Army brought a characteristic distinction to the chasing of paper. In the Forest of Fontainebleau (according to a correspondent of *Notes and Queries*), officers conducted the chase on horseback, with ladies following in carriages. The real object of the exercise was the *déjeuner sur l'herbe* at the end of the trail. The mounted hares performed their paper-strewing duties in very idle fashion, knowing that the hounds would not wish to catch them before the rendezvous was reached. It was essentially a social outing, with no nonsense about splashing through slime, and the motto might have been Talleyrand's '*Surtout, messieurs, point de zèle.*'

PASSING BELLS
To Speed The Soul

'What passing bells for those who die as cattle?' asked Wilfred Owen, and gave his own answer: 'Only the monstrous anger of the guns.' The rite of the passing bell, which was dying out in Owen's time, was authorised by the 65th Article of Canon Law: 'When any is passing out of this life, a bell shall be tolled and the Minister shall not then slack to do his duty.' For the death of a child, there would be three preliminary strokes on a 'teller' bell; for a woman, six strokes; and for a man, nine. Then would follow a series of strokes on the great bell to denote the number of years the dying person had lived.

The ritual occurs twice in Dorothy L. Sayers's *The Nine Tailors*. Going about his parish duties, the Rector stands still to count the booming strokes of Tailor Paul. After establishing that it tolls for a man, he fears it may be signalling the death of 'Hensman's boy', aged twelve and sickly; but this number is safely passed. Eventually he tells an enquirer: 'They have rung the Nine Tailors and forty-six strokes and I am afraid it must be for Sir Henry.' Some weeks later an unidentified male corpse found in the parish qualifies for fifty strokes (an estimate of the dead man's age) and then 100 more.

Strictly speaking, the bell was to be tolled as the sufferer was *in extremis*, not after death, the idea being to mark the soul's passing from one world to another; but very often it was not sounded until after death. Sometimes the big bell which was tolled at the hour of the funeral was called the passing bell. It was all work for the sexton. In a punning poem by Thomas Hood is the verse: 'His death, which happened in his berth, / At forty-odd befell; / They went and told the sexton, and / The sexton toll'd the bell.' In spa towns, and other places where the moribund gathered, the monotonous striking of the passing bell did little to raise the morale of the survivors. In times of war, knells of all kinds were suspended, since the ringing of church bells was reserved as an invasion warning.

PENS
'Excuse Blot'

Except in very old-fashioned offices and banks, or in gentlemen's clubs, quill pens hardly survived into this century. They were a shade affected even for the signing of death warrants or peace treaties. The quill may have been 'Nature's noblest gift', as Byron said, but the gift was obtained only by much mangling and mutilation of the goose population (fastidious writers preferred the feathers from the left wing, because they curved away from the writer's nose, and the second and third feathers were most coveted). The advent of steel pens greatly pleased humanitarians, though there was still a toothpick industry to be supported.

Steel pens, however, were by no means economical. Quills could always be reshaped with a pen-knife (a name which survives even though the knife has lost its original function) and a Dr Warner, to

173

show what could be done, wrote a two-volume ecclesiastical history and a one-volume dissertation on the Prayer Book with a single quill. No such feats were possible with a steel pen, but that did not stop the penmakers of Birmingham from taking extravagant pride in their nibs and showing excessive scorn of their rivals' products. The best of them offered boxes of assorted nibs free on request. There were pens designed especially, or so it was claimed, for bankers, for actuaries, for etchers and for ladies (Queen Mary graciously allowed a nib to be named after her, perhaps the original *plume de ma tante*). If one believed the advertisements, there were nibs so smooth that writing was like drawing the silk from a reel. It was impossible not to write noble sentiments with them, for the imagination soared into Miltonic realms as soon as the point touched paper. One nib was cut on the slant, to make it easier to keep up with the poet's teeming brain. These wonder-pens had variously designed, and patented, holes and slits which gave flexibility, or special hollows to act as reservoirs of ink. Some had snub or pellet points which supposedly made for smoothness. There was even a well-remembered night-mare of a pen which carried a long reservoir on its back and was supposed to hold 'enough ink for a letter with a single dip'.

Schoolchildren were given workaday Waverleys, untipped with gold, platinum, iridium, vanadium or palladium (such rare metals would have been wasted on an article destined to end its days straddled to make a tip for a paper dart or aeroplane). The nibs that children envied were the broad-tipped 'J' variety, or the still-broader 'B', which left a gratifyingly bold trace but were reserved for the more slapdash and emphatic writing of adults.

Writing exercises, as at dame school, were the source of much *angst*. Once we had mastered 'pot hooks', we were faced with copy-books in which improving maxims set out in copperplate had to be meticulously reproduced. Rudyard Kipling thought highly of the 'Gods of the Copy-Book Headings', whose teachings were sounder than those of the gods of the market-place or the fashionable pulpit. We had no views whatever on their worth. The Wages of Sin might well be Death, but what mattered was getting those 'hangers' right. The punishable offences were to leave unlooped those strokes which should have been looped and to loop those strokes which should not have been looped, as well as leaving unclosed those letters which should have been closed. Thick downward strokes were made by

pressing harder on the nib, when as often as not the ink ran out, or alternatively spattered in a constellation of tiny blobs, with perhaps one major blob for emphasis. 'Excuse blot' was a recurring feature of private correspondence. Mostly school ink was sludgy at the bottom, like Turkish coffee. Sooner or later an impurity, perhaps a hair, attached itself to the nib and left a trail as of a drunken spider.

With luck, one started the day with a new nib, which had to be moistened in the mouth so that the ink would 'take'. After use, it was cleaned meticulously on the pen-wiper, usually a stitched-together assemblage of bits of serge. Some grown-ups had highly covetable pen-wipers consisting of little silver jars filled with shot, in which the nib was dipped till clean.

The fountain pen was not for young children. It had come on a bit since the days of Fanny Burney, who wrote her court diary with a pen in the form of an ink cylinder with a cork which had to be eased to let the ink flow. Other early models worked on the squeeze-as-you-write principle. Gradually the fountain-pen designers devised cunning capillary channels, working in conjunction with flood barriers, to ensure a constant flow. It was a sophisticated instrument by the time Lloyd George signed the Versailles Peace Treaty with a gold-plated Waterman.

One way to fill a fountain pen was to unscrew the end and squirt ink into it with a rubber-ended tube like an eye-dropper, rather as one would feed a fledgling. Another had a side lever which compressed the rubber sac inside; then, on release, the ink was sucked in from the pot. Other models were loaded by pumping with a plunger or massaging the sac with one's fingers.

At home, ink was to be had only in an 'unspillable' pot, which could, however, be spilled if a boy put his mind to it. For travelling, adults had spill-proof silver ink-pots encased in plush and leather. The worst ink in the country was to be found, along with the worst pens (their points crossed, like the beak of a crossbill), in Post Offices. Anyone who nipped into a Post Office simply to fill his fountain pen deserved everything coming to him.

The business of writing called for much ancillary equipment. It was fashionable to seal envelopes with wax, which meant a whole apparatus of wax bars, lamp and set of seals; and there were special portable sealing sets for those who did not like to slacken standards on holiday. To children, the opportunity to create multi-coloured wax puddles on the backs of letters, and then stamp designs on them, was purest joy. Those stick-on paper seals afforded no comparable pleasure.

In the years just after World War Two, the fountain pen had reached such perfection as to function even in the cockpit of a supersonic fighter, in sub-zero conditions, during aerobatics at 40,000 feet. Obviously such a paragon had to be replaced; and replaced it was by the ball-pen, which made terrible messes in aircraft but could write under water. A Parker spokesman described it as the only pen which could make eight carbons and no original. Banks tried to ban the ball-pen for the signing of cheques. Teachers said it would be the death of copperplate writing and for once they were right.

POGO STICKS
For Bright Young People

In 1921, taking their cue from France, school children, undergraduates and Bright Young People fell for the pogo stick and began bobbing up and down like kangaroos, or Spring-Heel Jacks. The device was a stout pole with hand-grips at the top and foot-rests at the bottom, and inset into the base was a heavy spring covered with a buffer pad. Most people did not hop for long before falling, though show-offs put up some surprising records, egged on by popular newspapers. In Europe, pogo halls were opened up, on the lines of skating rinks, and there were pogo carnivals, with high-jump and long-jump contests.

Among British society leaders to welcome the pogo stick were Sir Oswald and Lady Mosley. Their son Nicholas has described, in *Rules of the Game*, how from a window at Savehay Farm, Denham, he watched the family guests pogoing merrily. Then one of them fell and broke his jaw, so all formed up in a solemn procession to throw the naughty pogo stick into the river.

In the 1970s the word pogoing was used to describe an ebullient jump-up dance, with optional salmon-like wriggles. Variations on this punk exercise were sometimes performed, arms-linked, before television cameras to celebrate radical victories.

PONDS
Lure Of The Bent Pin

The village pond was easy to sentimentalise. It might have been used, in cruder times, for 'floating' witches, or ducking scolds, or sobering up drunkards, or, in more recent days, for fighting fires or refuelling steam cars, but it lay secure in the affections of anyone who had ever gone fishing with a home-made rod or a scoop for frogspawn. So, when conservationists in 1974 began their campaign to reclaim ponds, they were careful to cry: 'Save the *Village* Pond.'

The green-scummy ponds of childhood, with their ducks and dragonflies, were not necessarily village ponds; some were tucked away in corners of fields and woodlands, none the worse for a notice planted in the middle, reading: 'No Fishing. No Bathing. No Nuisances.' These ponds eddied and twitched with a complex life of their own – a life of half-glimpsed fins, noses, legs and even fingers, of bubbles, scums and jellies; and, most tantalising of all, of inaccessible nests among the rushes.

Today, the city dweller wanting to 'do a Thoreau' and seek out a back-to-Nature pond would face a frustrating quest; nothing is more disheartening than to find a lonely silent pool where all is peace but the fish are floating upside down. All over Britain, farmers have mopped up puddles on their land like housewives with mops. Builders have drained ponds to put up houses and multitudes of frogs have died miserably in the drying mud. In wartime, many sheets of water – the lake in St James's Park, the ponds in Richmond Park – were emptied because they reflected moonlight and were thought to assist enemy bombers. These were restored afterwards and the wild life returned, but hundreds of ponds extinguished in peace are gone for good.

Trying to catch fish with a bent pin and a cotton reel for float was pure wishfulness, but 'fishing' was something which had to be got out of the system, like measles. At first the thrill of waiting for a tug on the line was intense; an actual nibble set up the equivalent of the huntsman's 'buck fever'. Always it turned out that the bait had been stolen or washed away. Transfixing grubs, worms and caterpillars on the hook was not the most alluring part of the game, though no one should underestimate a boy's natural talent for impalement. The pond-obsessed hero of George Orwell's *Coming Up For Air* reflects much of his creator's boyhood passion for fishing. In one pleasing episode the gang of young anglers call at the butcher's to beg a supply of gentles. He performs a ritual explosion at the suggestion that he allows blow-flies on his premises, then calms down and says perhaps they will find one or two in the back shop.

Orwell would presumably have applauded the volunteers who, a few years ago, began dredging village ponds and extracting old beds and bicycles. He might have been less happy about 'best-kept pond' competitions, the 'adoption' of ponds by primary schools and the creation of aseptic, concrete-edged pondlets at the base of office blocks. The lost ponds of childhood belonged to a private and personal world, not to be shared with others or made the subject of school projects.

POST HASTE
And No Drink For Postmen

'He does not bore me, no. I like of all things to hear about the Post Office. I had no idea it was such a wonderful institution. Do tell me more about it, Mr Flint.'

That was Miss Lillicrop, in *Post Haste, A Tale Of Her Majesty's Mails*, by the famous boys' writer, R. M. Ballantyne. Encouraged by Miss Lillicrop, Solomon Flint continues his paralysing recital of postal statistics: the number of stamps found loose in mailbags every year (52,856 – surely a criticism of Post Office mucilage); the total of letters posted without addresses; the number of receptacles for letters throughout Britain; the latest figures for deposits in the Post Office

Savings Bank; the number of postal workers serving in the Volunteers. Solomon Flint goes on like that in chapter after chapter; then, when it seems that the flow must be exhausted, he is given twenty-one uninterrupted pages to work off the text of a lecture on the history of the Post Office, delivered to members of a self-improvement society whose delight in statistics equals that of Miss Lillicrop.

Never one's favourite Ballantyne, *Post Haste* (first published in 1880) now seems, on re-reading, to be one of the worst books ever cobbled together, despite its splendid frontispiece showing a railway accident in which a number of postal sorters are being hurled from a coach in a snowstorm of letters. How could one's youthful regard for the Post Office have survived this turgid welter of statistics and sententiousness?

Of course, one allowed for pi-jaws in Ballantyne and skipped them. And there really was, as Miss Lillicrop said, so much to admire in the Post Office, notably in the head office at St Martin's-le-Grand – a splendid address for a Holy of Holies. This building had a 'mighty telegraph hall' where 1,200 telegraphists, male and female, 'flashed electric sparks broadcast over the land', and an even more fascinating basement where two steam engines produced the breath to blow messages through miles of pneumatic tubes.

Ballantyne drew his facts from official reports and also from the *Post Office Guide*, a handbook which sooner or later found its way into most homes. It laid down how bees, snakes and other live creatures were to be packaged for the post. Dead creatures, if despatched by the best people, were no problem; game birds could be sent just as they were, with a label round the neck, so long as they were 'not so high as to taint other packets' and were not exuding liquids.

The Post Office seemed unbelievably efficient earlier this century. It may be that postmen were abominably paid, but they wore their red-piped blue uniforms with pride and would have been horrified at the sloppy open-necked appearance of today's tripper-like breed. To its credit, the Post Office resisted all pressure, in Parliament or elsewhere, to make postmen deliver at the back door; the Royal Mail was the Royal Mail and it did not go through the tradesmen's entrance. Every Christmas the Postmaster-General urged the public not to ply the postman with liquor, surely a recognition of the man's popularity rather than an implication that he was a tippler who did not know when to stop.

Letters were collected and delivered throughout the day. Even as one was preparing for early bed, bills might rain through the door. Addicts of the correspondence columns in *The Times* and *Daily Telegraph* will know what wonders were achieved in the field of 'same day' delivery. It will be enough here to give one particularly poignant example: a free-lance writer, living in London, could post an article in the morning to *Punch* and, returning home in the afternoon, find it waiting for him with a rejection slip.

As anyone knows who has read his Sherlock Holmes or Bertie Wooster, the telegram service was unbelievably efficient too. An economist once complained that spendthrifts were telegraphing home for clean handkerchiefs, but as extravagances go this hardly seems censurable. There were, of course, minor irritations like having to count a name like Plunkett-Ernle-Erle-Drax as four words when Stow-in-the-Wold counted as one; but the Postmaster-General of those days would surely have resigned rather than charge 'Congratulations' as two words, a miserable innovation of 1981 which must have done much to kill off the telegram service. In *Post Haste*, Ballantyne reminds his readers that words underlined must count as two words, which was probably fair enough, since his contemporaries, notably Queen Victoria, were great underliners.

There were certain Post Office departments which were never written up, by Ballantyne or anybody else; for example, the department for reading people's postcards. The rules used to say that a postcard was to be charged at the full rate if it bore words of an informative or interrogatory nature, but at a lower rate for a message with an amatory or fanciful content. Occasionally Members of Parliament used to ask why 'Arrived safely' should cost more than 'Lang may your lum reek', but they never received a sensible answer.

Should they not rather have asked embarrassing questions like: 'How many staff does the Postmaster-General employ to read postcards written by Her Majesty's subjects?' Yet in 1921 we find Horatio Bottomley MP, of all people, demanding an extension of this snooping. As a recipient of a good many scurrilous postcards he asked the Postmaster-General whether the officials who franked the mail could not direct their attention to the messages on postcards addressed to MPs and eliminate those which were an affront to Parliamentary dignity.

PRIZE MONEY
For Hammering Bolsheviks

If a very old salt boasts in the public bar that he once picked up prize money for helping to seize Bolshevik warships, do not scoff; he could be telling the truth.

Prize money, or 'blood money' as it was once called, was last distributed after World War Two and the country was given to understand that this was the last time it would happen. Not that there was all that much to give away: £4 million for the Royal Navy, a little over £1 million for the Royal Air Force, nothing for the Army (capturing a port full of shipping from the land merited no reward). Shades of the days when an admiral could make a million pounds in a day by seizing the Acapulco galleon; when the loot of Mexico was marched in triumph through the City of London!

Possibly some can remember the notices which went up in the post offices after World War One inviting ex-Navy men to claim their prize money. The rate of distribution had been announced in April 1920: Commanders-in-Chief of the Grand Fleet would receive 1,000 shares, or £2,500; other commanders 850 shares, or £2,125 (with variations in respect of rank), captains in command £400 to £250, according to their position on the List, commanders £150 to £75, lieutenants about half of that, midshipmen and chief petty officers £25, able seamen £12 to £10, boys £10 to £7, supernumeraries and canteen staff £5. To qualify for a full share of fifty shillings, an applicant had to have put in thirty months' service. Crews of transports and hospital ships did not receive a pay-out, nor did deserters. Prize money was free of income tax.

That was the Naval Prize Fund, distributed by the Admiralty. For individual successes against the enemy, there was a bonus in the shape of a bounty from the Prize Court Fund, administered by the Accountant-General. Those who hoped for a big share-out for helping to sink enemy vessels at Jutland were disappointed, because so many ships and crews were involved. The rate was set at 160 shares for senior captains and five for ordinary seamen, which worked out at £8 and two shillings a head respectively.

In the Prize Court was seen the strange spectacle of solicitors, representing commanding officers of His Majesty's ships, laying claim to bounty in respect of U-boat 'kills' and being awarded modest sums – between £200 and £100 as a rule. Among the engagements qualifying for bounty were some which had never been heard of before. One involved a spirited fight in the Caspian Sea against Bolshevik warships in May, 1919. Five Royal Navy ships and 'certain airmen from the carrier *Alexander Yousanoff* destroyed eight Bolshevik armed vessels at Alexandrovsk and immobilised others, a feat which 'definitely curbed the Bolshevik naval power in the Caspian'. Another Caspian exploit which rated prize bounty was carried out by British warships bearing the names *Bibiabat* and *Orlianok* (the latter a seaplane carrier). Both vessels were commanded by lieutenants.

Over the same period the British newspapers were carrying advertisements of captured enemy vessels for sale – whole strings of prizes lying in British or European ports, with details of tonnage. Lord Inchcape was sitting in an office in Leadenhall Street to receive offers. The Allies seized the Kaiser's finest vessels for flagships. *Imperator* and *Bismarck* became *Berengaria* and *Majestic* – or did anyone think they were built on Clyde or Tyne?

In 1948 a House of Commons debate on the Prize Bill revealed a marked lack of enthusiasm, especially on the Labour benches, for the principle of paying prize money. It was being awarded, the House was told, only because the Royal Navy had been led to expect it. This time, to appease the spirit of egalitarianism, the fund was divided on the basis of ten shares for the highest rank and one for the lowest. An admiral, it was explained, would receive between £50 and £60, a captain between £24 and £20 and an ordinary seaman £6 to £5.

PROFESSORS
A Title For Anyone

How one relishes the professors of yesterday! In these pages, already, we have encountered a professor with a boxing kangaroo and a professor who was a competition solutionist. There were also professors of boxing, cricket, phrenology, conjuring, ventriloquism, wire-walking, ballooning, ballroom-dancing, Punch and Judy shows and flea circuses. There was a famous Professor Finney who dived in flames, either from seaside piers or from high platforms indoors.

Vendors of quack medicines have always called themselves professors. Whereas advertising codes discourage the use of 'doctor' when it is not justified, the mantle of professor may be assumed by anyone. And who can honestly say that the professorships listed above are more risible than some of those to be found in seats of learning, in one country or another: professors of mail-order advertising and dance and government, and (any moment now) of tourism and leisure. It would be a pleasure to record that the 'Hamburger University' run by the fast-food firm of McDonalds has a chair of hamburgerology, but that day too must be close.

PUSHER-UPS
Room For One More

Pusher-ups (or pushers-up) were employed to make people sit closer together in the 'gods' of old-fashioned theatres. There were no separately defined seats, simply long wooden benches stretching from one side of the auditorium to the other. When it looked as if a row was full, the pusher-up made his way along it, not merely urging people to sit tighter together but standing over them until they did, if necessary assisting them with a light shove. He was an able-bodied young man with a nice blend of authority and banter, well able to stand up to the sort of citizens who did not mind how many stood so long as they could sprawl in comfort.

It was hard to resent the pusher-up if he made one sit closer to a pretty girl. Not everyone in the 'gods' was nice to be near, but the pusher-up used suitable discretion. By curtain-up he had the audience in a well-compacted, steaming mass and deserved the ribald cheer which greeted his departure.

QUIFFS
A Bad Sign?

'The quiff, or lock of hair which some lads wear on their forehead, is a sure sign of silliness,' Sir Robert Baden-Powell told his Boy Scouts (he also believed that waxed moustaches worn by an adult denoted vanity and a propensity to drink).

Sir Robert was thinking of the brushed-down, even plastered-down, quiff as worn by the soldiers of the Queen. This boyish kind of quiff was also cultivated by the 'Napoleon of Fleet Street', Lord Northcliffe, who possibly copied it from the original Napoleon; critics of Lord Northcliffe's wilder vagaries may have seen no reason to dispute Baden-Powell's judgment.

A less controversial quiff was the brushed-up kind as worn, to the

 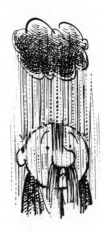 

joy of cartoonists, by Arnold Bennett and Herbert Morrison, and more recently adopted by Elvis Presley and Cliff Richard.

Dr Gordon Stables, of *Boy's Own Paper* fame, was not bothered about quiffs, but he warned that: 'If a boy's eye-brows meet in the middle . . . he ought to give all his time and thoughts to the cultivation of his mind.'

RECITATION
Hesperus, Ahoy

Field-Marshal Lord Wavell revealed that, when he was a boy, admiring aunts paid him threepence to recite 'How Horatius kept the bridge', while a wiser uncle gave him sixpence to do no such thing. In later life, recognising that 'repeating verse to others is seldom popular', he recited to himself when driving a car or riding a horse alone, but never when walking or in the bath. As a war-time Viceroy of India, egged on by his staff, he found time to empty his head of remembered verse and send the result to a publisher, whose reader described the manuscript as 'a familiar collection of schoolboy recitations advancing on a broad front' (a judgment passed on, perhaps inadvertently, to the Viceroy). Nevertheless the collection, suitably corrected and edited, became the extraordinarily popular *Other Men's Flowers*.

Was Wavell the last field-marshal capable of such a feat of recollection? How many remembered poems could the entire present intake at Sandhurst write down between them? Regrettably, the committing of verse to memory is right out of fashion. Learning anything by rote became a process to be despised and reviled; the chanting of the multiplication tables – which, at dame school, formed an enjoyable incantation, in which the strong carried the weak – was bitterly assailed. Yet even the pious sonorities of the Catechism could be memorised with pleasure. How very satisfying to 'renounce the Devil and all his works, the pomps and vanity of this wicked world, and all the sinful lusts of the flesh', whatever those might be; and to beg to be excused 'from lightning and tempest, from plague, pestilence and famine, from battle and murder, and from sudden death'.

But the real fun came from gulping, in great draughts, the heroic poetry in our class books. We were at war with the Kaiser and it was natural that we should be asked to subscribe to the sentiments of Thomas Campbell:

The meteor flag of England
　　Shall yet terrific burn;
Till danger's troubled night depart
　　And the star of peace return.

Which did not mean that we had hatred of the Hun rammed into us. The most rousing poems were those with echoes of far-off battles: 'Like a servant of the Lord, with his Bible and his sword, / The General rode along us to form us for the fight . . .'; 'If the Dons sight Devon I'll quit the port of Heaven / And drum them up the Channel as we drumm'd them long ago'; 'Sink me the ship, Master Gunner, sink her, split her in twain, / Fall into the hands of God, not into the hands of Spain.'

The question, posed by brave Horatius, 'How can man die better / Than facing fearful odds . . .?' was the burden of many of these poems. With the Gatling jammed and the Colonel dead, there was perhaps a case for a public schoolboy to rally the ranks, but it was never quite clear why the boy should have stayed on the burning deck, 'whence all but he had fled'. Yet in the Battle of Jutland sixteen-year-old John Cornwell stayed alone, mortally wounded, beside his gun – and we were not allowed to forget that Boy Cornwell was awarded the Victoria Cross. Doubts of a different order were raised by Longfellow's 'Excelsior'. It was a peculiarly haunting piece, a joy to commit to memory – but what possessed this youth, carrying his 'banner with the strange device', to press ever upward until, 'lifeless, but beautiful', he fell? Even the Light Brigade had a reason for pressing half a league, half a league onward. What, then, in the words of today, was this headstrong youth *trying to prove*? Poor Longfellow! His poems lent themselves fatally to schoolboy parody, notably 'The Village Blacksmith', 'Hiawatha' and 'The Wreck of the Hesperus'.

Much resented by the average child was the notion, which teachers were so keen to inculcate, that rhymes should be 'lost' or glossed over during recitation in order to avoid any tum-ti-tum effect. This offended against natural justice. What was the point of a poet racking his brains for a rhyme, and investing his lines with rhythm, if people were to go out of their way to smother his art? Some resentment is liable to resurface willy-nilly when one hears Shakespearean actors doing their utmost to disguise or disintegrate the blank verse of favourite passages.

Happily, the Victorian tradition that everyone should have a party piece was dying. By all accounts, the well-bred boy of an earlier day never flinched when called on to recite for his betters. A 'proud though child-like form', he stood firm and 'spouted' the stuff as taught, making the appropriate gestures for bewilderment, grief and disaster, impersonating the Count who 'threw the glove, but not with love, right in the lady's face', or the dying gladiator 'butchered to make a Roman holiday' or Eugene Aram 'with gyves upon his wrist'. With equal aplomb, little girls said their pieces about cuckoos and daffodils; or, if unlucky enough to be conscripted into the Band of Hope, gave all they had to 'Father, dear Father, come home to me now' or (for older girls) 'Lips that touch liquor shall never touch mine.'

In *The Spectator* of 4 September 1982, A. N. Wilson, commenting that children were now rarely expected to learn poems by heart, said: 'When you see the unmemorable "verse" they are given to read, this is perhaps not surprising. Who wants to memorise Ted Hughes?' In some schools, children are encouraged to write their own 'poems', with the assurance that they need not bother about rhyme or rhythm (or spelling) and that a poem is whatever one chooses to call a poem. Thanks to this offhand attitude to the Muses, now well established, we have a whole generation which does not know whether a line of metrical verse has two syllables too many or four too few. The odds are that almost any poem of yesterday, quoted in print, will be garbled; academic writers, sub-editors, printers' readers have all developed a tin ear for metre. None of which need have happened if they had been encouraged in youth to roll sonorous rhythms through their heads.

The most shameful epitaph ever incurred by mortal man is that which was bestowed on one Peter Robinson:

> Here lies the preacher, judge and poet, Peter
> Who broke the laws of God, and man, and metre.

Those lines are by Francis, Lord Jeffrey, but a stumbling variation of them, in the *Oxford Dictionary of Quotations*, is attributed to John Gibson Lockhart.

RESTAURANTS
Red Lights, Red Sofas

One of the hardest-worked seams of nostalgia has always been for Romano's, the Gaiety, the Cafe Royal, the Trocadero and other London West End resorts favoured by devotees of the 'Pink 'Un', or *Sporting Times*. All very innocent, of course; or was some of the sentiment inspired by memories of those private upstairs rooms?

Ann Veronica, in H. G. Wells's novel of that name, published in 1909, was taken by the lustful Ramage to a *cabinet particulier* in the Hotel Rococo in Germain (Jermyn?) Street. The couple were received by a bald waiter with whiskers like a French admiral and 'discretion beyond all limits in his manner'. Ann Veronica, the biological student, remarked that it was an odd little room, 'dimly apprehending that obtrusive sofa'. After the meal and the payment of the bill, the waiter 'closed the door behind him with an almost ostentatious discretion', after which Ramage off-handedly turned the key in the lock. It now turned out that the biological student imperfectly understood what was expected of her; she was in 'a world of unknown usages', 'a world of shabby knowledge, of furtive base realism'. However, she had not learned ju-jitsu in vain, and in the struggle on the intrusive sofa Ramage received a stinging injury. A drinking glass was noisily broken and the waiters standing under the red lamps on the landing outside were quick to enquire whether everything was all right. Ann Veronica was saved, but she had learned an important biology lesson in the Hotel Rococo, which Wells oddly describes as 'that remarkable laboratory of relationships'.

In Jean Rhys's *Voyage in the Dark* (period 1914), the chorus-girl heroine is taken to a private room in a restaurant in Hanover Square. There is a red sofa and all the lights are red-shaded. Screened by a curtain is a door to a bedroom, where there are more red-shaded lights. The waiter who brings in the meal gives 'a long elaborate knock' before entering, and when finally retiring shuts the door 'as if not coming back'.

These facilities were popular with officers on leave from the Front in 1914–18, as one may see from Stuart Cloete's memoirs, *A Victorian Son*. The elderly waiters in this catering Special Branch were, according to Cloete, unshockable. Mark Tellar, author of the autobiographical *A Young Man's Passage*, describes a type of Soho hotel which had no public rooms or bedrooms, just rooms for dining à *deux* and a bed behind folding doors. The Eiffel Tower restaurant, haunt of Bohemia, had a red dining-room upstairs (reached by way of a discreet side entrance for ladies) and bedrooms on the top floor.

Presumably at some point the London County Council put the *cabinet particulier* out of business, along with the music-hall promenades for tarts and other survivals from the Belle Epoque. It is not hard to see why the etiquette books forbade unmarried girls to lunch or dine with gentlemen in restaurants, even as late as the 1920s. Today the private upstairs rooms of restaurants are hired for advertising promotions and trades-union festivities.

RIDDLE-ME-REES
Time For Come-Back?

Before crosswords became the universal puzzle, during the 1920s, children's papers used to be stuffed with modest teasers like this:

My first is in quiet but not in hush;
My second's in robin and also in thrush;
My third is in fiddle but not in flute;
My fourth is in pretty but not in cute;
My fifth is in Ella and also in Nell;
My whole is a food – and rubbish as well.

The answer is a five-letter word which the reader will have no trouble in disentangling. As puzzles go, it was neither too hard nor too easy and almost any child could make them up. Why did the riddle-me-ree vanish into oblivion?

'SHAVE, SIR?'
No Scope For Sweeney

In Evelyn Waugh's *Brideshead Revisited*, the narrator, Charles Ryder, travelling in the *Queen Mary*, sends for a barber to remove his beard when the ship is pitching and rolling in a tempest. This scene is wasted in the television version, for we are given no proper idea of the man's dexterity in wielding a cut-throat razor at a time when Ryder admits he dared not have used a safety razor. Instead we simply see this sure-footed professional forced to stand impassively by while his client, soapy and supercilious, talks intimately on the phone to a lady.

The scene is a reminder that the spectacle of one man shaving another has become nearly as rare as those old barber-shop practices of letting blood, lancing boils and pulling teeth. For the client it was a half-voluptuous, half-humiliating ordeal, with the elderly barber (no Antoine he) holding the sitter's nose as it protruded from an expanse of white foam, scraping away with a long-bladed razor, wiping the unwanted soap on a sheet of toilet paper, then smothering the patient with steaming white towels, leaving him for a few moments to parboil, before freeing him with a pink, lobster-like look, as if from a Turkish bath. Assisting at this sixpenny (or even four-penny or twopenny) ritual might be a lather boy, who was allowed to soap the customers' chins. (For a brief period the young Charlie Chaplin was a lather boy in Kennington, a trade obviously designed for a budding slapstick comedian; more surprisingly, Greta Garbo was a back-street lather girl in Stockholm, but she was not really one for soft-soaping men.)

No doubt it is all those 'amazing shaving revolutions', making self-shaving so swift and trouble-free, which have caused public shaving to be phased out; always assuming it has not been deliberately priced out by the Antoines of the Barbers' Guild, on the grounds that scraping chins is no part of their Art and Mystery. Or it may be that men are no longer attracted by the idea of being held by the nose, kissed by cold steel, smothered and dabbed by a styptic pencil.

Americans used to complain of the scruffiness of British barber shops. Over there the clients had their own ornamental shaving mugs ranged on the shelves. There was a tradition of camaraderie and even song, highly enough regarded to warrant forming a Society for the Preservation of Barber Shop Quartet Singing. Ironically, barber shop singing has now become a minor cult in Britain, where it has no roots at all. Sweeney Todd would have jumped at the prospect of turning a whole quartet into meat pies.

SHIPS' NEWSPAPERS
No Barmaids Under Fifty In Prague

The Atlantic crossing, between the wars, took a good week out of one's life. A strong-minded novelist could shut himself in a cabin and knock out a whodunit, starting at the Lizard and finishing at the Ambrose Light, thus earning himself a publisher's Blue Riband. An alcoholic could spend the week in a state of suspended animation and know he would be well looked after. A philanderer could test for himself whether it was true that the ocean air, or perhaps the vibration, had an extraordinary effect on women. But the rest prepared themselves for seven days of non-stop social life

and there was a ship's newspaper to make sure they knew what was going on. It listed Rotary meetings, Sunday masses, sweepstakes and fancy-dress balls. It warned that there might be gamblers on board and even alerted passengers to the presence of Oxford Groupers. And in its limited way it reported the news from the world's capitals.

In the pleasure-ground at Alum Bay, in the Isle of Wight, stands a monument to the Marconi station (1897–1900) from which news items were first transmitted to a ship's newspaper, the *Transatlantic Times*, published aboard the United States liner, *St Paul*, thirty-six miles off shore. If it was anything like the ships' newspapers of a later generation, the *Transatlantic Times* would have contained brief snippets of 'hard news', a few market prices and the baseball scores, and a great many pages of pre-set stories from all over, plus items like 'There are no barmaids under the age of fifty in Prague.'

It was a poor ship which could not produce its own newspaper. Even if one was the only passenger sailing first-class from Glasgow to New York – something which occasionally happened in the off

193

season – one was entitled to a copy of the *Anchor News*, just as one was entitled to an evening's screening of a pre-release Hollywood film (assuming one did not go slumming in Tourist for the sake of company).

Under headlines like 'Beauty's Day on the Ocean', the ship's newspaper described how a woman could spend her time applying 'youthifying' herbal masks and scraping them off again (a keen wind from the ice-pack near the St Lawrence could play havoc with the skin of an English rose). What with all this, and changing her clothes for every meal, a woman had little time for the roving philanderer.

The newspaper's chief advertisements were for health salts, designed to correct that much-feared condition resulting from 'the unusual latitude of meals and the unusual longitude of hours'. The day's eating began with fruit in the cabin on waking. Then came a multi-course breakfast (with steaks on demand), sandwiches and *bouillon* at eleven, a multi-course luncheon, afternoon tea with sandwiches and cakes, a multi-course dinner and (on a German liner) sausages at midnight.

Under foreign flags the ship's newspaper went bilingual or trilingual. The *Lloyd Post* on the *Bremen* carried no Nazi propaganda – just hard news written in American and pre-set stories like the one about the farmer at Sargenroth who was inadvertently carried for a ride on a pig. If anyone wanted Nazi propaganda, there would be an unobtrusive pile of leaflets somewhere headed 'National Socialism and World Relations' (like those political leaflets to be found today in Russian airports). There were one or two copies of *Mein Kampf*, undisplayed, in the library. And there were tiny swastikas on the flags marking the day's progress on the chart of the Atlantic.

No matter what flags they sailed under, the great liners were basically the same, though service was decidedly 'buddy-buddy' under the Stars and Stripes. They were not so much ships as a collection of cinemas and swimming baths, set in a row, with a hull wrapped round them (and what else is a Jumbo jet but three cinemas in a row?). At the time it seemed like truly gracious living, with baronial smoking-rooms, squash courts and pigeon-shooting; no conservatories, but banks of blooms tended by the ship's gardener. Even in Tourist Class the social standards of the day were maintained. Four men, strangers to each other, sharing a common cabin, would struggle into dinner jackets and emerge in the public rooms

194

looking as if, like Lord Curzon, they dined at Blenheim once a week. Secretly, they might be cursing the purser for assigning them to a table with four or five crashing bores – the same faces, meal after meal, day after day.

If one disliked fresh air, it was possible to cross the Atlantic without once breathing the stuff, or without once being subjected to natural light. The public rooms were as cut off from the outside world as the halls of a casino; only when they began to tilt was it apparent that there were tiresome natural elements at play. To be thrown from one's seat while watching a film of the San Francisco earthquake was a strange experience indeed. Was there any truth in those tales about passengers being killed by grand pianos out of control? Probably not.

There were occasional dull trips, of course, and nail-biting moments when it looked as though one's crowded four days in New York, spending dollars at the rate of five to the pound, would be cut, by bad weather, to three or even two, or even to an instant turn-round. But it was without doubt the best way to arrive at New York, with the spires of Manhattan at last springing from the mist, and real newspapers borne on board, with headlines like AXMAN SLAYS SIX. Unless, of course, one was landing at Quebec, when the head-lines, to everyone's surprise and irritation, were in French.

To some, the passenger list was of more interest than the ship's newspaper. It told the confidence trickster who was worth cultivating; it supplied the Mayfair hostess with the names of possible cocktail guests. Under 'First Class' were delightful entries like these (from the maiden voyage of the *Queen Mary*):

> Miss Frances Day
> and chauffeur

> The Rt. Hon. Lord Inverclyde
> and manservant.

It had been the same on the *Titanic*. According to Walter Long's *A Night to Remember*, the passenger list included:

> Carter, Master William T.
> and manservant

Master Carter and his parents were saved, but, alas, not his man-servant nor Mrs Carter's maid.

SHOCKS
From Cats And Coils

The highly-charged Lady Sackville – highly charged in more senses than one – had a party trick which she practised at Knole (according to her 1978 biographer Susan Mary Alsop). On frosty nights she would shuffle along the carpet generating electricity and then light a gas jet with a spark from her nose. Is it any wonder that she was able to fascinate such diverse figures as Sir Edwin Lutyens and J. Pierpont Morgan? (Morgan's nose was large and notoriously rubious, but hardly suited to lighting gas jets.)

The trick of extracting sparks from the nose was known in George I's day. Speculative philosophers used to practise it on charity boys at the London Charterhouse, hoisting them up with insulating cords and touching them with rubbed glass (see Ronald W. Clark's *Benjamin Franklin*). Another party game of the period involved wiring up a lady and a gentleman in such a way that, when they attempted to kiss, their heads would jerk apart. How to electrify small boys by the carpet-shuffling method was described in the *Boy's Own Book*, that Victorian *vade mecum*. It also had this description of how to get shocks from a black cat (without saying why the cat had to be black):

> Place the left hand under the throat, with the middle finger or the thumb slightly pressing the bones of the animal's shoulder; then on gently passing the right hand along the back sensible electric shocks will be felt in the left hand. Very distinct discharges may be obtained too by touching the tips of the ears after applying friction to the back of the cat. It will be hardly necessary to hint how requisite it is that good understanding should exist between the experimenter and the cat.

The shocking coil, with its two tingling hand-grips, was being marketed well into this century as an aid to curing gout, neuralgia, lumbago, insomnia, headache and – yes – constipation. 'Every home should have one', said the advertisements, and nearly every home did. The apparatus could be adjusted to give anything from a light tingle to a really nasty shock. To children it was simply an exciting toy and the thing to do was to see who could withstand the strongest charge. To adults it became just something else to be relegated to the attic.

The electric quacks were still flourishing in the inter-war years. There were hairbrushes and combs wired for electricity, to promote the growth of hair; the current was supposed to revivify the roots, 'like life-giving water on parched soil'. For women, there were electric face-massage instruments, guaranteed to build up the original line of face and neck and eliminate wrinkles. For the bath, there were 'magnetic sponges'.

Perhaps everybody's favourite electrical quack was the moustachioed, flamboyant Dr Walford Bodie, Laird of Macduff, who performed shocking feats on the stage, sitting unharmed in electric chairs amid spectacular showers of sparks and flashes of lightning. Between the wars his star was beginning to fade, but he still returned in triumph to Glasgow, scene of the 'Bodie riot' in 1909 when medical students, indignant at his slurs on doctors, pelted him with the sort of filth they normally reserved for their own Rectors. His lady accomplice, La Belle Electra, did not escape the barrage. It was the Doctor's custom to 'cure' members of the audience and some theatres allowed him to festoon their frontages with discarded leg-irons and crutches. He ran a factory which distributed, among other things, Electric Liniment.

SILLY ASSES
Cult Of The Chinless

The cult of the 'silly ass' flourished exceedingly in the early decades of this century, both on the stage and in light literature; it even overflowed into real life, as Nature began to imitate Art. When the actor Claude Hulbert died in 1964, the obituarist in *The Times* defined the 'chinless wonder brigade' as 'elegant in appearance, affable in manner, well-bred, well-to-do and well-intentioned, but absent-minded and always a little weak in the intellectual stakes . . . the old grey matter tended to move a little sluggishly under the well-groomed hair. The breed is now dying out . . .' Add to this specification a falsetto chuckle, difficulty in pronouncing the letter R, a

197

monocle and spotless spats. The silly ass might have been devised to convince foreign powers that Britain was in the extremities of decadence; cartoonists in Paris, Berlin and New York used him as a substitute for John Bull. At home, at least, it was a convention that silly asses had unexpected inner reserves and were to be relied on in an emergency.

How did the cult start? Twittering fops have always been with us, not least on the Restoration stage. Baroness Orczy's Scarlet Pimpernel was an affected fellow who exclaimed 'La!' and 'Lud!' and dusted his sleeve with a lace handkerchief, but who showed that an apparently half-witted English *flâneur* was worth a dozen dark-jawed foreigners; surfacing as he did in 1904, he was a valuable recruit to the silly-ass cult. Twittering fops had abounded in Victorian cavalry regiments, exclaiming 'Haw-haw' at every opportunity and saying 'bwigade'. Then Wodehouse, who knew a good thing when he saw it, produced his memorable nest of silly asses at the Drones Club. In 1937 he wrote to *The Times* to point out that Wooster's chin, compared to that of (say) Sir Roderick Glossop, was 'definitely episthognathous', but that, compared with such Drones as Augustus Fink-Nottle and 'Catsmeat' Potter-Pirbright, the Wooster chin 'will seem to stick out like the ram of a battleship.' Inevitably, drawling silly asses turned up in Frank Richards's Greyfriars (Lord Maule-verer) and St Jim's (Arthur Augustus D'Arcy).

In pre-1914 days it was fashionable to be a 'nut' or 'knut', a variant on the silly ass whose hallmark, according to Sir Osbert Sitwell, was 'an air of concave and fatigued elegance'. The fate of the knuts, was to be wiped out in Flanders; among them died Basil Hallam, who had portrayed 'Gilbert the Filbert, the Knut with a K' on the stage. A West End success of that war was *The Man Who Stayed At Home*, the hero of which was a chinless wonder who frivolled about attracting white feathers but who was actually working to frustrate a gang of German spies.

Between the wars the stage seemed never free of silly asses. The variety theatres had their Burlington Berties; the actor Ralph Lynn sported his monocle through all those Aldwych farces by Ben Travers (an even more languid performer was Kenneth Kove). Mean-while detective-story writers equipped themselves with inane-seem-ing sleuths, among whom Lord Peter Wimsey was not, perhaps, the most rebarbative. In one unflattering description (in *Whose Body?*), his 'long amiable face looked as if it had generated spontaneously from his top-hat, as white maggots breed from Gorgonzola.' Margery Allingham's Peter Campion was launched (in *The Crime at Black Dudley*) with 'an absurd falsetto drawl', 'foolish pale-blue eyes', 'vacant and peculiarly inoffensive features', tow-coloured hair and a slightly receding chin; but by the end of the 1930s he had shaken off most of these unhappy characteristics.

The silly-ass cult collapsed in World War Two. A misguided at-tempt to represent William Joyce, who made traitorous broadcasts from Berlin, as the silly ass to end all silly asses fell flat, though the name 'Lord Haw-Haw' (once bestowed by a novelist on Lord Cardi-gan of Light Brigade fame) stayed with him. Jonah Barrington, radio critic of the *Daily Express*, wrote early on of Joyce: 'I imagine him with a receding chin, a questing nose, thin yellow hair brushed back, a monocle, a vacant eye, a gardenia in his button-hole. Rather like P. G. Wodehouses's Bertie Wooster.' In fact Joyce's voice summoned up no such comic vision; it had nothing of the aristocratic neigh, it was both supercilious and sinister. Rebecca West thought it 'rasping yet rich'.

What sort of sex lives, if any, the silly asses were supposed to enjoy can only be conjectured. They were not portrayed as effeminate, or epicene; they did not mince or put their hands on their hips. They enjoyed the company of bits of fluff at country houses, but valued their bachelorhood and bolted for their clubs if feminine nets looked like tightening. Their relations with their butlers and valets were as innocent as those of Sexton Blake and Tinker. It is perhaps unnecessary to say that the silly ass had no connection with today's 'Hooray Henry', a heartier and more obnoxious type who is not content to throw bread rolls but must needs wreck the restaurant.

SKIPPING
Bring On The Matrons

Salt, mustard, *vinegar*, PEPPER!

The long rope turned ever faster as the successive condiments were called and few contestants survived more than a few seconds of PEPPER. Boys who ran in and began jumping in a show-off spirit rarely distinguished themselves. Skipping was a girls' game because only girls were any good at it. It is true that the *Guinness Book of Records* lists staggering male feats of skipping – 120,744 non-stop turns, 330 turns in one minute, 108 in ten seconds – but one would rather not know about such things. We are talking about childhood.

Small girls with big bows in their hair were never so innocently employed as when skipping concentratedly by themselves, exercising their new ropes with ball-bearings in the handles, counting 'One, two, three, O'Leary, Four, five, six, O'Leary' and now and then crossing their arms while still skipping.

The game of jumping in and out of the long rope had many an inconsequential song to help it along, often ending in a numerical chant to test jumping power: 'Charlie Chaplin drove to town / How many kids did he knock down? / One, two, three, four . . .' Or there was the doggerel to regulate jumping in and out: 'On the mountain stands a lady, / Who she is I do not know. / All she wants is gold and silver, / All she wants is a nice young beau. / Jump in, sister Mary, / Jump out, So-and-So . . .'

What we seem to have lost is the Bank Holiday spectacle of long ropes being turned, by rough men in search of pennies, for the benefit of agile ladies on the loose. Six fat matrons a-leaping and a-shrieking made a more memorable sight than twelve fat matrons playing ring o' roses round the traffic policeman.

SLANDER OF WOMEN
What, No Action?

In Honor Tracy's hilarious novel *The Deserters* (1954), Sergeant Pratt of the military police gives as her reason for not being too outspoken about an infection suffered by Lady Clarissa, in custody, that 'There's such a thing as the Chastity of Women Act, which prevents one speaking out. And I've no wish to take away another's character, even if she does move in high society where those things don't matter.'

The 'Chastity of Women Act' referred to is presumably the Slander of Women Act, a curious and almost unheard-of measure which was introduced in 1891 to rectify what Lord Macnaghten called 'a very cruel state of the law'. It laid down that anyone falsely calling a woman a whore, a slut, a trollop, a soiled dove, a demirep or anything else in that class was liable in damages. The Marquess of Salisbury wished it to be made clear that only modest women would be eligible to sue. Lord Selborne forecast that the courts would be flooded with frivolous actions arising from tittle-tattle. No such flood occurred, nor, so far as one can discover, was there even a trickle. Probably women just did not fancy being hectored by counsel on the lines of 'Do you really stand there and tell the court you are a modest woman?' Be that as it may, feminists should note that the law, however misguidedly, was really trying to do women a favour, even in those days of male oppression. There was never a Slander of Men Act, to protect them from being called rakes and goats.

201

SLOT MACHINES
Twenty-two Letters For A Penny

An ambition of childhood was to run a chain, or preferably an
empire, of slot machines. What more agreeable way of making
a living than to go round with a black bag and a bunch of keys,
collecting coins from weighing machines, try-your-strength machines
tell-your-fortune machines and the like?

The favourite of all these machines was the one which contained
an almost endless roll of aluminium tape on which names could be
stamped out. No decent railway station was complete without one. It
was a solidly-built apparatus, with a heavy metal pointer which was
rotated to the desired letter and a substantial handle at the side to
operate the punch (the letter E, which tended to be worn, needed an
extra-positive strike, which left it worse than ever). In the 1920s the
tariff was twenty-two letters for a penny, but by the early 1960s the
rate had been cut to ten – and inflation had not yet taken off. There
was another machine which used to produce medallions instead of a
strip of metal. Helpfully, the makers listed a few purposes for which

medallions were suitable; among them were identifying tool boxes, dog collars, plant labels and plumbers' kits.

The name-plate machines were among the very few which enjoyed parental approval. Those which sold 'sweetmeats' gave poor value and were deemed unhygienic. At the seaside, there was no question of being handed a bag of pence for the amusement machines. An occasional look through a telescope was permitted, but the lens was usually fogged ('Didn't we tell you?'). When, at last, we were able to get round to the pier machines, the most fascinating of them proved to be the automata which showed 'The Execution', 'The Vampire' and 'The Haunted Churchyard'. The standard of finish might be unsophisticated, but the ingenuity of the mechanism had to be admired. No doubt the machinery could have been used, with little or no modification, to animate a scene called 'The Confirmation Class' or 'The Sunday School Prize-Giving', but the makers knew their public. Very disappointing were the mutoscopes showing 'What The Butler Saw'. The long-awaited naughty pictures which flipped over to give an illusion of motion were as feeble as they were faded and the stench from the viewing aperture, where so many hard-breathing faces had been pressed, was like that of an uncleaned telephone.

Between the wars the slot-machine operators began to be reviled as enemies of society. They provided machines from which boys could obtain cigarettes and adolescents could buy contraceptives (yes, these were on the streets in big cities in the 1930s). There was also open warfare over the proliferation of 'fruit machines' in which so much public-assistance money was supposedly lost. In Glasgow the sound of havoc which arose from police stations was caused by young constables in shirt-sleeves pounding confiscated fruit machines with sledge hammers, showering the Devil's cogs and cams in all directions. In America the machines were loaded on to barges and sunk at sea. Over there the 'coin-op' men were up against devious entrepreneurs who marketed cheap discs the size of dimes helpfully inscribed 'Not to be used in vending machines'.

Somehow, in the slot-machine race, America and Europe always seemed a jump ahead of Britain. Well before 1914 Germany had 'automats' serving hot and cold meals; there was even a brandy-and-soda machine, which however failed to appeal. Automats were flourishing in Holland between the wars and it was not long before dropouts found they could get cheap meals by hanging about the machines when stocks were due to be cleared.

After World War Two, while slot machines in British dance halls dispensed whiffs of scent, those in Paris gave whiffs of oxygen. In due time even London fell for a coin-operated booth in which the tired shopper stood on a metal plate which vibrated to massage the feet; but by that time American motels had introduced a coin-box beside the bed, with a notice: 'For your added comfort this bed is fitted with the famous MAGIC FINGERS massaging assembly. It quickly carries you into the Land of Tingling Relaxation and Ease.' It did nothing of the sort; and how lucky we were, as youthful cyclists, to be spared this cunning cash-call in our bed-and-breakfast stop-overs.

SPECIAL TRAINS
A Rocky Ride For The Rich

S pecial trains were of three main types: those laid on for Cook's tourists and day trippers; those provided for the nobility to proceed from one estate to another with full retinue of servants, horses and coaches; and those whistled up in emergencies to enable persons of consequence to keep appointments.

Such emergency trains were to be had even in the dawn of railways. When Queen Victoria's fourth child, Prince Alfred, was born at Windsor in 1844, a succession of Great Officers of State all hired 'specials' to convey them from Paddington to Slough, since witnesses to royal births could hardly be expected to take an ordinary train. The first party, consisting of the Lord Chancellor, the Home Secretary and three others, covered the eighteen-and-a-quarter miles in eighteen minutes. A second special containing the Prime Minister was delayed by a down train. The Duke of Wellington, starting late in a train all to himself, clipped half a minute from the time of the first train. It is not clear whether the Great Western, that magnificent line, kept a shed full of specials, with steam up, at Paddington ready for all occasions, or whether the stationmaster had been forewarned of the impending *accouchement*. Anyway, he laid on an excellent service; and it is noteworthy that the first of the day's specials to return from Slough to Paddington completed the journey

in fifteen minutes ten seconds, a speed of over 70 mph and a Great Western record.

In later years the Prince of Wales (Edward VII) put up some good times in special trains, but then one expects tracks to be cleared for royalty. Newspapers occasionally headed their reports 'By Special Engine'. The stupefyingly rich 'Bendor', Duke of Westminster, hired specials for hunting parties and funerals, though not, it seems, for one-man journeys. His friend Winston Churchill, early in the 1914-18 war, set him an example, travelling to France by special train to Dover and thence by warship. On 11 January 1915, Asquith, the Prime Minister, acidly notes that Churchill has returned from the Front 'in his usual regal fashion', keeping his special waiting all morning while he reports. When Kitchener visited the Front, Churchill provided a special to take him from Charing Cross to Dover.

Between the world wars, specials were only for the very flamboyant. The ill-fated financier James White hired one to carry himself and a friend from London to Manchester for the opening of a play he had financed, and at midnight he was seen distributing £5 notes to the station staff (*The Long Week-End*, by Robert Graves and Alan Hodge).

To most of us, familiarity with special trains comes from old detective stories. In one of Sir Hugh Greene's anthologies is a tale in which a medical jurist hires a special in order to lose no time in ripping from a woman's jaw a tooth he believes, correctly, to have been filled with hyoscine, lightly stoppered by a slow-melting plug. In a Sax Rohmer story, Wayland Smith, pitted against Dr Fu-Manchu, barks at Inspector Weymouth: 'Jump in a taxi and pick up two good men to leave for China at once! Then go and charter a special train to Tilbury to leave in twenty-five minutes.' The Inspector is 'palpably amazed' by these orders, as well he might be. Because Wayland Smith is 'invested with extraordinary powers by the authorities', the line to Tilbury is immediately cleared and railwaymen watch in astonishment as the police party races through, 'for a special train was a novelty on the line.'

Too rarely are we told what these trains cost, or whether the money had to be paid in cash, or whether the footplate crew expected a tip. We do know that Sexton Blake, in his early days, always carried enough money to take him round the world and that his boy assistant, Tinker, excelled at nipping out and chartering a ship.

Although Sherlock Holmes was normally content to use public transport, it is from a story by his creator that we glean some practical details about hiring a special. Set in the year 1890, Sir Arthur Conan Doyle's 'The Story of the Lost Special' deals with a Monsieur Louis Caratal who arrives at Liverpool from America, just misses the express to London, and goes to the superintendent of the Central London and West Coast Station to hire a special, since his presence is urgently required in Paris. Money, he says, is of no importance; the company can make its own terms. 'Mr Bland struck the electric bell, summoned Mr Potter Hood, the traffic manager, and had the matter arranged in five minutes.' The special, however, could not start for three-quarters of an hour – 'it would take that time to ensure that the line should be clear.' The train was made up of a locomotive called Rochdale, attached to two carriages and a guard's van, the first carriage being necessary to cut down oscillation. The second carriage had four compartments: first-class, first-class smoking, second-class and second-class smoking. The cost for the hire was £50 5s, 'at the special rate of 5s a mile', which Caratal must have found remarkably reasonable. Before the train could leave, another traveller arrived and demanded a special. Conan Doyle, who seems to have done his homework on all this, says that 'a request for a special is not a very uncommon circumstance in a rich commercial centre', but a call for two in one afternoon was certainly unusual; to supply a second was out of the question as the first had already deranged the service. How Caratal's special vanished on the first leg of the journey to Manchester does not concern us here, fascinating though the explanation is.

From a novel by the popular writer Richard Marsh, *The Beetle* (1897), it is clear that a ride in a special train could be a bracing experience. An Arab carrying a Thing in a bundle on his head, and accompanied by a kidnapped young woman in a hypnotic trance, has caught the midnight train from St Pancras to Hull. His pursuers engage a special to follow and overhaul the express. There is a short delay in starting because St Pancras cannot provide a special saloon, only an ordinary first-class carriage. The driver, a man with that 'semi-humorous, frank-faced resolution' characteristic of his calling, is told 'not to spare his coal' and that there will be £5 to be divided between himself and his fireman if they catch up with the quarry at Bedford (the guard is offered no inducement). This means that they must travel at a mile a minute at least. 'Journeying in a train which consists of a single carriage attached to an engine which is flying at topmost speed is a very different business from being an occupant of an ordinary train which is travelling at ordinary express rates,' the reader is informed (which makes one wonder how the Duke of Wellington enjoyed that rapid run to Slough). The carriage swings and jolts to such a degree that the passengers are flung from their seats and talking is out of the question because of the tremendous racket. Driver and fireman are determined to earn that fiver, the thought of which has inspired them to near-dementia; and it is all they can do to stop the special's mad career when they find that the train containing their quarry has crashed.

Today, one fears, the engine-drivers of ASLEF, not all of whom have semi-humorous, frank faces, would put immense difficulties in the way of operating special trains of this type. One of the most gratifying forms of transport ever devised seems to have vanished.

STRAW ON THE ROAD
The Parting Luxury

'You could always tell when a happy event was expected in the better-class neighbourhoods by the straw used to deaden the sound of the horses' hoofs,' writes Gilbert Frankau, self-styled 'Britain's most voluble author', in his *Self-Portrait*. When his first wife was lying in, he dutifully ordered up straw in 'van loads', unenthusiastic though he was at the prospect of paternity. Monica Dickens has revealed that, when she was born, her mother received the straw-in-the-road treatment in Notting Hill.

More often, the sight of yellow straw meant that someone was dying, or at least seriously ill. The deadening material might be flakes of tanners' bark or even sawdust, as laid down in Great Russell Street, London, by Ruskin for Burne-Jones's wife when she was suffering from scarlet fever. This must have left the street in a fine old mess; but so did the crushed and mildewed straw which had survived its purpose – like the melancholy drifts which blew about Mr Dombey's stricken residence after the *châtelaine's* decease (*Dombey and Son*).

According to Reginald Pound's biography of Arnold Bennett, the last time straw was laid down in central London was in 1932 when the novelist was on his deathbed in Chiltern Court, a block of flats uncomfortably close to the noisy Marylebone Road. The local council gave the necessary permission. Shortly after Bennett died, a milk float skidded on the wet straw and shed its load with a hideous din.

The solace of straw was more likely to be accorded to the Forsytes than to the Pooters. It was for householders with tradesmen's entrances and white stone balls on their gateposts. No one explains how this supreme parting luxury was organised. Did one need a doctor's certificate and the authority of a police superintendent, as well as the council's permission? Did the butler ring the nearest livery stable, or perhaps Harrods, and say: 'Send two vans quickly – the master's had a relapse?' And how did the patient feel on realising, in moments of consciousness, that the traffic sounds had suddenly, ominously, become muted? Did he then strain his ears for the sound of the passing bell?

STREET LIFE
Muffins And Music

When the last horse cabs died out (and in some towns they hung on tenaciously), so did the last of the haggard, panting men who ran behind them, all the way from the railway station to the suburbs, hoping to earn a shilling by helping to unload the luggage at journey's end and perhaps to carry it upstairs. Sir Compton Mackenzie says he tried hard to persuade his father to pay a particularly gaunt specimen two shillings, but his request fell on stony ground.

The muffin man gnawed at nobody's conscience. Ringing his handbell, he patrolled the likelier suburbs with a cloth-covered tray of porous delights balanced on his head. Many remember the sound of the bell, few remember actually buying muffins. There was a report that the muffin man had died out in World War Two, a victim of food rationing, but he may well have made a comeback later.

The lamplighter was something of a trick cyclist. He could tilt his lance at the switch on the gas lamp and turn it on without dismounting, returning to the attack if he failed the first time. This agile public servant was replaced by mechanisation, which ensures that street lamps go on at full noon.

The peep-show man, with his pole-borne box of scenic wonders, hardly survived the Victorian age; a fellow casualty was the 'Happy Family' man, who displayed a cage of mutually antagonistic creatures – cat, dog, bird, mouse, rabbit, monkey – living in apparent amity. But one remembers a bird man with a pole-borne box in which tame birds performed tricks on see-saws and swings, a real child-puller.

Among the aristocrats of the street were the sturdy horse-handlers who stood with their draught horses at the foot of long inclines, ready to give an extra pull to vehicles with heavy loads. Sometimes their horses wore straw hats and ear covers. When a horse fell in the shafts, these were the heroes who helped the threshing, frightened beast back to its feet.

There were colporteurs, the curious name given to men who sold religious tracts from one public-house to another; they had a gift for insinuating themselves into company, like the Army Scripture Readers who used to infiltrate barrack-rooms. There were knife-grinders and scissors-grinders galore, and men who screwed patches over holes in kettles. In shopping streets there were sometimes touts, indefatigable young men who stood in the doorways of tailors' shops (notably in Glasgow) and all but ran the passer-by into the shop by the scruff of the neck to be measured.

The amount of music-making in the streets, mostly by foreigners, was prodigious. Until 1914 much of it came from German bands, which were made up of not-too-young men in peaked caps and uniform of a sort, playing mainly brass instruments and equipped with music-stands. For contributions in towns they relied heavily on coins thrown by children from windows. Considerate donors saw to it that the coins were wrapped in paper to make them easier to find. In the streets, urchins ran about helping to trace errant coins.

The German bands were popular in town and countryside alike, despite a notion in rural areas that their coming presaged rain. That famous Cockney anthem, 'Down at the Old Bull and Bush', contains (or used to contain) a line: 'Dear little German band, la, la, la, la, la, la.' Not even the Northcliffe press accused the German bandsmen of being spies for the Fatherland. However, in August 1914 they were smartly rounded up and interned, first in a camp at Frith Hill, near Camberley, and then in the Isle of Man, where they played 'The Watch on the Rhine' to their fellow inmates for the duration.

The Italians were the other great music-makers, their young men relying heavily on a Latin line of blarney. In London, barrel organs, with monkeys, were hired for the day. The poet C. S. Calverley apostrophised the hurdy-gurdy man, holding the streets to ransom:

> Grinder, who serenely grindest
>   At my door the Hundredth Psalm,
> Till thou ultimately findest
>   Pence in thy unwashen palm . . .

Calverley was reasonably well-disposed towards the organ grinder and his monkey, unlike Charles Babbage, 'father of the computer', who devoted much of his ferocious energy to denouncing them, and estimated that one-fourth of his entire working power had been destroyed by audible nuisances. Among these he no doubt included banjo-twanging black minstrels (pushing their own miniature pianos), Welsh choirs, one-man bands and old men blowing penny whistles.

After 1918 the music of the streets underwent a change. Most of it was now provided by British ex-Servicemen, many with empty sleeves and empty trouser-legs and all with empty hopes. And, if George Orwell is right in *Coming Up For Air*, they were joined by masked women singers; masked presumably to conceal their shame.

STRUWWELPETER
And The Scissor-Man

Hilaire Belloc's *Cautionary Tales* deal with children like 'Rebecca, Who Slammed Doors for Fun and Perished Miserably' and 'Henry King, Who Chewed Bits of String and was early Cut Off in Dreadful Agonies'. The tales appear to owe a literary debt to Heinrich Hoffmann's *Struwwelpeter*, the English version of which was still read in old-fashioned households earlier this century, as it had been for generations. The tone of this work was deplored by the new wave of parents, who underestimated their children's natural love of grue.

Struwwelpeter, or Shock-Headed Peter, was always portrayed with long matted hair and immensely long finger-nails. He would seem to have been an ideal target for a pair of shears, but it was little Conrad who attracted this treatment. Cautioned by his mother not to suck his thumb when she went shopping, he disobeyed, whereupon:

> The door flew open, in he ran,
> The great long red-legged scissor-man.
> Oh, children, see! The tailor's come
> And caught out little Suck-a-Thumb.
> Snip! Snap! Snip! the scissors go,
> And Conrad cries out – Oh! Oh! Oh!

Kindly Mamma, returning home, notices Conrad's bleeding stumps of fingers:

> 'Ah!' said Mamma, 'I knew he'd come
> To naughty little Suck-a-Thumb.'

An even harsher fate overtook Harriet, who continued to play with matches when ordered to desist:

And see! Oh! what a dreadful thing!
The fire has caught her apron string;
Her apron burns, her arms, her hair;
She burns all over, everywhere.

A spirited colour illustration depicts this scene, but in case it has not been fully visualised the author continues:

So she was burned, with all her clothes,
And arms, and hands, and eyes, and nose,
Till she had nothing more to lose
Except her little scarlet shoes.

Other children condignly punished were Frederick, who pulled the wings from flies (savaged by a dog) and a pack of boys who taunted a blackamoor for being black (dipped in a giant bottle of black ink).

If there are anticipations of Belloc in Hoffmann, there is also a clue as to where John Pudney may have found the name Johnny Head-in-Air. But Hoffmann's Johnny Head-in-Air is just another boy who refuses to look where he is going and deserves all that happens to him.

212

SUCKERS
Limpet On A String

In Jerome K. Jerome's *Three Men in a Boat* is an urchin with 'something on the end of a string, which he let down on to every flat stone he came across, and then pulled up again, this producing a peculiarly unattractive sound, suggestive of suffering'. The urchin was using a sucker, which the dictionary defines as 'a toy consisting of a leather disc and a string, for lifting stones &c'. The leather was thin and soft, readily obtainable from any father who did the family cobbling, and the string was threaded through the centre and knotted to prevent it coming out. A good sucker, moistened and pressed down on a stone, would grip like a limpet and lift quite substantial 'stones &c', including loose tiles from a kitchen floor. Only when the weight was too heavy did it make that peculiarly unattractive sound as it reluctantly forsook its grip.

SWEETS
A Power To Annoy

Who remembers stickjaw, chew-chew, Jap Nuggets (founded 1822), Conversation Lozenges, Cupid's Whispers, Traffic Lights, Hundreds and Thousands, Penny Prize Packets, Paradise Mixture (otherwise window clearings), snowballs, aniseed balls, brandy balls, sugar bacon and those white sugar mice with string tails which always turned up in the toes of Christmas stockings? Who remembers when chocolate came unwrapped in corrugated sheets, from which the shopkeeper broke off a single ridge for a halfpenny and two ridges for a penny? Who remembers the Radium Super Chocolate of the early 1930s – 'Actually Contains Radium: Ideal for Sportsmen, Invalids, Children'?

'There is no place today for the shabby sweet shop we knew in childhood,' says *Sweet Shop Success*, published by Cadbury Brothers (who advise the shopkeeper: 'Endeavour to sell a bigger quantity than is asked for at first'). Well, there is still a place in memory for that shabby little bow-windowed shop run by some-body's grannie. At least she did not stock pornography, as they do at today's sweets 'outlets'. Nor did she have a notice in the window saying: 'No More Than Two Children Admitted At Once'.

The well-remembered sweets tend to be the down-market 'cheap-ies' which were recommended in childhood by word of mouth, in so far as recommendation could emerge from mouths filled with deli-quescent jelly babies and the severed heads and legs of chocolate belles.

To be a real success a sweet had to have the power to annoy adults. Did it contain a powerful dye enabling one to redden the lips and spit blood? Or to give one a 'sore throat'? Would it render the tongue black like the tongue of a plague victim? Would it taint the breath with dubious eastern odours? Would it pull out new fillings from teeth? When it had been drained of colour and flavour, could it still be extruded noisily in a hundred offensive shapes – or chewed endlessly with the mouth open? Look at the perennial success of the humble sugar cigarette, which has not yet lost the power to provoke questions in Parliament. Look at the gobstopper, the very name of which outraged fine ladies who preferred to stop their gobs with French fiddle-faddle like *fourrés, confits, dragées, pralines* and *non-pareils*. Look at candyfloss, which had no sooner been invented than it became a contemptuous synonym for the nation's economy. And look – to bring the record up-to-date – at the success reportedly enjoyed, in 1983, both at home and overseas, by the Fifeshire makers of Skull Crushers, described as 'a white flavoured chocolate skull which oozes blood-red fondant when bitten'.

Adults tried to insist that, when something had been put in the mouth, it should not be removed, inspected, shown around, laid aside, recovered from under the sideboard and put in the mouth again. The rule was most unfair to those white-coated scientists who had gone to the trouble of investing sweets with rainbow colours, even with ghostly pictures of the Tower of London and spies' mess-ages which came and went. And how else, other than by experiment, could a child hope to answer the songwriter's question: 'Does the Spearmint lose its flavour on the bed-post overnight?'

Adults had to be dissuaded, if possible, from buying wholesome, 'no nonsense' sweets – usually 'boilings' or butter-scotch. However, those amber twisted pillars of barley sugar were by no means to be rejected and ranked well above acid drops. There was small juvenile demand for 'winter sweets', flavoured with horehound and eucalyptus, though in principle the notion of fighting illness and disease by sweet-sucking was acceptable enough. A medicated sweet was particularly unpleasant when it stuck in the throat, as boiled sweets sometimes did, taking an age to dissolve and inhibiting further intake.

If there were winter sweets, there were also summer sweets. Adults went to the seaside for whelks and winkles, but children looked for a diet of pink peppermint rock, in the fattest bars available. By nibbling along the sides one could see the long shafts of the red letters in 'Prestatyn' stretching mysteriously. Why were we never told who invented this masterpiece? John Mackintosh was allowed to boast, 'I Am The Toffee King', but any fool could make toffee. Who was the Rock King? Who ensured that it was the same shrill pink everywhere? It was not to be confused with Edinburgh Rock, brittle, very sweet and easily dissolved, a surprising choice for Scots who liked things to last; indeed, Edinburgh Rock was a bit precious, like the Edinburgh accent. Regional sweets, like Berwick cockles and Harrogate toffee, tended to disappoint; nothing could beat cheap, universal, anonymous trash. (Some of our sweet towns could have learned a thing or two from Montelimar, in the Rhone Valley, where the inhabitants line up for miles waving boxes of nougat at the motorist; a scene never recorded at Bournville.)

One expects readers of *The Times* to reminisce from time to time about their favourite dabs and suckers. They did so in 1951, when war-time sweet rationing was still in force and memories had obviously been quickened by deprivation. Correspondents asked what had happened to the Kalibonker, a coloured creamy toffee of 'ambrosial gooiness'; or to Kruger's Whiskers, consisting apparently of cocoanut-ice part-coated with chocolate to 'a villainous brown'; or to the Farthing Turnover, in which a threepenny piece might very occasionally be found.

One reader described the gobstopper as 'that magnificent off-spring of a cannonball and a mothball'. By 1973 financial journalists were reporting that the greater gobstopper was on its way out; it had become too costly to turn out at a realistic price, whatever the realistic price of a gobstopper may be. Today's gobstopper-substitutes still change colour, but one would wager a bag of Skull Crushers that they would hardly stop the gob of a ferret.

When the next nostalgia outbreak occurs in *The Times*, perhaps someone will write in recalling a report of 1964 which said that a Blackpool firm had accepted an order from America for ten million Beatles records made of toffee. Was this magnificent export order faithfully fulfilled? Were there many complaints about sticking needles from the more humid states of the Union? And what was the greatest number of times a record was played before the purchaser grew tired and began stuffing it into his gob? (See also LIQUORICE.)

TAXIDERMY
Anyone For Spolia?

The taxidermist's window was decidedly worth a detour. It might not show a grizzly rearing on its hind legs, or a lion leaping on to the neck of a terrified horse (for these one had to go to the big window of Rowland Ward in London), but it would have a snarling otter or two, a kingfisher in a glass pool, a cuckoo in its usurped nest, a row of wise old owls and a cosy domestic scene in a rabbit warren. How the taxidermists in small towns kept going as long as they did is something of a mystery, but there were always prize pike to be stuffed, foxes' masks to be mounted and the occasional domestic pet to be immortalised.

The Sussex village of Bramber for long housed an Exhibition of Humorous Taxidermy by Walter Potter, a local inhabitant, whose life work included tableaux showing rabbits at school, squirrels behaving as clubmen, guinea pigs at cricket and rats playing dominoes, watched by the dog which killed them. Potter's masterpiece was 'The Death and Burial of Cock Robin', in which a hundred little birds mourned the victim; also present was the fly which, according to the rhyme, saw him die. Whether it was all very humorous, or poignant, or dreadful depended on one's age and the prejudices on which one had been nurtured. Apparently the creator of this display (last reported at Arundel) was unrelated to Beatrix Potter, of even greater anthropomorphic fame.

The firm of Rowland Ward specialised in great jungle set-pieces for international exhibitions – 'A Trying Moment', or 'Nature in the

Raw'. In 1957 its craftsmen tackled their first elephant since 1908; the demand for entire pachyderms was, and remains, slight. The firm once turned the Sangers' boxing elephant into a hall porter's chair. Elephants' feet turned up in the better stores as liqueur stands, umbrella holders, humidors, wine-coolers and door-stops. Such 'spolia' can now be found, less and less frequently, in junk shops. A table with legs made from real snakes was very much an acquired taste; so was a crocodile with a locked cigar chamber in its belly (a rival to the famous statue of the Venus de Milo with a clock in her navel). One of the Rowland Ward lines was binding worth-while books (e.g. game books) in lion skin. It never turned out cheap hyena-backs.

Do-it-yourself taxidermy was encouraged in the *Boy's Own Paper*. Suggested subjects for the boy's own charnel-house were birds, foxes, otters, stoats, weasels, moles, squirrels, water rats, small horned animals – and cats. *Cats?* Yes: 'Let us begin by imagining that the keeper has brought in a fine large poaching cat . . .'

Readers of the *Boy's Own Paper* really *did* dabble in this hobby,

217

using dangerous arsenical soap in the process. However, the boyish urge to reconstruct Nature seems to have dwindled. In the late 1960s the Museums Association was offering bursaries to young would-be taxidermists – 'they should be good field naturalists and have some artistic ability.' Without artistic ability it would surely be wrong to attempt to counterfeit the brilliant hues of a mandrill's rump.

TELEVISION
The First Pale Blink

On 1 September 1939, with war imminent and families being evacuated to the country, Britain's first television service – the first in the world – went off the screen, in the middle of a cartoon film showing Greta Garbo making up to Mickey Mouse. There was no announcement, no apology. Somebody just pulled out the plugs and that was that. It was like drawing a curtain across the cage of a tiresome parrot. The television transmitter at Alexandra Palace could have been a navigational aid to enemy bombers, but the public was left to deduce that for itself.

The only tears shed for television were by those who had recently bought expensive sets. Most of the 20,000 viewers had other things on their minds. The tears withheld then may freely be shed now; tears for lost innocence; tears for a clever, precocious child nobody had really wanted; tears for Lord Reith, who was sure this child would grow up wicked and wanted nothing to do with it. (Was he, perhaps, right?)

A great many citizens had seen demonstrations of television during the 1930s – in big stores, at museums, at exhibitions, in the waiting-rooms at Waterloo Station – and what they had seen was a small picture of fuzzy people groping in a fog. As entertainment it could not compare with wall-to-wall coloured pictures in a cinema. It was a clever toy, but was immediacy all that important? Other countries did not seem in any great hurry to start public service television. America put out limited experiments in 'visio', as some called it; Germany had transmitters on the Brocken and the Grosser Feldberg, but these sent pictures only to a few viewing-rooms, and there seemed very little

prospect that television would ever work for the greater glory of the Führer.

Such was the lack of interest in television in the upper echelons of Broadcasting House that it is astonishing the service was ever launched. The first blink of 'the milk-coloured eyeball' (an American newspaperman's phrase) came on 2 November 1936 and was seen in only about a thousand homes, mostly within twenty-five miles of Alexandra Palace. Nobody knew what to call these early set-owners – lookers? watchers? scanners? gazers? – but eventually the BBC's choice of 'viewers' was grudgingly adopted. Many called them fools for spending up to £200 to see a fourth-rate picture. The cheaper the sets, the smaller the picture, and some had screens little bigger than a postcard. All that viewers received, at first, was roughly an hour's service in the afternoon and another in the evening, with a total shut-down on Sunday. It was hard to watch the screen for even an hour, but that did not stop viewers complaining they were not getting their money's worth.

What they did get for their money was an astonishing number of plays. This, surprisingly, was an economy measure, since photographing a play in a studio was cheaper and less time-consuming than distributing resources over a number of outside functions. Leslie Mitchell, better known as the voice of the Movietone news-reel, was the first of the brisk, brash young men to live dangerously before the cameras, making much of it up as they went along. The press had told us that he and his two women presenters would wear bright blue lipstick and orange face cream. In *Leslie Mitchell Reporting* he has written entertainingly of those early days, when so much that was to be photographed had somehow to be dragged into, or staged within, the grounds of Alexandra Palace. At the receiving end the results were often boring to a degree, but there were periodic glimpses of big sporting events as they happened (television, when perfected, would make sports commentators unnecessary, thought 'Peterborough' of the *Daily Telegraph*). For what it was worth, television viewers saw Neville Chamberlain stepping from the Munich plane at Heston and waving that sheet of paper before cinemagoers did.

By then the quality of the television picture was much brighter and sharper. To their surprise the staff at Alexandra Palace received postcards from satisfied viewers well outside the twenty-five-mile radius, even from as far away as Ipswich. With relay stations, what might not the future hold? Quite a few citizens formed the view that television was bound to kill radio stone dead and that it was not worth buying a new radio set. The manufacturers of radio sets were still bemoaning this attitude when war began.

When Britain's television service was resumed in 1946, a handful of citizens were able to resume viewing on their pre-war sets. They were shown the rest of the Mickey Mouse film which had been cut off seven years earlier.

TICKLING STICKS
And Ladies' Tormentors

At fêtes and fairs, on Bank Holidays and Victory Nights, there were pedlars who sold aids to introduction in the form of feather-ended ticklers, back-scratchers and 'ladies' tormentors' of various kinds. Among these was a rudimentary tube and plunger which would squirt water, or, better still, a jet of 'perfume' at the lady of one's choice. A well-splashed dress then became a target for rice or confetti, which would be difficult to dislodge. However, ladies' tormentors were also used by girls to break the ice with men. As we are so often reminded, people made their own amusements in those days.

The 'tickling stick' survives as a wand of office in the hands of the comedian Ken Dodd.

TIME GUNS
Boon Or Barbarity?

A guide-book to Edinburgh describes as 'an amusing barbarity' the one o'clock gun which is fired from Half Moon Battery at Edinburgh Castle, causing Festival visitors to jump out of their skins. This armament, serviced by the military, is the survivor of a number of time guns which once performed for the benefit of shipping in British ports, notably at Newcastle-on-Tyne, South Shields and Liverpool.

The Merseyside gun was still banging away after World War Two. Supposedly it once embarrassed an American author who was orating in the city. His audience, hearing the bang, took out their watches to check them, which the speaker assumed to be a concerted intimation that he had gone on long enough.

Edinburgh's gun has been sounding off since the middle of the last century. Its inspiration may have been a cannon in the gardens of the Palais Royal in Paris, which was fired by the sun's rays. Edinburgh also installed a visual signal in the form of a ball on a mast, which

dropped at the appointed hour like the one at Greenwich. There was another time-ball overlooking Trafalgar Square and a rather special one on the ramparts of Norwich Castle, which fell with a loud report.

Overseas, time guns abounded. The cannon on the Janiculum Hill in Rome was operated with the aid of an old astronomical clock in the Church of St Ignazio. Fortresses of the British Empire punctuated the day's rituals with gunfire, as at Gibraltar and the Citadel at Halifax, Nova Scotia. Now the most famous of the overseas guns is the one at Hong Kong. For weaving it into a song – 'In Hong Kong they bang a gong / And fire off a noon-day gun' – Noel Coward was allowed to pull the lanyard himself. Traditionally, the taipans of Jardine Matheson had got a bit above themselves and taken to firing salutes to their own merchantmen, so the Royal Navy exacted re-tribution by ordering the firm to fire a time gun in the colony in perpetuity. At noon, two company servants in white duck suits arrive at the saluting base under the Excelsior Hotel, carrying a transistor radio to give them the signal. As the moment nears they motion to the old women in the sampans huddled below to block their ears. But the din in Hong Kong is such that hardly anyone now hears the bang.

TIPPERARAY
Why Not Tobermory?

Tipperaray is an Irish town with a population of about 5,000, noted for dairy products and linoleum. Of the millions who have sung yearningly about Tipperaray ('My heart's right there') how many have ever bothered to visit the place? Would they not have sung with equal yearning about Inveraray, or Aberconway, or Tobermory, or any other euphonious place-name with the right number of syllables?

It is the mischievous way of song-writers to have us professing nostalgia for places we have never seen or wanted to see and which they have probably not seen themselves. So long as they give us a good tune, we go along with them and play the sighing game. Then, as the years go by, we transfer our nostalgia to the tune itself. A film showing marching men singing 'Tipperaray' as they head for the jaws of death can be a real tear-jerker for the generation which remembers the Kaiser's war.

The song-writers, and especially the American breed, try us pretty hard at times. Is there any State of the Union for which we, the former title-holders, have not been invited to yearn? Carry me back to old Virginny, to my old Kentucky home, to old Alabammy, to the whispering pines of Nevada; put me back home in Tennessee, deep in the heart of Texas; California, here I come, O Carolina moon . . . and wasn't there somewhere called Oklahoma? We have sung about America's mighty rivers, about the Chattanooga Choo-Choo and the two tattiest and most over-rated streets in America, namely Broadway and Forty-Second Street.

It is when Americans start writing nostalgic songs for us to sing about our own landmarks that we are entitled to grow really restive. 'There'll be bluebirds over the White Cliffs of Dover' – what an ornithological nonsense that was! Yet many of the generation which remembers those years find it as big a tear-jerker as their elders find 'Tipperaray'.

TOILET ROLLS
A Surprise On Every Sheet

It was in the Depression years that a leading manufacturer of toilet rolls decided to brighten the smallest room by printing a different joke on every sheet. Thereafter, anyone who told a funny story was liable to be met with a chorus of: 'We know where you got that.' Anti-social individuals sat on unreasonably in lavatories going through the jests like brokers looking at tapes.

The firm was Izal. In 1932 the cartoonist Heath Robinson visited the factory and produced a series of drawings purporting to show how the firm's germicide was made. Some of these were incorporated in a roll 'published' in the summer of that year. Later came rolls with a potted nursery rhyme on each sheet. In the Jack and Jill rhyme, the emphasis was on germicide for head injuries rather than 'vinegar and brown paper'. Then, when World War Two broke out, there was a try-out of anti-Hitler illustrations.

Pre-dating, and outlasting, this fashion were the well-loved jokes on 'England's Glory' match-boxes, which were first seen just after the turn of the century. A numerical code, which puzzled many, showed which jokes were being run a second, third or fourth time.

TOPS
A Vanished Skill

It seems extraordinary that the whipping of tops – a diversion mentioned in Aristophanes and Plato – should have passed into limbo, in the course of a couple of generations. In part, the reason is that top-whipping was indulged on metalled roads which were not, at that time, inundated by fast traffic. There was not enough room to whip tops on pavements, while school playgrounds tended to be too rough or congested. Yet, in Shakespeare's day, English villages kept tops for the exercise and stimulation of youth in cold weather. On what smooth surfaces were they whipped? Frozen ponds?

Top-whipping seemed to come round in seasons, like marbles. There were two main kinds of top: a drum-shaped one with a conical base and a 'peg top' shaped like a champagne cork running to a pointed metal tip. The first was launched by winding the string of the whip round it and then throwing it, when with luck it would spin as it landed and could be lashed into continuous gyrations (ideally the whip was not of string but of fish-skin). Alternatively it could be launched by twirling it between both hands. The peg-top was usually activated by propping it up in soft earth, coiling the whip round it and then flicking it into action. Some boys were extraordinarily skilled at whipping tops, others extraordinarily incompetent. Normally, the feat of keeping a brightly coloured top briskly turning before an audience of admirers was reward enough, but there were sometimes contests to see who could whip a top fastest over a given distance or cause it to knock down a rival's top.

A specialised form of top was the teetotum, or small gambling top, inscribed with instructions. In the early 1920s there was an astonishing craze for the 'Put and Take' top, with faces reading 'Put One', 'Take One', 'Put Two' and so on. Children spun it to win tiddlywinks, adults for coins. For preachers it was a useful peg for homilies on trying to take more out of life than one put in.

TWO MINUTES' SILENCE
Even In The Air

On 11 November 1922 the pilot of a Daimler air express flying from Manchester to London saw rockets exploding over Rugby. He throttled down his engine and began to glide. 'Glancing round', reported *The Times*, 'he saw that his passengers had risen from their seats and were standing with heads bared.' Eight thousand feet above Lichfield a pilot of the Berkshire Aviation Company shut off his engine.

That gives some idea of how seriously, and perhaps how dangerously, the Two Minutes' Silence was taken in the early 1920s. Nobody who, as adult or school child, lived through those years will forget the intense poignancy of it.

The first Silence, in 1919, fell on a week-day. The King had appealed for 'the complete suspension' of all normal activities. 'During that time, except in the rare cases where this may be impossible, all work, all sound and all locomotion should cease, so that in perfect stillness the thoughts of every one may be concentrated in reverent remembrance of the Glorious Dead.'

In cities, maroons were fired or sirens sounded to initiate the Silence; in the country the signal was given by church clocks or bells. Trains stopped, except in tunnels. In the streets, bus conductors and drivers stood beside their vehicles, while the passengers rose from their seats. The great stores were 'like the petrified city of Pompeii'. Selfridge's had its own maroons, its own flags to lower, its own buglers to sound the Last Post. Harrods sounded the fire alarm at the start and finish. Inevitably, Lloyds rang the Lutine Bell, while gongs halted the Stock Exchange and Baltic Exchange. In Northampton, a murder trial stopped. No telephones rang, for the exchange staffs were all standing. For that brief period, Britain was cut off from the world.

The streets were not wholly silent. Dogs yelped, wondering what was happening. Striking clocks, as always, kept their own time. Car engines were not always shut off. But the stillness was strong enough to show up the half-muffled sob, the cries of the overwrought. When it was over, 'women powdered their noses and moved on'.

In schools, pupils stood and for once there was no larking, no fidgeting. The teacher looked out of the window, impassively. Would we get through it without nervous giggles? We did, but it was a tremendous strain and the two minutes seemed interminable.

Abroad, all garrisons and warships observed the Silence. Australia came to a halt. The Prince of Wales's train stopped between Baltimore and Washington.

For the next two or three years the Silence seemed to grow even more dramatic. Then unhappy incidents began to occur. Too many trains kept running; motorists and taxi-drivers were in trouble for failing to stop; in Croydon a vendor of Communist leaflets kept shouting his wares and was mobbed.

In the High Court, in 1924, the eminent barrister, Marshall Hall, made unworthy use of the Silence to support his defence of a newspaper accused of libel. He had reduced the plaintiff, Lady Terrington, to tears and (according to his biographer, Edward Marjoribanks) his bullying was failing in its purpose. Then, as he was making his final speech, the sirens sounded. At once he struck a theatrical pose, with head bowed and 'on his fine ascetic face an expression uncontrollably sad'. Afterwards he resumed speaking as if with an effort. The nation, he informed the jury, had once again celebrated the greatest national sacrifice the world had ever seen, a sacrifice in which they had all been involved, and now they had to address themselves once more to 'the trivial grievances of this lady'. Opposing counsel jumped up to protest but the judge did not see Hall's behaviour as foul play. Lady Terrington lost her case.

The day came when the pilot of an aircraft, far from shutting off his engine, was fined for towing an advertisement banner during the Silence.

UNDERGROUND
The Lost Stations

A 1914 map of the London Underground is a fascinating study. The pattern of the rail network is very different and quite a few of the halts indicated have vanished. It is an odd thought that the uncaring metropolis sits on a dozen or so abandoned stations, whose walls once bore posters for 'Tatcho' and 'Scott's Emulsion' and (no doubt) graffiti about President Kruger, and whose entrances are built over or cunningly concealed against inquisitive eyes. Sometimes the alert Tube traveller can spot these gutted stations as the train rattles through, just as the traveller by underground from West to East Berlin can spot the darkened halts which the Communists have ruled are no longer to be used.

Between Hyde Park Corner and Piccadilly Circus used to be two stops, Dover Street and Down Street. Dover Street was developed into the present Green Park station and Down Street became a railway headquarters. During the 'Blitz' on London, Winston Churchill spent some nights there, seventy feet below ground. The British Museum once had its own Tube station, but someone decided that pilgrims to the Elgin Marbles must be made to trudge there from Holborn or Tottenham Court Road. Off Bloomsbury Street, at the time of writing, is a disreputable waste site where the entrance stairs to the old Museum station are said to be concealed.

Other vanished stations include Tower, Park Royal, Hounslow Town, South Kentish Town, Brompton Road and Lord's. The reasons for their disappearance are various: some were casualties of competition before the lines were brought under unified control; others were built for special purposes, for example to serve exhibitions; others became redundant through rationalisation and expansion.

One of the lost stations, when under construction, went into service for a purpose other than that which was intended. This was Clapham Deep, planned as an ultra-deep station in a chain linking North and South London. During World War Two it was enlarged into a transit camp for troops, with a quarter-mile network of galleries 120 feet below ground, capable of holding 5,000 men. It could be reached by a special staircase from a platform of South Clapham

Station, intended as an emergency entrance for bombed-out families.

Those beady investigators who are fascinated by the subterranean ramifications of London's emergency defence system have their own ideas of what purposes some of these lost stations may be serving (*see* Peter Laurie's *Beneath the City Streets*). We are fortunate, perhaps, that no gangs of robbers, or terrorists, have as yet set up house in these hide-outs. Applications to view old stations are not encouraged; one can only hope for a power breakdown when the train reaches an appropriate spot. Surely Sir John Betjeman should have been invited down into one of these grey ghostly caverns, to dream appropriate dreams of cloche-hatted minxes in silk hose tit-tuping up the stairs, clutching their *Peg's Papers* and screeching their 'Cheerios' . . . with an honourable mention for that one-time hero of the Underground, the man with the wooden leg who was hired to sprint up and down the new-fangled escalators to show the able-bodied how easy it was.

VENTRILOQUISM
The Ever-Elusive Secret

'Boys! Throw Your Voice into a Trunk, under the Bed or Any-where! Lots of fun fooling teacher, policemen, or friends.' The advertisement, by a well-known firm of magic-dealers, appeared regularly in boys' papers between the wars, and probably still does. It was illustrated by a drawing of a man carrying on his back a heavy load from which emerged cries of 'Help!', 'Police!', 'Murder!' and 'Stop Thief!' All you needed was a book of instructions and a voice instrument which could produce bird trills or 'raspberries' as and when required.

Well, why should we not have believed the advertiser? The notion that voices could be thrown about like tomatoes, causing the same degree of havoc, had been bred in us from late infancy. In some of us, ever groping for the secret of this black art, the belief never really died at all.

Who was historically responsible for spreading the idea that voices

229

could be *thrown*? Really thrown, that is, not just transferred to a dummy on one's knee but hurled on suitable trajectories across public gatherings to create maximum confusion? The finger points firmly towards the Victorian comic novelist, Henry Cockton, author of that perennial best-seller, still appearing this century, *The Life and Adventures of Valentine Vox*. (In the belief that Valentine Vox is a name to conjure with, a present-day performer has adopted it, with much success.)

Once Cockton had launched his voice-throwing fantasy, the editors of boys' papers latched on to it and nourished it from generation to generation. So did editors of magazines for grown-ups. In Sir Hugh Greene's anthology of magazine stories, *The Rivals of Sherlock Holmes*, is a tale by William Hope Hodgson, 'The Horse of the Invisible' (1913), in which the terrifying sounds of neighing and gobbling by a spectral horse in the grounds of a country mansion are produced by ventriloquism from inside the house. If adults were ready to swallow that sort of thing, why should not schoolboys believe that classrooms could be thrown into glorious anarchy by the same means?

230

The Life and Adventures of Valentine Vox, which The Times recommended as a cure for the melancholy, had a preface in which the author professed his eagerness to shed light on social evils, in particular the unscrupulous practices of private lunatic asylums desperate for customers. Stuffier readers may have thought that Valentine Vox, the hero, was something of a social evil himself. Having mastered the art of voice-throwing after six months' practice in the fields, and often astonishing himself in the process, he started operations in a small way by shouting 'Mad dog!' behind old ladies and then transmitting ferocious growls. To punish a girl who had snubbed him at a dance he attended her wedding, called out in disembodied tones, 'I forbid the marriage', and had the satisfaction of seeing her carried out senseless. In a restaurant he alarmed diners by causing two chimney boys to call out to each other in a hot flue. At a Guildhall banquet he initiated a discussion between Gog and Magog and from the gallery of the House of Commons he created pandemonium down below. In the British Museum he induced the Memnon to shout threats at tourists (the old Egyptian talking gods, no less than the Witch of Endor, were possibly animated by priestly ventriloquists). At a Victuallers' Fancy Fair he caused portraits on the walls to speak. And here he is at a phrenological lecture:

'Now,' continued the learned professor, taking up a very singularly formed skull in both hands and looking at it very intently, 'this is the head of Tim Thornhill, the murderer.'
'The what?' cried Valentine, pitching his voice into the skull. The startled professor dropped it on the instant, and as it rolled with peculiar indignation upon the rostrum, the audience simultaneously burst into convulsive roars of laughter.

As may be supposed, the trick came in useful in exposing wrongdoing in those private asylums. Eventually Valentine married a nice girl called Louise who persuaded him to grow up.

Cockton did not deign to explain how the trick of throwing the voice was done. It was just one of the 101 things a boy could do – or couldn't do. However, in the late Victorian years, would-be ventriloquists could buy handbooks describing how to manipulate the glottis and the buttock muscles, and above all how to dodge the labials – those tiresome letters B, F, M, P and V, which involve movement of the lips. The ventriloquist Frederick MacCabe explained that 'Mind what you are about' should be rendered "ind what you are awout' and 'I'm here up the chimney' as 'I'ng here uck the chingney.' For a beginner, making a speech ('ngaking a skeech') was pretty hard going, but if one had a talent to 'angyuse' one kept at it.

The late Patrick Campbell wrote an admirable piece – to be found in Paul Jennings' *The Book of Nonsense* – about the day when, as a schoolboy fortified by the instructions of a Dr Farvox, he set out to play voice-throwing pranks in class. The result was not the mirthquake it always is in the comics. Under the schoolmaster's mocking eye he was forced to entertain the class with his rendering of Dr Farvox's test sentence: 'A pat of butter moulded into the shape of a boat' ('a cat of gutter noulded into the shake of a goat'). The experience can have done little to cure that famous stutter.

To revert to Frederick MacCabe. He squarely blamed the creator of Valentine Vox for popularising the idea that voices could be thrown. The secret was simply to direct the audience's eye and ear to the selected spot and leave the rest to the imagination. As an example he told how the great Alexandre was walking along the Strand with a friend who requested a demonstration of his skill. In no time Alexandre convinced passers-by that cries for help were coming from underneath a load of hay on a passing cart. As one man, they fell on the cart and scattered the load, leaving the carter to stack it up again and reflect on the folly of driving down the Strand when clever people were about. Time was when one would gladly have believed that story.

The stage ventriloquists of McCabe's day used rows of dummies for their 'throwing' displays. Then came the fashion for a single cheeky homunculus sitting within inches of the performer's lips and the question of throwing scarcely arose. The audience now concentrated on trying to spot lip movements. Surprisingly, the 'vents' flourished as never before with the coming of radio, talkies and television, where any throwing could be assumed to be the work of sound engineers. What chiefly mattered now was a funny script.

Some of those macabre films about ventriloquists had the faithful worried. The mannikins were taking over and driving their masters along the road to madness and murder. Many a dummy has much too knowing a look, like that of a page-boy who has opened too many bedroom doors, and the touch of exophthalmia does not help. Who would be surprised if ventriloquists, suffering from split minds and identity crises, sometimes end in those private asylums that Henry Cockton was worried about?

232

WALL OF DEATH
With Or Without Lions

For those who grew up in the 1920s this was an exhilarating spectacle, as exhilarating as its name. Some unknown genius decided that motor-cyclists could not be better employed than careering with a deafening din round the inner vertical walls of a giant drum, or round the lip of a saucer, or even over and over inside a Globe of Death made of steel lattice. The act, originally performed by pedal cyclists, was sometimes staged at flower shows (for example, in the Quarry at Shrewsbury) and as a spectacle for boys it compared very favourably with a tent-full of begonias. In fairgrounds the set-up was different: spectators stood on the top of the wall and looked down into the pit, where the riders sat in their elegant breeches waiting for a quorum to assemble. Girls rode not only pillion but on the handlebars – fierce flashing-eyed creatures who would otherwise have been spinning by their teeth in a circus tent or perhaps just doing the splits in a chorus line. It was the riders' custom to swerve up and down the side of the pit, forcing the spectators to step back from the safety wire.

In the 1930s small motor cars began to appear on the Wall of Death and then someone had the rather horrible idea of carrying a lion in the passenger seat, or in an attached side-car. There were interventions and prosecutions – one at least, in 1932, at Lough-borough was successful – but the act continued. The Wall of Death was staged in variety theatres too, sometimes in a saucer which, as a spectacular climax, was lifted into the air.

Today one has to go a very long way to find a Wall of Death. Instead, motor-cycle daredevils are expected to leap chasms or soar over a row of double-decker buses.

WATCHES
And Visible Trinkets

A small child perched on grandfather's knee was faced by an irresistible display of paunch ornaments. The gold watch-chain, or 'albert', or 'dog chain', led to a fine hunter or half-hunter watch, capable of chiming the time when a spring was pressed or even when it wasn't. The owner of this portable Big Ben would open the lid, apparently, by blowing on it, while stealthily releasing the catch, and invite the child to do the same; a time-honoured game which rarely palled. At the other end of the chain, which was threaded through a button-hole in the waistcoat, might be a locket with a portrait, or a sovereign-case in the form of a round silver box from which the gold coins could be slid out one by one, against the pressure of a spring. Or there might be a seal, dangling free from the chain, for imprinting the wearer's monogram (cut in cornelian, bloodstone or agate) on sealing-wax. A gentleman did not wear too much in the way of stomach jewellery, but hobbyists attached to their watch-chains all sorts of gadgets, from compasses and light-meters to pedometers and watch-shaped barometers.

The neat albert was the Prince Consort's reply to the more osten-tatious fob adornments of the eighteenth century (it was the practice in those days to balance a real watch with a false one). The statesmen

who gave us both world wars wore alberts of one form or another and so did the union leaders who gave us the Gerneral Strike (their chains might be of silver, brass or even iron). The public figure most famous for his midriff adornments was Arnold Bennett, friend of the cartoonists, who would no more have discarded his chains and fobs than he would have cut off his quiff. His friends tended, or pretended, to deprecate his taste.

The wrist-watch, once a suspect adornment for men, justified itself in active-service conditions on the Western Front, notably in the Royal Flying Corps, and its worth was attested afresh in World War Two. Field-Marshal Lord Montgomery, however, wore a watch-chain between his upper breast-pockets, whether in battle dress or service dress, which would appear to have infringed the King's Regulation against the wearing of visible trinkets. After World War Two, the waistcoat went into steep decline and the watch-chain vanished with it. The generation which sported stomach jewellery would never have descended to ear-rings, or medallions worn against the chest hairs.

WATER CARTS
Pink And Fragrant

The old horse-drawn water-cart, throwing out its crystal curtain of rain, leaving the dusty streets smelling country-fresh, was one of the more delectable engines in the municipal stable. What small boy did not wish, at some time, to be a water-cart driver, with the chance to spray other small boys and fussy elders?

In Bloomsbury, it appears from the memoirs of Frances Partridge, water-carts sprayed pink rain and children could pick up little specks of a red substance which, put in water, turned it a delightful hue. Bloomsbury was a haunt of pinkish people and it is tempting to think the colour was specially added for them.

As for the country-fresh fragrance left by the water-cart, could it have been that elusive petrichor, the strong romantic smell of rain falling on hot earth, as exhaustively discussed by Dr Magnus Pyke in *Butter Side Up*? Apparently this smell is so prized in Uttar Pradesh that it is bottled and sold as 'earth scent'.

WEMBLEY
The Fade-Out Of Empire

There should have been an Eiffel Tower at Wembley, topping the one in Paris by 175 feet. It was begun in the 1890s, when tower-building was in vogue, and the driving force was Sir William Watkin, who laid the Snowdon Railway and was a keen Channel Tunnel man. Unfortunately, or fortunately, funds ran out and only the first stage of the tower was erected. This, for what it was worth, was opened to the public in 1896 and demolished in 1907. New Brighton, on the Mersey estuary, had a complete Eiffel-style tower from 1897 to 1921; the Blackpool version, half the height of its Paris prototype, dates from 1896.

To see its dreams of architectural fame fulfilled, Wembley had to wait until 1924, when the British Empire Exhibition (minus a tower) was staged there. This city-in-a-suburb was to be a boast, a celebration, a dedication and a sacrament; a grand fusion of tribal and

national loyalties; a hymn to industry; a spectacle much greater than the Great Exhibition of 1851; and indeed it was all these things. Yet somehow the vision of lake-reflected palaces in an intoxication of styles was too much for an imperial people to take in. Their attitude was not far from that summed up by 'Evoe' in *Punch*:

> They praised the huge pavilions,
>   But one and all confessed –
> And so will several millions –
>   They liked the Dolls' House best.

The Queen's Dolls' House certainly registered in the minds of children and adults alike (it is now at Windsor Castle). But what seized the minds of adolescents taken up to Wembley from the country tended to be, not the way of life in kraals and log-cabins, but the life of the Fortunate Ones in the capital, as luminously and tantalisingly seen through the windows of Park Lane and Kensington. Here were the real beneficiaries of Empire, here were the inheritors of the Power and the Glory, here in short were the people to be emulated, and the sooner the better.

How could one have remembered the chandeliers and canopies and cockaded hats of the West End and forgotten all the purpose-built gorgeous palaces? And all the other wonders of Wembley? One now discovers that there was a coal mine there, complete with pit-head gear and a two-decker cage in which people descended into the ground, to discover real pit ponies and tracts of pitch masquerading as coal. Did we go down the mine? Surely we could not have forgotten that? There was also a factory in which Ford cars were assembled; once again, no memory of it remains. Anyway, what had Henry Ford to do with the Empire? There was an exciting (if, as many said, cruel) rodeo, an event chiefly associated with the American West, though Canada had a West too. Again, it seems there was a full-scale reconstruction of Tutankhamen's tomb. The original of it did not lie within the Empire, though other nations might have been pardoned for thinking that it did. One dimly remembers seeing the Prince of Wales carved life-size from Canadian butter, beside a butter horse, but not the pen-knife with 1,924 blades, 'one for each day of the Christian era'. How could one forget a preposterous object like that?* And what on earth could it have looked like? Another forgotten masterpiece was the electrically controlled reconstruction of the raid on Zeebruge, with warships moving to their destination on under-water rails, and real smoke and sparks pouring from *Vindictive's* funnels. Probably the reason one cannot recall these wonders is that many of them cost more money to view than was available for a family outing.

The amusement park was dominated by unnatural heights from which the uninhibited slithered or whooshed down to a welcoming mat. Royalty went on the roller-coaster but probably not on the Caterpillar, where a green cover came down over the riders' heads and fierce jets of air blew up the ladies' skirts (an un-imperial idea presumably imported from Coney Island). And was there not a riveting cock-shy in which the object was to 'Tip the ladies out of bed'?

All too soon the name of Wembley was to be synonymous only with football and greyhound racing. By the end of the decade the shoppers of Britain were being berated in Government advertising campaigns for not supporting the products of Empire so expensively promoted at Wembley.

---

* Apparently it is still sighted from time to time on display in the sort of shops which sell multi-bladed Swiss Army knives. It is said to resemble a huge glittering porcupine.

WHISTLING
By Scouts And Ladies

'A Scout smiles and whistles under all circumstances . . . When you just miss a train or someone treads on your favourite corn . . . you should force yourself to smile at once and then whistle a tune . . . A Scout goes about with a smile on and whistling. It cheers him up and cheers other people, especially in time of danger . . .' Thus Baden-Powell, in *Scouting For Boys*.

There was far more whistling in days gone by, whether caused by Boy Scouts or not. If an errand boy on a bicycle failed to whistle it was as if an Automobile Association patrol failed to salute – a sign that there was something wrong. Inevitably there were urchins who whistled not so much from a desire to cheer other people as to exasperate them. And whistles from the gallery did nothing to cheer actors.

Adult whistling was the worst. Here is a *Daily Mirror* editorial from the stressful year of 1916, when cabs and taxis were becoming scarce:

239

Watch the cab-whistlers. Note the blank idiotic face of the firm parlourmaid or bounder butler. Observe the impossible club servant in uniform. Look at the lady behind him waiting. She wants a cab. She must have a cab. How can she get home without a cab? So she whistles. Or she commands that the whistling shall go on! What to her the war, or the wounded? She wants a cab . . .

A week after that appeared, a ban was imposed on whistlers for cabs between ten p.m. and seven a.m. Ladies, it should be noted, did not whistle by putting two fingers in the mouth, but used a referee-type instrument.

Old ladies sometimes carried police whistles, for use in emergency. Borne on the night breeze, the deep-throated sound of a police whistle – now largely superseded by the car siren – set the pulses tingling. 'If you hear a policeman's whistle sounding, run and offer to help him, it is your duty, as he is the King's servant,' commanded B-P. Girls could do their bit too. The Chief Scout praised by name three young women who, in three separate street incidents, rushed up and blew the whistles of policemen who were being attacked. What an example for today!

WILL O' THE WISP
'The Earth Hath Bubbles'

When did anyone last see a will o' the wisp? This question was being asked a hundred years ago and not many hands were then upraised. Thanks to deep drainage and high farming the mires were vanishing from the English scene and with them went the Tinkerbell of the swamps (alias Jack o' Lantern). However, sightings were still reported early this century.

We forget what a soggy land this used to be. The great bog at Solway Moss 'burst' in 1771 and poured wet filth over fields and villages, until the region reeked like the Pit of Tophet. When the earth could perform tricks like that, what apparitions might it not release? But the will o' the wisp did not wait for dramatic convulsions. It would perform at any sizeable swamp, or even (as some

240

said) above old plague-pits or slaughter-grounds. *Ignis fatuus*, as it was contemptuously called by those who could not agree on a scientific explanation, was supposed to lead travellers to their doom, or to shatter (by explosions?) the lanterns of those who tried to pry into its haunts. Its malign attentions could be offset by turning one stocking, or an entire vest, inside out. The pale, dancing fires appeared in swamp-lands after hot autumn days and were the size of candle flames; sometimes they would balance like soap bubbles on the tips of reeds or grasses, or cluster round horses' ears, causing no apparent discomfort. As the traveller moved, so did the will o' the wisp, retiring before him, advancing behind him, presumably in the eddies he created. The manifestations were not optical illusions, for people would stand watching the scene for long periods. The Waveney marshes, near Syleham, in Suffolk, used to be famous in pre-drainage days for 'Syleham lights'.

Why are there no will o' the wisp sightings in Irish boglands? It would be sad to think that this phenomenon had vanished for ever into the realms of political metaphor.

X-RAYS
A Peep-Show For Children

In *As We Were*, E. F. Benson recalls the fears of those who thought the invention of X-rays in the 1890s would allow 'the un-scrupulous scientist to direct his baleful ray on to the walls of your solid-seeming house and discover you in your bathroom'. Quite a number of citizens shared this delicious dread. In America, notices in theatres forbade the use of X-rays in opera glasses. On both sides of the Atlantic X-ray-proof underclothes for women were marketed.

As it turned out the dangers were physical rather than moral. Science, as usual, did not quite know what it was up to; nor did Commerce. In the 1930s, leading shoe-shops introduced X-ray machines, into which customers inserted their toes to see whether the fit was too tight. For children it was a new shop toy, like sitting on a rocking-horse. It took the General Medical Council until 1956 to decide that the X-raying of feet was of 'dubious value' and that

241

multiple exposures might even be dangerous to children. Two years later – there was no urgency, of course – came an announcement that shoe-shop machines were to carry a warning against X-raying the feet more than twelve times a year (something else to mark in one's diary). It was also announced that shoe shops would employ trained X-ray operators. Soon after that the machines rapidly dwindled in number; the skeletonic peep-show was over.

YELLOW PERIL
Evils Not To Be Named

Rumours of plots to dominate the world spiced the early decades of this century. As if Imperial Germany and Bolshevik Russia were not bogeys enough, we were invited to sweat over the Yellow Peril (annihilation of the West by the East) and the monstrous ambitions of world Jewry (see next entry).

The novelist Sax Rohmer was thought to have done more than anybody to keep the Yellow Peril going. His Dr Fu-Manchu appeared in 1913 and proved a villain suitable for all ages. In 1924 he was introduced to the youthful readers of *Chums* as 'the Yellow Peril Incarnate in One Man'. The artist who illustrated the series was required to depict a fiend with 'a brow like Shakespeare and a face like Satan'. Fu-Manchu held the key which 'unlocks the heart of the secret East' and his hand was stretched out to recover the lost gardens of China. Like the author of *Mein Kampf*, he proposed to move when his enemies had destroyed themselves; then 'the golden dawn of the East will come.' Film producers lost little time in playing up the evil Doctor.

Bret Harte had told us that, 'For ways that are dark / And for tricks that are vain / The Heathen Chinee is peculiar . . .' Innumerable popular authors developed the Harte-Rohmer line. They represented the yellow men as devils roosting in the least savoury reaches of western seaports, where – pending the call to action – they dedicated themselves to drug-running, pimping, crimping and 'nameless vices that we never mention, but which are not so unfamiliar to our private understandings' (Edwin Pugh, in *City of the*

242

World). It was not the best of training for world domination; for, debauched by opium, bhang and betel, they periodically 'saw red' and set about each other with cleavers, in the hope of seeing more red than ever; or, as a variation, set fire to each other's property to destroy evil jinns. For the rest of the time they would glide, slink, shuffle or shamble in and out of shuttered dens, either pretending to cringe at westerners or upsetting them with the hard stare of unfathomable eyes. The prolific Thomas Burke, whose *Limehouse Nights* (1916) caught the popular fancy, mocked his fellow journalists who sensationalised London's Chinatown, but the Limehouse characters he portrays are far removed from Sing Hi and Sing Lo in *The Rainbow*. Here (as described in *Nights in Town*) are drug-wrecked men, five in a bed . . . drunk, loose-lipped girls in the fan-tan house with its 'huge scorbutic proprietor' . . . everywhere a scorn for the age of consent. Here contemptuous 'Chinks' look coldly (as well they might) on whites who come to smoke an opium pipe in a filthy room to round off a West End night out. Burke tries to convince himself that Limehouse is really no worse than the West End, but harps on 'things not good to be talked of'. There is one wickedness in particular that nobody writes about. 'Even if this wickedness were known I doubt if it would be mentioned. It concerns – but I had better not.' (This was fairly typical of the fearless social investigators of the period.)

Outside the Chinatowns, the Chinese were sometimes seen in little groups being marched across seaports by junior Merchant Navy officers, looking like anything but a master race. They were the coolies of five continents and it was in that capacity that thousands of them were recruited into labour battalions to serve behind the Allied lines in Flanders. In times of peace the Chinese took in the world's dirty washing. What happened to all those Chinese laundries, by the way? In George Formby's song, Mr Wu had 'a naughty eye that flickers / When he's ironing ladies' blouses', but perhaps his eye was really flickering at thought of that golden dawn?

In 1925 the Chinese suddenly began to insult 'foreign devils' in Shanghai. People remembered their earlier insolences, when they tried to drive the West's robber barons from their shores. Would it be necessary to sack their palaces again? Fortunately, a 'distinguished anthropologist', Dr A. Legendre, chose this moment to announce that the Yellow Peril was non-existent. The yellow race was (as the

243

Illustrated London News reported) 'quite incapable of the sustained effort of organisation necessary for conquest or for any other kind of achievement'. What, after all, was the yellow race but a blend of black and white? Chinese art and philosophy were derived from other lands and any yellow men of distinction had always possessed Aryan characteristics.

So long as the West could produce anthropologists like this, there was nothing to fear. However, Dr Legendre did concede that China might well roll up the West if a renegade white nation stepped in and organised its population.

ZION'S PROTOCOLS
A Really Bad Joke

In 1921 that outrageous hoax, 'The Protocols of the Learned Elders of Zion' – setting out the supposed plans of the leaders of Israel's Twelve Tribes to corrupt and conquer the world, with Freemasons as their junior allies – should have received its comeuppance. The Protocols had been published in Imperial Russia and were a favourite of the Czar's secret service, which tried to interest Allied intelligence in them during the 1914–18 war.

The Learned Elders were supposed to have met twenty-four times in secret conclave to exchange their ideas. These involved getting hold of all the world's movable capital, controlling stock exchanges and financial houses, buying up estates, abolishing all laws in restraint of usury and easing the laws on bankruptcy; seizing and suborning the press; infiltrating all schools; destroying the military classes; and ruining the Christian Church by encouraging freethinking and scepticism. As if this programme was not inflammatory enough, there was a recommendation that Jews who wished to commit adultery should invariably choose Christian mistresses.

The Protocols were exposed, in 1921, by two independent investigators. One was an American, Herman Bernstein, who in a book called *History of a Lie* traced the Protocols to a work of fiction published in 1868 by a disgraced German postal official, Herman Goedsche, writing as Sir John Retcliffe: his novel, *To Sedan*, had a chapter in which the Leaders of the Twelve Tribes met at midnight in the old Jewish cemetery in Prague, with the Devil in attendance, to plot world domination. Then Philip Groves, *The Times*'s man in Constantinople, published a series of articles showing that the Protocols echoed the text of a work by Maurice Joly, *Dialogue Aux Enfers Entre Machiavel et Montesquieu*, published in 1864 as a satire against Napoleon III. It was now obvious that Goedsche had plagiarised this work and given it an anti-Semitic slant. For Jew-baiters the Protocols were an irresistible attraction and they were used, with suitable embellishments and perversions, to reinforce Czarist pogroms in Russia.

After 1921 the Protocols should have been laughed off as a bad joke, as they tended to be in Britain – at least, by those who remembered that they had been debunked. In America anti-Semites were reluctant to believe the plans were bogus; Henry Ford's *Dearborn Independent* endorsed them, but by 1927 Ford had retracted and apologised. Others acknowledged that the Protocols might be false, but thought they indicated well enough what was going on.

In Nazi Germany the Protocols were gratefully received and used in the Jewish persecutions, proving that it is impossible to keep a bad hoax down. Even 'Sir John Retcliffe' might have been appalled by what he had started.

ZOOT SUITS
A Stormy Birth

This was the over-sharp suit of the post-1945 spiv generation, broad-shouldered, long-jacketed, with wide-flared trousers, designed to outrage. Few who laughed at it were aware of its lurid history. Said to have been originated by the youth of Puerto Rico in the early 1940s, it provoked riots in 1943 in down-town Los Angeles, where bands of American sailors and marines roamed the town beating up young Mexican 'zoots', ripping off their grotesque gear and sometimes leaving them naked. In one round-up by the authorities, 500 combatants were gaoled and 150 injured, and Los Angeles was put out of bounds to Servicemen. The troubles also

spread to San Diego. Supposedly the 'zoot suiters' had been robbing and molesting troops and insulting their women.

Thomas Sanchez's novel, *Zoot-Suit Murders* (1978), has a zoot leader saying things like: 'You got to be tricking yourself out like the dude, get yourself up in some pants with stuff-cuffs, reet-pleats, look like a Zoot, walk like a Zoot, talk like a Zoot.' Weapons used in the Los Angeles 'slugfests' included steel chains, brass knuckles, knives and 'tire-irons'. According to Sanchez, the American Government outlawed the zoot suit not because it was provocative, or because its wearers were manipulated by anti-American groups, but because it wasted cloth in war-time.